www.profrose.eu

Six intellectual companions united at a Committee on Political Sociology conference at Villa Serbelloni, Lake Como, Italy; about 1970. From left to right, Giovanni Sartori, Juan Linz, Mattei Dogan, Karl Deutsch, Richard Rose and Stein Rokkan

Learning About Politics
in Time and Space

Richard Rose

University of Strathclyde Glasgow

Only connect
E. M. Forster, *Howards End*

© Richard Rose 2014

First published by the ECPR Press in 2014

The ECPR Press is the publishing imprint of the European Consortium for Political Research
(ECPR), a scholarly association, which supports and encourages the training, research and
cross-national co-operation of political scientists in institutions throughout Europe and beyond.

ECPR Press
University of Essex
Wivenhoe Park
Colchester
CO4 3SQ
UK

All rights reserved. No part of this book may be reprinted or reproduced or utilised in any form
or by any electronic, mechanical, or other means, now known or hereafter invented, including
photocopying and recording, or in any information storage or retrieval system, without
permission in writing from the publishers.

Photograph permissions
The Old Court House, page 25, by TJR (Own work) [CC-BY-SA-3.0
   (http://creativecommons.org/licenses/by-sa/3.0)], via Wikimedia Commons.
The Vienna Staatsoper Opera House page 41 courtesy of Archiv Wiener Staatsoper.
*The Memorial in Montgomery, Alaba*ma page 98 courtesy of John O'Hagan
Reform Club, page 186, by M. T. Walters.

Typeset by ECPR Press
Printed and bound by Lightning Source
British Library Cataloguing in Publication Data
A catalogue record for this book is available from the British Library

ISBN: 978-1-907-301-47-6
Kindle ISBN: 978-1-907-301-80-3
PDF ISBN: 978-1-907-301-12-4

www.ecpr.eu/ecprpress

Dedicated to

ROSEMARY

Thig crioch air an t-saoghal ach mairidh gaol agus ceol

Though the world shall end, music and love will endure

Series Editors:
Dario Castiglione (University of Exeter)
Peter Kennealy (European University Institute)
Alexandra Segerberg (Stockholm University)
Peter Triantafillou (Roskilde University)

ECPR Essays:

Croce, Gramsci, Bobbio and the Italian Political Tradition (ISBN: 9781907301995)
Richard Bellamy

From Deliberation to Demonstration: Political Rallies in France, 1868–1939 (ISBN:
9781907301469) Paula Cossart

Hans Kelsen and the Case for Democracy (ISBN: 9781907301247) Sandrine Baume

Is Democracy a Lost Cause? Paradoxes of an Imperfect Invention
(ISBN: 9781907301247) Alfio Mastropaolo

Just Democracy (ISBN: 9781907301148) Philippe Van Parijs

Maestri of Political Science (ISBN: 9781907301193) Donatella Campus,
Gianfranco Pasquino, and Martin Bull

Masters of Political Science (ISBN: 9780955820335) Donatella Campus, and
Gianfranco Pasquino

The Modern State Subverted: Risk and the Deconstruction of Solidarity (ISBN:
9781907301636) Giuseppe Di Palma

ECPR Classics:

Beyond the Nation State: (ISBN: 9780955248870) Ernst Haas

Comparative Politics: The Problem of Equivalence (ISBN: 9781907301414)
Jan W. van Deth

*Citizens, Elections, Parties: Approaches to the Comparative Study of the Processes of
Development* (ISBN: 9780955248887) Stein Rokkan

*Electoral Change: Responses to Evolving Social and Attitudinal Structures in Western
Countries* (ISBN: 9780955820311) Mark Franklin, Thomas Mackie, and Henry Valen

Elite and Specialized Interviewing (ISBN: 9780954796679) Lewis Anthony Dexter

*Identity, Competition and Electoral Availability: The Stabilisation of European
Electorates 1885–1985* (ISBN: 9780955248832) Peter Mair and Stefano Bartolini

Modern Social Policies in Britain and Sweden: From Relief to Income Maintenance
(ISBN: 9781907301001) Hugh Heclo

Parties and Party Systems: A Framework for Analysis (ISBN: 9780954796617)
Giovanni Sartori

Party Identification and Beyond: Representations of Voting and Party Competition
(ISBN: 9780955820342) Ian Budge, Ivor Crewe, and Dennis Farlie

*People, States and Fear: An Agenda for International Security Studies in the Post-Cold
War Era* (ISBN: 9780955248818) Barry Buzan

State Formation, Parties and Democracy (ISBN: 9781907301179) Hans Daalder

The State Tradition in Western Europe: A Study of an Idea and Institution
(ISBN: 9780955820359) Kenneth Dyson

Please visit www.ecpr.eu/ecprpress for up-to-date information about new publications.

Contents

List of Photographs

Introduction

Reflections From Experience

Everyone is supposed to be able to write one interesting book: the story of his or her own life. This implies that for the past half century I have been writing more than 40 books that are uninteresting because they are impersonal. Social scientists are expected to emulate natural scientists, setting aside personal experiences rooted in a particular time and place, and concentrating on timeless and universally applicable phenomena. Yet the sociology of knowledge emphasizes that what we write reflects who we are and what, if anything, we have experienced outside as well as inside the walls of academe. In practice, much of the best political science is written by people who combine a broad experience of life, a passion about what they do, and a willingness to take intellectual risks (*see* Munck and Snyder 2007: 3).

History imposed a broad experience of life on anyone like myself, born in 1933, the year that Adolf Hitler and Franklin D. Roosevelt each came to power. My first political memory is listening to a radio broadcast of Hitler accepting the surrender of France by Marshal Pétain in June, 1940. I was fortunate in being American, and thus having an ocean between my home and Europe's battleground. That saved me from the scourge of an occupying army demonstrating that even if you are not interested in politics, it is interested in you. Before I was old enough to vote, I was on a boat to experience Europe. Since then research has led me to experience what politics is about in places as different as England and Russia, Western and Eastern Europe and the United States.

I have always been passionate about writing. Initially, the question was: What to write about? At the age of eight I taught myself to type in order to write about baseball. The newspapers that reported baseball games also reported politics, which in those days was more than a game. I wanted to become a reporter on the St. Louis *Post-Dispatch*, a Pulitzer-Prize winning newspaper in the city in which I was born. In 1955 I succeeded in doing so. But after two years I decided to combine my passion for writing with my passion for study by getting a PhD. Since then I have written many books and articles about dozens of countries and given talks in 45 countries on six continents.

Because I care about what governments do and do not do, I have spent more than 60 years writing about politics as it exists in the streets as well as in books. I did not learn about racial and religious discrimination from being taught about democracy in school but from living with it in my youth. I did not learn about the importance of freedom from political theorists but by talking to people who had suffered or fled from Nazi and Communist dictatorships. I have been tear-gassed by police at the 1968 Democratic Party convention and a year later at the Bogside Rising in Londonderry. Seeing the gun re-enter Northern Ireland politics when researching there, I put a proposal to act to a Labour minister. She said with surprise, 'Why Richard, you care'. I was surprised that she did not seem to care.

I have taken many risks in seeking knowledge from life as well as from books, but at the time choices were made they did not seem risky. My career has developed by doing what I felt right to do at the time. In the belief that studying politics as well as literature would improve my work as a reporter, I became a postgraduate researcher in international relations at the London School of Economics in 1953 although I had never taken a class in international relations. After a year I dropped out to return to St. Louis to work as a newspaper reporter. However, I soon realised that I had too much or too little education, and quit to go to Oxford to get a doctorate. I stuck with the decision to look for an academic job after being turned down for post-doctoral fellowships at Oxford and the LSE. A month after my student grant had run out, with no job and my wife pregnant with our second child, I was offered a job at the University of Manchester. When universities expanded all over Europe and my contemporaries were taking chairs in the South of England, I chose to become a professor in Scotland in 1966. When offered a chair at MIT a few years later, I turned down the opportunity to leave Europe for the United States. The choices I have made have not been calculated career moves; each was made in hopes it would further my education.

People who have heard me tell anecdotes about my experiences of places, people and times have suggested that I collect them in a book. This memoir is my response. Unlike an autobiography, a memoir is an extroverted book; the object is to characterize what has been observed as well as the observer. Evoking events from the past is a reminder that countries not only differ from each other today but also that every country differs from what it was when I started travelling more than 60 years ago. I can remember what places such as Oxford, Mississippi and Oxford, England were like when they were wrapped in their pasts. Comparing past and present emphasizes the truth in the maxim: the past is another country.

In accumulating the experiences encountered here I had the advantage of becoming involved in politics when politicians were more accessible. Leading politicians were accustomed to talking to other people without being protected by handlers. When I wrote to former prime minister Clement Attlee requesting an interview for my doctoral thesis, he replied in his own writing. Television cameras and YouTube had not yet intruded in what were then private discussions. Very few doctoral theses were written on contemporary (that is, 1950s) politics. Experience as a newspaper reporter taught me where to look for information, how to get access to policymakers who knew things I wanted to find out and how to establish empathy with the people you are talking to. Enjoying the visibility of a bylined Fleet Street journalist and a television election expert gave me a status among policymakers independent of that conferred by a PhD. This explains why much of what follows is set in the corridors of power or in streets where the rubber, that is, government, hits the road, that is, citizens.

A Memoir

This book is written for people curious about politics, people and places. Reflecting my long life and varied times, each chapter offers a different mixture of the three. As a sequel to my book *What Is Europe?* (Rose 1996), the opening chapters give an explanation of what sort of European I am. Chapters about universities refer to institutions that professors and students know today, but few experienced what they were like before the transformation of academic life began in the 1960s. Instead of offering readers an impersonal discussion of social science methods, chapters present my own approach to turning words and numbers into ideas for articles and books. With careful attention to words and examples, both statistical and anecdotal, it is possible to communicate to all kinds of audiences from undergraduates to an Oval Office incumbent. The style is inspired by Sir Philip Sidney, who emphasized *In Defence of Poesie* that writing can both inform and entertain.

Socialization of a Social Scientist

In geographical terms, almost all of my adult life has been lived in Europe but my mind naturally travels across national borders or continents almost hourly. My roots, described in Chapter 1, are in the border state of Missouri, a slave state held in the Union during the American Civil War. However, in its chief city, St. Louis, there was a sense of *Kultur* reflecting the enlightened influence of 1848 German immigrants, including my father's family. Cleavages of race, religion and ethnicity were evident and accepted. This gave me a good grounding in applied sociology. My schooling had disadvantages and advantages. Almost all the teachers had attended teacher-training colleges rather than having an academic education. This left me with lots of free time to educate myself. I could explore the streets of a big city and listen to jazz in bars and to Bach in more formal settings. I began learning about the world outside St. Louis by prowling the stacks of a well stocked public library.

Of the three places where I initially sought to further my education, only Johns Hopkins in Baltimore was a university in the deepest sense of that term. It was founded on the German model in 1876. This gave it a Central European vision of humanistic scholarship that attempted 'to reconstruct the civilization which had been in disarray since 1914' (Donnelly 1978: 137). I made the most of its library and of the streets of Baltimore and took my degree in comparative literature and drama in two years. In the year following at the London School of Economics, I learned about British politics by going to political meetings and about English society by talking to people who gave me lifts when I hitchhiked around the country. I explored European cities and countries that no one in my family had ever seen. Then it was back to St. Louis to continue my education as a newspaper reporter. I learned to get information by telephone, by knocking on doors, and by interviewing all kinds of people from policemen to the poet W. H. Auden.

The founders of modern political science in Europe were necessarily amateurs, for they could not be trained in a subject that did not then exist. I was the youngest and most amateurish among the group described in Chapter 3. When I was at the

LSE there was engagement with politics but not political science. Oxford was almost seven centuries old when I entered and the professor of modern history could be an expert on the 13th century. There was suspicion and even denial of the idea of social science. It was only after I was appointed a lecturer in government at Manchester University that I found myself in a political science department. It shared intellectual interests with the small band of political sociologists led by Stein Rokkan and Marty Lipset. I happily threw in my lot with them.

The explosive expansion of universities in Europe in the 1960s removed traditional academic barriers to change and made possible the institutionalization of political science as a profession. At the age of 33 I gained a chair at the University of Strathclyde in Glasgow. Chapter 4 sets out the programme of training that I developed while head of department there. The foresight of Stein Rokkan, the energy of Jean Blondel, and the generous confidence of the Ford Foundation made possible the founding of the European Consortium for Political Research (ECPR) in 1970. However, decades of effort were still required to create what we have today. When the ECPR first met, there were only eight of us in the room.

Experiencing history forwards

History viewed forwards is much less predictable than history in retrospect. The starting point of each chapter in the second section of this book shows a world very different from what we now know; it was unclear what the future would bring to places such as England under rationing, to Eastern Europe under Stalinist control or a Germany that ten years earlier had been governed by Nazis. Such uncertainties were not due to a lack of theoretical understanding by social scientists; they reflected the consequences of the Second World War.

England as it was when I arrived in 1953 still bore marks of Queen Victoria's reign. The Prime Minister, Winston Churchill, had been born in 1874, the leader of the Opposition in 1883, and people could be put in their class as soon as they spoke. When I read the expurgated version of *Lady Chatterley's Lover* I took it as an excellent novel about relations between classes. The prosecutor who sought to ban publication of the unexpurgated edition agreed; he asked the jury: 'Is this a book that you would even wish your wife or your servants to read?' (Rolph 1961: 17). My experience of the transformation of England is recounted in Chapter 5. Over half a century political change has been reflected in successive editions of a book of mine that first appeared with the title of *Politics in England* in 1964 but in the 2014 edition is called *Politics in Britain*.

I made for Washington, only an hour by train from Johns Hopkins in Baltimore, at the end of my first month at university and happily walked its streets. I still go to Washington now that I live 3,000 miles away. My interest in jazz made me very conscious of race. Chapter 6 records how I practised desegregation by following musicians and the changes that I have witnessed since first visiting the Deep South in 1953. It also records the changes I have witnessed in Washington. Working as a freelance British journalist I covered presidential nominating conventions from Lyndon Johnson to Jimmy Carter. Working as a professor, I have written books about the presidency and introduced the comparative study of presidents and prime ministers to an academic field that had remained parochial while national leaders were going global. Washington has changed from being a small Southern town to a city global in impact, its politics remains true to Congressmen Tip O'Neill's dictum, 'All politics is local'; the locale is the world inside the Washington beltway.

My academic friends thought it odd to study Northern Ireland in the mid-1960s, because nothing was happening there. But that was the point: I wanted to learn how a political system created in the aftermath of civil war could persist when it was supported by a Protestant British majority and rejected by a Catholic Irish minority who wanted to be part of the Republic of Ireland. No sooner had I completed an ambitious survey of public opinion there than civil rights marches began to disrupt the status quo. By the time my book on *Governing Without Consensus* was published in 1971, the killing had started in a three-sided civil war. Friends now thought it odd that I continued to research while thousands of people were being killed. Chapter 7 explains why the term civil war is a great misnomer and spells out my experience of politics when it became deadly.

As a byproduct of being on committees of the International Political Science Association, in the 1970s and 1980s I visited many countries in the Soviet bloc. I had no illusions about how its citizens were subjugated. When the reforms of Mikhail Gorbachev demonstrated that a seemingly powerful ruler can miscalculate, I was in residence at a West Berlin think tank. The fall of the Berlin Wall was a great challenge to social scientists to learn how ordinary people responded to the collapse of institutions that, like them or not, were integral to how they lived. In 1991 I launched the New Europe Barometer, nationwide sample surveys that systematically collected data about how people coped with the transformation of their polity, economy and society. Since then, more than 100 Barometer surveys have been conducted in 17 countries, some now in the European Union and others in a more or less post-Communist state. Fortunately, the questions I asked made sense both to political scientists and to the people who were interviewed. The experience of researching post-Communist countries at political ground zero is recounted in Chapter 8.

Learning to compare

Anglo-American comparison starts for me at the breakfast table, for my wife, Rosemary, is English. I have always sought to go outside this comfortable but narrow world to study un-American and un-British countries. In the course of time I have done fieldwork and published on many countries across Europe from Ireland and Portugal to Turkey and from the United States to Colombia, Korea and Japan. The third section of this book not only discusses issues central to seminars on the comparative method, but also things that are not taught there, such as how to find the black market up the Amazon and how to tell the President of the United States that he is following a policy in Iraq that is doomed to fail.

The more experience you have, the more necessary concepts are to categorize what is seen. Just as abstract concepts such as Gothic and Renaissance enable architectural historians to compare buildings, so we need concepts to turn anecdotes into data and transform what is observed into what is meaningful. Chapter 9 emphasizes a basic logical rule: We must name things before we can count them. Whereas learning to understand the society in which you are born usually occurs unthinkingly, comparative research requires soaking up knowledge of foreign countries and poking around unfamiliar cities and talking to people who live there. Years of going to the theatre have trained me to watch how people behave and what they say and to reflect on what I see and hear. This helps write questions that make sense to the people asked them in surveys of public opinion, as well as to those who want to extract conceptual meaning from what they say.

Up to a point, writing is a discipline: graduate students learn the rudiments of making a PowerPoint as I once learned the rudiments of drumming. Making a PowerPoint 'sing' requires both application and inspiration. After 70 years of writing, I still have to write each article and book line by line. I do not care for free form jazz or prose. I start by thinking about the theme and title before I write the first line of text. Since writing involves communication, one first has to find the right voice for a given audience. In Chapter 10 I draw on the experience of writing everything from television scripts to University press books to suggest how writing skills can be cultivated and how it is possible to communicate an idea in three minutes to a president as well as in 300 pages to an academic audience.

The concluding chapter is about the difference between the study of politics and of political science and how I try to be an intellectual arbitrageur combining the two. I founded the Centre for the Study of Public Policy (CSPP) at Strathclyde in 1976 to relate the undisciplined problems that politicians find in their in-trays to the problems that academics find in books. Like medicine, public policy can be scientific in searching for evidence and diagnosing a problem through cause-and-effect analysis. Whether its prescriptions will work is even more uncertain than in medicine. In addition, there are also conflicting views about what constitutes good health in the body politic. In my public policy work I have developed distinctive social science tools for analysing the growth of government and learning lessons from other countries. I have also learned that your ideas about the future consequences of current political activities can be politically unwelcome and take decades or longer to have an impact.

The Perspective of the Author

In the course of my career, I have drawn inspiration from two fellow Missourians, Mark Twain and T. S. Eliot. Twain's Huckleberry Finn rejected the idea that he should conform to conventions by going to school and wearing shoes. Instead, he explored the frontiers of knowledge in America's then Wild West. T. S. Eliot left St. Louis in the opposite direction, embracing the civilizations of Europe. However, this embrace was not uncritical. His writings also reflected the injunction of his Idaho-born mentor, Ezra Pound, to 'make it new'.

The political views that I hold are in the tradition of nineteenth-century liberalism in which the first freedom is freedom from the state (Berlin 1958). I

Signed photo of a Missouri Democrat, Harry Truman, before he became a statesman. Sent to myself as a Truman Democrat

have known enough refugees from authoritarian and totalitarian political regimes not to take freedom for granted. My commitment to liberty and law led me to join the American Civil Liberties Union when Senator Joseph McCarthy was riding high and to have a continuing concern with abuses of the rule of law in the United States and the United Kingdom. Reading Reinhold Niebuhr re-enforced what I had learned from tragic dramatists, namely, that moral men and immoral societies can and do co-exist. Governments can 'miss the mark' or, as in the case of Nazi Germany and the Soviet Union, hit the wrong mark. My political preferences are disciplined by the belief that social scientists should try to understand parties that win elections, whether or not they would vote for them. The judgments embedded in the chapters that follow will make clear that, to quote Winston Churchill, there are also some things up with which I will not put.

My initial party identification bespeaks my time and place; it is that of a Truman Democrat. Like Abraham Lincoln, Harry Truman was a self-educated farmer. Instead of looking charismatic, he looked and talked like people I could see any day on the streets of St. Louis. The only presidential vote I ever cast was for Adlai Stevenson in 1956. I would not have voted for John F. Kennedy in 1960 because the position he and his brother held on McCarthyism was the opposite of a profile in courage. Moreover, even in the White House he sought to avoid addressing the challenge of desegregation, a challenge that Lyndon Johnson understood and accepted.

While I have views on political issues, I find it difficult to imagine that there would ever be a political party that would consistently agree with me or that I would want to join. I have friends in all parties and none: the godfather of one of our children is a former Labour parliamentary candidate and of another was a leading figure in the Conservative Research Department. Although I am a European by residence and choice, my citizenship remains American. I appreciate the benefits that the European Union has brought to Europeans, myself included, but am ineligible to vote in the election of the European Parliament. After writing a book about how EU institutions do and do not represent Europeans (Rose 2013), I feel no more deprived of a voice in Brussels than the average European citizen and, through the access that my expertise has earned, probably have more voice there.

This memoir is not a straight-line narrative, because my life has not conformed to a plan mapped out in youth. It started as a trial-and-error search for something that would challenge my abilities and it continues to take novel turns in response to fresh thoughts and opportunities. In consequence, my list of publications covers fields that are normally kept apart by the boundaries of social science disciplines today. A Google search of 'Richard Rose' can be confusing. It yields some 188,000,000 results that refer to a number of Richard Roses, including a dead California mystic and a second-division English football player. Searching 'Richard Rose politics' reduces the number to 71,000,000 in which I appear in a variety of guises: Rose the writer on parties and elections, Rose the Russianist, Rose the author of studies in medical sociology, Rose the Northern Ireland scholar, and so forth. The diversity of my interests led to my absence from a Japanese introduction to political science with chapters that presented the big idea of a number of Western political scientists. The author assigned to write the chapter about me could not reduce what I wrote to a single theme.

As is customary in a memoir, the chapters that follow are organised topically rather than chronologically. Since many readers will not be familiar with the full course of my career, in the appendix there is a short curriculum vitae. A website, www.profrose.eu, has bits of journalism written when events discussed herein were happening; other materials not easily fitted into the text; and some photographs. Details of citations in the text are given in references at the end of the book. A full list of my academic publications is given as part of the lengthy CV on the website. While this is hardly my first book, it is a first in another sense: it is the first in which the only table is the table of contents!

Multi-cultural references reflect the way that I think and talk. Since no reader of this memoir could share all my experiences, this should make the book more interesting. I have tried to provide enough information in the text so that a reader not familiar with an allusion to Charles Gomillion or to Ernest Bevin can turn to Google for details. This avoids interrupting the flow of the narrative with detailed descriptions of what will be familiar to some if not all readers. Given the autobiographical nature of a memoir, I have followed the *Dictionary of National Biography* practice of drawing on private knowledge as well as on what is in print. A retentive memory for a revealing remark is the source of many quotations in this book. In addition, I have a set of pocket diaries that summarily record where I have been since 1953 and what I have written since and sometimes earlier.

An academic inevitably learns from those who have gone before. When starting my career, I was fortunate in becoming friends with many giants whose shoulders were broad. A number are pictured in the frontispiece of this book. I have also funded a doctoral dissertation prize at the European University Institute, Florence, in the name of Juan Linz and Stein Rokkan to reward the doctoral thesis that best exemplifies their broad and deep scholarship. I have learned too from people who have had to endure the effects of politics gone wrong in America's Deep South, Northern Ireland, Central and Eastern Europe and the Soviet Union. Michael Goldsmith, Karen Howes, Edward C. Page, Toby Sanchez and Donley Studlar made detailed comments on the manuscript as it progressed.

As a succinct form of acknowledgment, I am pleased to recount names of many to whom I have dedicated books, starting with my father, my mother and her family in rural Illinois, and Mrs W. A. Bemis, a teacher who introduced me to the study of global geography at the age of 14. My fourth book I dedicated to those from whom I learned early on: Bob McKenzie at the LSE; the tough taskmasters who edited my copy at the St. Louis *Post-Dispatch*; two Oxford dons, Saul Rose and David Butler; and my Manchester professor, W. J. M. Mackenzie. Successive secretaries, Margo McGlone, Isobel Rogerson and Ohna Robertson, have shown the capacity to cope with any load. Stein Rokkan, who learned about politics avoiding Germans in Northern Norway, has deservedly had two books dedicated to him. A book each has been dedicated to Rudolf Wildenmann, formerly of Mannheim, and to Heinz Kienzl, Vienna; their commitment to democracy was forged by keeping their inner beliefs alive when conscripted into the *Wehrmacht*. Richard Neustadt and William Mishler, friends as well as scholars, have also received dedications. *What Is Europe?* is dedicated to Juan and Rocio Linz, who first pondered this question in the shadow of the Spanish civil war. Appropriately enough, this is the fourth book that I have dedicated to my wife, Rosemary, who has been there since midway in Chapter 2.

Part I

Socialization of a Social Scientist

Chapter 1

The Roots of a Political Scientist

If someone asks — Where are you from? — almost everyone has more than one answer. You can name the city where you were born or where you live now; Londoners can give the name of their borough and a Viennese the number of their district. If travelling in the United States, saying you are from Europe can be sufficient to explain your ignorance of what the World Series of baseball is about. Saying you are from America can invite Europeans to ask if you know their friend who lives 2,000 miles from your home. History and politics have dealt older peoples of Central and Eastern Europe a more complicated choice: they can either give the name of the city or country in which they were born, for example, Breslau, then in Germany, or Wroclaw, the name it now bears as one of the largest cities in Poland. Naming your birthplace explains the soil in which you are rooted and nurtured, whereas your current residence shows where you have got to through choice or the vicissitudes of work and politics.

When asked where I am from, the answer I give depends on who asks, where, and why. The simplest answer, because of its multiple overtones, is to say that I come from a border state. If a precise answer is appropriate, then I say that I come from the States. This can then be elaborated by adding that I am from St. Louis like T. S. Eliot, and that Miles Davis came from across the river in East St. Louis. My explanation for not living in America now is that, since I couldn't get spit out of a trumpet, I went to Oxford. If asked in America where I am from, then I reply Missouri or St. Louis. If asked by a St. Louisan where I come from, then I reply, Clayton, the suburb of 15,000 in which I grew up.

If a cab driver in a European country asks me where I am from, the answer is usually Scotland. It is where I have lived for almost half a century and though not a state, it is an internationally recognised place. If a Scot asks me where I am from, the answer is Helensburgh, where the Highlands come down to the sea west of Glasgow. In pursuit of clearer international recognition, my academic base, the University of Strathclyde, has modified its name. Since few people know the meaning of 'strath'(a broad valley in Gaelic) and not many more know that the Clyde is the river that Glasgow straddles, it now calls itself the University of Strathclyde Glasgow.

The epigram — the past is another country — becomes more relevant the older one gets. Since I was born in St. Louis, the population of the United States has grown by more than 150 million people, while the British Empire, which once had upwards of a billion people nominally subject to its King and Emperor, has disappeared. Of the 28 countries that are now EU member states, most have experienced one or more changes of political regime, France has had four regimes, and Germany has become a paradigm example of a good European democracy.

The past is not so much gone as it is under foot. In the evocative German phrase it is one's *Grund das Wesen*, that is, the ground of one's being. It is the starting point for learning about politics. Socialization involves learning how to fit into your place of origins and what to make of the opportunities it offers. This is not only a question of what will grow best in the soil, but also what individuals make of their surroundings. Marcel Proust turned a small child's bedroom in his grandmother's house in a small French village into the first pages of his multi-volume search for time past. Aaron Wildavsky (1971) celebrated the fact that nobody ever told him he was wrong to go to a low-prestige local school, Brooklyn College, because it gave him the educational foundation to become a world famous academic. Only afterwards does one branch out.

Everyone, including people who become professors, learns about life in many ways besides reading a set list of books and crunching numbers in a computer. One learns from family and friends before going to school, and from books discovered in libraries as well as from textbooks. If you have eyes and ears and intelligence, there is a lot that can be learned by getting out of the familiar setting established by family, friends and school to see what else is happening in your native city. If all these resources are drawn upon, by the time one starts the academic study of social science, there is a fund of experiences against which the concepts and insights in books can be tested. To supplement the limited education offered in my school, I went to the library and explored the streets of a big metropolitan area.

Growing Up in a Border City

St. Louis is on the west bank of the Mississippi River at its convergence with the Missouri River. Together, the two rivers have a length more than twice that of the Danube and five times that of the Rhine. They drain the great mass of land between the mountains that separate the American Middle West from the once colonial cities of America's East Coast and what was in my boyhood the lightly populated Pacific Coast. St. Louis was founded by the French in 1763 and briefly under the Spanish flag. President Thomas Jefferson took advantage of local difficulties in Europe, that is, the Napoleonic wars, to buy from France the whole of the Louisiana territory, which included the great bulk of the lands west of the Mississippi. St. Louis was never under a British flag nor were there large waves of immigrants from England.

St. Louis boomed in the 1840s, making it a magnet for two groups wanting to leave Europe, Irish fleeing the famine and liberal Germans frustrated by the failure of the 1848 Frankfurt Parliament to unify Germans peacefully (Rippley 1984). My father's family were South St. Louis Dutch (that is, *Deutsch*). His grandparents were born in Alsace, whatever country it was then in. The family had arrived in St. Louis by 1860, for one of my great-great uncles served with Union troops in the American Civil War. When I was growing up, the bakeries, the beer advertisements, the turns of phrase and the surnames of many people were German in origin. Thus, the phone book entries under Sch- were as numerous as those for Mac in Scotland. When I visited Mannheim for the first time in 1965 I was struck by the faces of the older women I saw on the street; they reminded me of people I had seen at my grandmother's funeral. When I shut my eyes listening to an operetta on a hot summer night in a Budapest park in 1989 I was almost back at the summer opera in St. Louis a half century earlier.

America's entry into the First World War in 1917 on the British side led to a massive repression of German connections. Street names such as Berlin Avenue, Kaiser Street and Bismarck Street were replaced with American names. Helen Traubel, later to become famous as the first American to sing Brünnhilde, was growing up in St. Louis in a family in which even the dog was a German-speaker (Traubel 1959). After America entered the First World War on the British side, German became *verboten* as it were, and Traubel learned that her grandmother could speak English. On the Illinois side of the river, a young German-born baker was lynched by a mob stirred up by anti-German sentiment. Nonetheless, the late nineteenth-century statue of a great German liberal, Friedrich Schiller, remained in place by the City Hall.

My father, Charles Imse Rose, was born in 1901, too young for the First World War and too old for the Second. He went to the University of Illinois to study ceramic engineering, which was then developing innovative uses that were later superseded by plastics. He took a first class degree in chemical engineering and then a postgraduate degree (Rose 1923). Initially he worked as a research chemist for Union Carbide Corporation in Buffalo before deciding that the family coffee business suited him better than being the employee of a large bureaucracy. My father remained an applied scientist all his life. If you spilled something on your clothes, he would give you a lecture about what chemicals would remove the spot as well as spot remover. Later in life I realized that his engineer's interest in how things work is reflected in my curiosity as a social scientist (www.profrose.eu/about.php).[1]

My mother, Mary C. Rose, was born on a farm in Macon County, Illinois in 1901. Abraham Lincoln had lived in the county (Kyle 1957) and was buried in the next county a year after my grandfather was born. Her parents' families had come from England to New England before and after the Napoleonic wars and had migrated to settle on farms in Michigan and Illinois when there was free land there. My grandfather was a farmer and when he died in 1941 he owned five 80-acre sections, the historic unit in which free soil was platted. My mother's mother was born just after the Civil War in a part of Kansas where Indians were still around. Her mother died on the prairie and her father came back to Central Illinois, where she trained as a schoolteacher. To go to secondary school my mother had to board in Decatur during the week. A high school classmate was Harold Lasswell, who went on to the University of Chicago to become one of the founders of the behavioural revolution in political science. My mother went to the University of Illinois to take a degree as a domestic science teacher, where she met my father.

---

1. Here and subsequently, the citation www.profrose.eu calls attention to the availability of additional relevant material on this book's accompanying website.

Neither of my parents showed any interest in Europe nor had they seen the Atlantic Ocean until they drove me 900 miles east to start university in Baltimore.

I had the good fortune to be brought up in a home that was very secure. My father had not only kept a family business going through the depression but also built a house. He showed his businessman's disdain for politics by not registering to vote, so he would have no responsibility for any government nor would he be liable for jury duty. My mother voted but she never mentioned her party preference. When Decatur, Illinois, built two new high schools in the 1950s they named one after General Dwight Eisenhower and, for political balance, the other after General Douglas MacArthur. I infer she voted Republican. The absence of any political cues from my parents was balanced by the absence of any pressure to go into the family business or to pursue any particular professional career. Their policy of non-interference kept us close together until my father died at the age of 102.

Borders in many dimensions

The schema that Marty Lipset and Stein Rokkan (1967) devised to map political cleavages in Europe fit St. Louis with one fundamental addition. Race was the first dividing line. Missouri was a slave state that had been held in the Union in the Civil War, thanks to the Northern orientation of St. Louis and the federal desire to control the strategic waterway of the Mississippi. The 125,000 blacks were about 15 per cent of the city's population; the surrounding suburbs were virtually 100 per cent white. Schools were segregated by law and housing was segregated by real estate operators, but black St. Louisans could register to vote and had their own patronage machine. The rhetoric of politics was not that of the race-baiting South, but for blacks there were clear lines that could not be crossed and ceilings on aspirations.

There was also an East/West divide reflecting America's geography and the ethnic divisions of immigrants from different parts of Europe. To the west was the cowboy and Indian country of the Great Plains while to the east was the culture of New England. In politics St. Louis was Democratic and the Democratic Party was run by Irish Catholics. In my day, all the police captains were Irish, even though the Irish were less than half the party's vote. When I was growing up the Midwest twang of Harry Truman was familiar to me and so were Southern accents like that of Lyndon Johnson. New York and Brooklyn accents came from what was then almost a different world. When I first heard Jack Kennedy's voice on the radio, it sounded to me like that of a Boston cabdriver.

The city's religious divisions reflected the Reformation and Counter-Reformation, with some distinctive American twists. The gender division between the leisure centres of the Young Men's and Young Women's Christian Associations were less significant than the fact there were parallel Ys or their equivalents for white Protestants, black Protestants, Catholics (who were almost exclusively white) and Jews. The Catholic Church financed a separate school system and class differences were evident in the co-existence of separate parochial schools

St. Louis, old and new. The Old Courthouse, where Dred Scott was sold as a slave, and the Gateway to the West arch by the Finnish-American architect, Eero Saarinen, commemorating the 150th anniversary of the United States purchasing vast territories west of the Mississippi River

and high-prestige schools run by Catholic orders. Protestants were divided first of all by race. As one black clergyman explained to me, while Billy Graham was respected, 'He's a bit tame for our people'. German Lutherans had their own school system as well as a belief in their faith alone. The Southern influence produced many Presbyterians and lots of Baptists; there were a limited number of adherents of the Church of England. The churches were not in competition with each other. Religion was an ascriptive social characteristic that could be modified by abandoning it but not by converting to another religion. St. Louis reflected its 1848 German origins in being a stronghold of liberal Judaism. The chief division in a substantial Jewish community was not on matters of doctrine but ethnicity and class: there were even two Jewish country clubs, one for Germans and one for post-1905 fugitives from the Russian Tsar.

St. Louis was an urban island in a largely rural state. The difference of rural and urban outlooks was brought home to me through visits to my mother's family in central Illinois. Although my grandfather had retired to the city of Decatur, he had a chicken house in the back garden and would kill a chicken fresh for Sunday dinner. My father started buying Missouri farm land in the depression as a hedge against war and his investments turned unproductive land without electricity into good farmland. As a consequence, I now own some 165 acres of farmland and 60 cattle. It keeps me up with a different way of talking and thinking than found in academic seminars. It also encourages a respect for the uncertainties of nature and of markets, for an investment in farming cannot confidently be reduced to a mathematical formula.

Insofar as I grew up with an ethnic identity, it was that of an unhyphenated American. More relevant was my local identity. Within a multi-dimensional matrix of suburbs, the one in which I grew up, Clayton, was distinctive. It bordered Washington University and was prosperous. Most families had two cars and many had bought new homes there during the Depression. I never heard anyone talk about what the Depression had done to them. Although Clayton was named for a Virginia farmer who settled there before the Civil War, its distinctive feature was being the suburb of choice for the city's liberal Jewish community. This set its 15,000 residents apart from other suburbs and neighbourhoods. I had never been on the Hill, the nearby Italian neighbourhood that was home to Yogi Berra and good Italian restaurants, until after I had been to Italy.

Learning in Spite of School

The Clayton schools were a problem for me and I was a problem for my teachers. The schools were comprehensive in the sense that classes integrated pupils of all levels of ability. The school system's philosophy was life adjustment, which meant adjusting advanced pupils to fit middle-mass standards. This was meant to be progressive; for me it was regressive. Whereas Arend Lijphart's (1997: 243) small town Dutch gymnasium required him to study five foreign languages for a total of 26 class years whilst specializing in mathematics and natural science, the Clayton schools offered only three languages for two or three years each. To have something to do, I would take a book to school; my worst day in elementary school was the day I left my book at home.

Without knowing it, the school system was involved in a *Kulturkampf* and I was a leading *Kampfer*. Teachers were often raised on a farm and becoming a teacher was a way to escape the dreariness and drudgery of that life. They could teach us how to read and do arithmetic, but with few exceptions the teachers could not instil a love of learning for they did not know what the world of learning was about. A job teaching in Clayton was a big prize in terms of social mobility, for it meant a good salary and escaping the boredom of a small town. However, it opened up a big gap with students, who could look down on teachers as hicks from the sticks who could not relate to the pupils who, bright or not, were urban and mostly Jewish.

The great advantage of my schooling was that I was free to do whatever I wanted. Primary school teachers unwittingly introduced me to the horrors of Communism. In Lenin's terms, they were 'useful idiots' whose naive idealism and dislike of successful businesses led them to speak well of the Soviet Union. In 1948 they favoured Henry Wallace, the Popular Front presidential candidate. Their views made me go to the library to find books written by refugees from Stalinist

Russia. Their accounts of the inhumane methods used in pursuit of totalitarian Soviet goals gave me reason to value freedom from the state, whether the threat came from a megalomaniac Nazi or a dictatorship of the proletariat. The tolerance often shown for European intellectuals enamoured of the Soviet Union makes me wonder if they would be treated so kindly if instead they were apologists for National Socialism.

To escape the boredom of school, at the age of 14 I thought about entering the University of Chicago, which at that time offered very early entry to precocious youths who were mired in the wastelands of schools like mine. However, the syllabus was dogmatic, requiring every student to read Mortimer Adler's choice of one hundred great books, and I only wanted to read half of them. So I decided to go to secondary school in Clayton. Secondary school offered more variety: a few teachers were racial bigots but one was a Quaker pioneer of non-violent protest against segregation (Kimbrough and Dagen 2000). Another had Dutch parents and a knowledge of classics of literature; she helped guide my desire to learn more about everything. By the time I was 16, teachers were encouraging me to stay away from class and I was glad to do so. I took required courses in American history and sex education by correspondence. The most useful class I attended in person was teaching how to drive and park a car.

My schooling offered a very wide choice of extra-curricular activities and friends. I edited the school newspaper and was educated in the arts of hot metal type by printing craftsmen. I led the school debate team and won prizes in public speaking. The three pillars of the school's SES system were Sports, Education and Sex. I was active in the first two until being knocked out of football by a foul. We could read and talk about whatever interested us. We read Freud not Marx. Four-fifths or more of the school entered college. The bulk went to Washington University when it was a local rather than an international institution. Another large group wanted to get away from home and went to the University of Missouri, often dropping out without a degree. As one drop out explained to me, 'I was either going to have to start studying or become an alcoholic'. Four classmates went to the Missouri Penitentiary. Half my close school friends went east to university, for example, Harvard, MIT and the Wharton School of Business at the University of Pennsylvania. Classmates who turned to authorship have produced books on Henry James, Janis Joplin and Malcolm X. The other half have remained in St. Louis and made careers in such business as real estate, wholesale bakery supplies and selling chemicals to rural sanitation districts. Having such friends has helped keep me in touch with the a world very different from that of academics.

No one I grew up with was interested in religion for its own sake. It was simply a marker by which people sorted themselves, like class in Europe. One summer a friend got me a temporary job as a mail clerk in the local Jewish hospital. This taught me 50 useful words of Yiddish, all of which were expressive and half of which were printable. In one respect I was the odd boy out: all my friends were Jewish but I was not. Ironically, not being Jewish in Clayton may have given me some of the intellectual advantage that Thorstein Veblen (1919) ascribed to Jews, being more sensitive to society because of being an outsider. On more occasions than I wanted, my parents dragged me to services of the Presbyterian Church of the USA (Southern). Its headquarters were in Richmond, Virginia, as a consequence of a split occasioned by the Civil War. The Sunday School teachers dripped Southern accents and perfume. They gave me a familiarity with Biblical stories and texts that I find useful in understanding architectural monuments that happen to be churches and in following the texts in Bach's sacred music. But it did not alter my humanist beliefs any more than did studying Latin convert me to becoming a follower of Zeus. The unseen things I am most committed to are in the world of aesthetics.

Learning from the Library and from the Streets

Crooked teeth, a by-product of being born with a cleft palate, required making regular trips to an orthodontist with an office across the street from the local library. At the age of ten I had my library card changed to that of an adult so that I was not limited to checking out books for children. In my case, some of the books that I read were not suitable for adults, because of the difficulty of their content or their unconventional points of view. My parents subscribed to three weekly news magazines and these, plus the St. Louis *Post-Dispatch,* enabled me to follow the Second World War and much else. My older sister subscribed to *The New Yorker* and as a young teenager I read every issue almost cover to cover. My introduction to English literature was to read and re-read the 1,323 pages of the complete stories of Sherlock Holmes.

My choice of reading reflected a shotgun approach to the library's open shelves and a readiness to devour the works of any author who was interesting and wrote well. Instead of reading childhood classics, a central guide to my reading was H. L. Mencken, a polymath who left school at 18 to work as a newspaper reporter in Baltimore. He applied his formidable talents to writing scathing descriptions of politics and politicians; to promoting European writers who were then virtually unknown in America; and to producing a philological magnum opus about what he rightly called the American language. By the time I had left primary school I had read more than a dozen of Mencken's books, including his major philological work. Although not sharing Mencken's politics, I was influenced by his interest in European playwrights such as Ibsen and Shaw and respect for traditional German music and *Kultur*. Reading Mark Twain was a natural choice for a Missourian. His irreverence and wit were immediately appealing, for example, in his novel about *A Connecticut Yankee at King Arthur's Court*. This reading encouraged me to include vivid and pungent American phrases when speaking or writing English. One of my favourite examples is from the humourist Ring Lardner, who put down what the English would call a chinless wonder with the phrase, 'I would have punched him in the chin only he ain't got no chin'.

St. Louis was on the circuit for touring Broadway plays, so in addition to acting in secondary parts in school plays I was able to see what are now classics when they were fresh. Tennessee Williams grew up in Clayton and plays such as *The Glass Menagerie* are particular favourites because I know the kind of people he brought to life. Arthur Miller's politics were of no interest to me but the force of *Death of a Salesman* was undeniable. On occasions when under pressure from others to sign something I disapprove of, I think of the stiff-necked integrity of his protagonist in *The Crucible*. St. Louis has also produced a lot of writers (Cuoco and Gass 2000). The father of a friend of mine taught English literature to William Burroughs, who reacted by writing *The Naked Lunch*.

My introduction to Europe was through film. The immediate impression it conveyed was that Europe was about war, even though both heroes and villains usually spoke with American accents. A small art theatre imported classics from Europe. The films that remain in my mind were tragedies: the *Blue Angel* with Marlene Dietrich; *Open City*, an account of resistance in wartime Rome; and *Kanal*, a study of doom in the Warsaw ghetto, for which Andrzej Wajda's *Ashes and Diamonds* and *Katyn* are apt successors. John Ford's *The Informer* was a melodrama with a clear message: an Irishman who informs to the British gets shot by his fellow Irishmen.[2] An early introduction to tragedy on stage and film prepared me to appreciate accounts from Europeans about how they survived the Second World War and to recognise that one only meets those who survive such trials with courage and luck. This background has made me reject the liberal faith that if the right policies are adopted, or if our candidate wins an election, the outcome will always be a happy one.

Learning from the streets

In Dickens' *The Pickwick Papers* the elder Weller explains to Mr. Pickwick that he took great pains with the education of his son: he let him run in the streets of London from a very early age. The streets of St. Louis were nothing like so grand or so disorganised as those of Regency London but were still full of people and things to be seen if you had the curiosity to explore your environment and a mind to reflect on what you saw. Just as art college students are presented with an *objet trouvé* and told to look hard and paint what they see, so social scientists should be able to look at the lives of others and think about what they see.

My father was an unusual combination of being street smart and school smart. He needed this because the family business was selling coffee. Prohibition closed taverns and created a big demand for lunch counters that sold coffee. Some also sold alcoholic drinks made with chemicals that he had been taught were dangerous in a laboratory. Many places were run by immigrant owners who counted the cash in the till at the end of each day and preferred to keep it as long as possible before paying their bills to Rose Coffee Company. My father did not need to read Viennese philosophers to be a positivist: good intentions and promises to pay were nothing compared to cash on the table. Applying this maxim meant that when

---

2. Two movies that belong in this group I only saw long after I came to know the cities where they were set: the Vienna shown in *The Third Man* and *Odd Man Out*, set in Belfast. The comparable American movie is Clint Eastwood's *Bird*, an account of the life and early death of Charlie Parker.

President Roosevelt closed the banks in 1933 my father had hundreds of dollars of cash in his pocket.

My earliest venture in seeing the world was looking out street car windows during an hour-long trip to the baseball park; the views were less leafy and prosperous than my suburb. By the age of 10 I could go downtown on my own and rummage around second hand bookshops looking for old baseball books. My secondary school was a short walk from an old fashioned pool hall and I could go there after school. Shooting pool gave me an introduction to what Robert Merton (1957) would call 'theories of the middle range'. Instead of starting out with a theory of how I would sink all the balls on the table, I concentrated on getting in a good position to sink a second ball if my first shot was successful.

National radio networks opened my ears and my mind to a wider world. In terms of Merton's (1957) distinction between locals and cosmopolitans, radio turned me into a precocious cosmopolitan. I listened to Ed Murrow reporting from London during the blitz and the panorama of American states casting their votes in the roll calls that then determined decisions in presidential nominating conventions.

Local St. Louis radio stations offered a much wider choice of music than the two-party political system. As a small boy I liked hillbilly music played by the local Jesuit station in order to secure advertising revenue that helped it carry on through the depression. The local Lutheran station played Bach, Beethoven and Brahms and a network station broadcast the Metropolitan Opera live from New York on Saturday afternoons. One local radio station had jazz programmes for white audiences and another station played all kinds of black music for its audience. When I was asked to do a BBC Radio 3 broadcast on my musical interests, it opened with a tune that some people would call *Tannenbaum*, others *The International,* and a third group, *Maryland, My Maryland*. The music calls all three sets of words to my mind. The version I know best was written by a Marylander calling on people to support the Confederacy during the Civil War, because Maryland, like Missouri, was a border state divided by that war.

I started to learn to play the drums at the age of ten and for the next eight years stood in the back of the school band keeping up a steady beat. Band music gives a good sense of dynamics, and drumming makes one sensitive to rhythm and accents in prose as well as music. In the school orchestra I counted almost innumerable bars of silence waiting for the moment to give a cymbal clash. Since we practised music five times a week, this has made me familiar with the voices of a great range of instruments and conveyed a sense of orchestration useful in weaving together the themes of an article or book.

The big breakthrough in my street education came on my 16th birthday. This meant I could get a license to drive a car. Once I had actually learned to drive — this was not necessary to get a license — my parents let me use a family car in the evening and on weekends, no questions asked. Instead of listening to music on the radio or on records, I could go anywhere in the city, be it a symphony hall or a black bar to listen to what I liked and to see what the players, the place and the audiences were like.

In my youth bebop and New Orleans musicians competed for attention. St. Louis was the city of the ragtime piano of Scott Joplin and there were black musicians who had come up the Mississippi on riverboats and settled into menial jobs in St. Louis. When the Louis Armstrong revival took off in 1947, they got out their horns and started playing in the evenings in middle-class white venues. Young black musicians wanted to play cool as well as dress cool. In consequence, black bars would book white musicians on tour; this enabled me to strike a blow for racial integration in order to listen to tenor men such as Stan Getz and Charlie Ventura. Billie Holiday was an exception: she was a black musician who sang in a black St. Louis night club. She was neither hot nor cool; she was striking and she was sad. Charlie Parker was full of anguish. I will always remember how he would play long solos at Jazz at the Philharmonic concerts and then sweat profusely at the edge of the stage.

I lobbied my high school band master to arrange home-and-home concerts with a black high school and he did so. However, we did not share any conversation with our fellow musicians. My first meeting with black youths was in a Youth Group organised by the local chapter of the National Conference of Christians and Jews. For that group, religion was a bigger obstacle than race. Neither the Catholic diocese nor the local Lutheran synod would tolerate their youths mixing with tolerant Protestants, because faith and error did not belong together. Both black and white public schools did allow pupils to participate in planning an annual Brotherhood Day conference for youths from all over the then segregated city. Instead of talking about race relations, the organisers concentrated on common concerns such as the atomic bomb.

Unlike a European city, there were no channels for conventional political activity in St. Louis. There must have been a Democratic Party, since it nominated candidates, but it was a closed corporation that did not seek members. When I brashly went to an address the phone book gave for the local Democratic Party organisation, my request to join was met with a bewildered response. A few years later, when one of John F. Kennedy's family flew to St. Louis to urge Democrats to register black St. Louisans to boost the party's vote, they listened silently and dismissed the suggestion with contempt. Doing so would have broken the power of the local green (that is, St. Louis Irish) machine. In 1964 I was at a local civil rights meeting at which poll watchers paid tribute to the machine's capacity to deregister black voters so that they could not vote in the Democratic primary for black candidates and oust candidates with names such as Dwyer.

Before graduating high school I had met three tests for becoming a political scientist. For my age, I had had a wide range of experiences. I had developed a passion for writing and finding out things that could stand a political scientist as well as a newspaper reporter in good stead. Moreover, I was inner-directed rather than other-directed; I read what I wanted to read and did what I wanted to do without any idea that it was risky not to conform to the behaviour of a group (Riesman *et al.* 1950). The one thing I lacked was a normal academic education.

Chapter 2

Discovering Learning

Up to a point omnivorous reading is an asset. However, the very diversity of my reading meant that I was simultaneously digesting ephemeral journalism, political polemics and serious scholarship, sometimes from the same source. Moreover, being an autodidact carried with it the problem of having no one else to learn from. To learn from others you have to look up to them. This was not so much a problem for many of my European contemporaries, for English grammar school or German *Gymnasium* teachers were usually well educated graduates whom pupils could respect and learn from.

I needed a University that not only had a big library and a readiness to let me read as I liked but also professors that I could look up to as scholars. I enrolled at Johns Hopkins University in 1951; it suited my needs exactly and Baltimore was a city that suited my taste. Johns Hopkins allowed students to select courses according to their own interests. On my application form I said that I wanted to study the humanities and did so with lasting benefit. Because it was a research-oriented university, it was promoting a plan to allow undergraduates to proceed to a PhD as rapidly as they were able to do so.[1] The class list jumped from broad survey courses to postgraduate seminars with little in between. Progress was determined by what you had learned rather than how long you sat in classes. Thanks to my previous reading and taking classes morning, noon and in the evening college, I earned a degree in less than two years — and was hungry to learn more.

Under the guise of becoming a postgraduate student at the London School of Economics, I sailed for England in September 1953, thinking it was part of Europe. I made the most of the LSE's location in Central London, and it was a great base for a *Wanderjahr*. However, the London School of those days was much better suited for an undergraduate education. The big bonus, and the big surprise, was that in spring 1954 I met an English girl starting a thesis on 17th century New England shipbuilding; we became and remain close. My first priority then became finding a newspaper job and getting married. After an accelerated start to an academic career, I dropped out of study at the LSE and returned to St. Louis.

Becoming a reporter on the *Post-Dispatch* in 1955 fulfilled my childhood ambition and greatly expanded my education on the streets. However, after acquiring the very research-relevant skills of finding information and reporting it accurately, I concluded that I had had too much education to be satisfied with

---

1. The idea of letting Hopkins students proceed at their own pace had been introduced in the 1920s when Frank J. Goodnow, an early president of the American Political Science Association, was president of Johns Hopkins. It died for lack of student demand.

being a reporter and too little to quench my thirst for learning. After three years I dropped out of newspaper work and headed to Oxford to discover what I could learn there.

An Old-Fashioned University Education

Discovering education. Johns Hopkins was founded as the first research university in America. Harvard was then a college and Oxford was a collection of colleges that had considered and rejected the idea of becoming a research university (Green, 1957). Hopkins took Germany as its model for a University, and classics was an integral part of the curriculum. The entrance to the library had an imposing portrait of the founding professor of Greek, a native of South Carolina with a doctorate from Göttingen (www.profrose.eu/writings.php#america). There is a bust of Friedrich Schiller in the section of the library where I spent many happy hours reading. The rise of the Third Reich gave Hopkins a fresh infusion of Central European scholars. Refugees taught every subject from classics to economics. There were also home-grown scholars, such as the Biblical archeologist William Albright, a Methodist with glasses so thick he would turn a Talmud scholar green with envy. When the Dead Sea Scrolls were found, Albright could read and date them at sight.

Since Hopkins at that time had only 1,300 undergraduates and more than half were in pre-medical courses or engineering, humanities classes were small and undergraduates were immediately in contact with senior scholars. As well as practical briefings, every freshman orientation group had one lecture by a professor. My group was lectured by Leo Spitzer, a great Viennese philologist who looked like Einstein and could cantilever a cigarette ash out to lengths that would puzzle an engineer. Drawing on his knowledge of more than two dozen languages, Spitzer read bemused 18-year-olds a paper about stylistics in Romanian poetry (Wellek 1960). I realized with wonder and pleasure that I had finally found a place of learning.

In the humanities faculty Hopkins emphasized teaching through the historical method. History and literature started with the Greeks and the first-year history class stopped at the end of the Middle Ages. Because the political and cultural divisions of Europe were so different then, this approach was inherently comparative across time and space. Boundaries were contingent rather than fixed by the Iron Curtain or by the European Union or even by the Reformation. This evolutionary and comparative approach has been of lasting value in researching twentieth-century Europe, especially since the fall of the Berlin Wall and the expansion of the European Union. Studying architectural history, art history and the history of music further enriched my understanding of what Europe was like at different times and places. It has given me a stock of knowledge about who was creating what and where over more than 1,500 years of history, starting with the Copts. In addition, it encourages detours from the motorways and airports of Europe to see what Europe was like before there were cars or trains and it helps put in context the many places where I have given papers from Palermo to Umea and from Ankara to Dublin.

One of a pantheon of portraits that made me feel I was on the right path when walking down the corridor to the library as a freshman. Basil Gildersleeve, 1831–1924, professor of classical languages and philology, Johns Hopkins U. 1876–1915

My undergraduate major was in the Department of Writing, Speech and Drama. It was a pioneer in offering a master's degree to people who wanted to write novels or poetry and attracted students on that basis, such as the novelist Jack Barth. I didn't get to know him because he exempted me from the freshman composition class after reading my first essay. At that time the Department emphasized that the way to become a good novelist or poet was to study great writers of the twentieth century, whatever their country or language. The approach was thus inherently comparative. Professors not only knew the cities of Europe but also many authors, including the youthful T. S. Eliot, Thomas Mann, Federico Garcia Lorca and Sigmund Freud. The Department pioneered the study of Southern authors such as William Faulkner and Thomas Wolfe; lecturers had grown up in Charleston and Oxford, Mississippi, the homes of DuBose Heyward and William Faulkner (Rubin and Jacobs 1953).

I did not have the urge to write a novel or a play, but I did have the desire to read authors whose works formed the Departmental canon at that time. The literature seminars mixed American and European authors; thus, I was simultaneously introduced to Thomas Mann and Ernest Hemingway, and to Franz Kafka and Thomas Wolfe. I devoured them all, and then some. Among many images that captured my imagination was Proust's depiction of a fictional author, Bergotte, transcending mortality by writing books. Another came from Mann's story of Tonio Kröger, whose name symbolized a mixture of cultures, artistic and bourgeois. I empathized with Mann's readiness to leave his excessively bourgeois home in Lubeck for the bohemian world of Munich.

Aesthetic theories, starting with Aristotle and Longinus, were an integral part of my undergraduate education. This has given me a hinterland outside the linear worlds of time and space and independent of the politics of those whose works have specially moved me such as T. S. Eliot and Richard Wagner. The Greek tragedies of Aeschylus and Sophocles made a lasting impact. I can still remember the excitement of debating in class whether or not the protagonist of Arthur Miller's *Death of a Salesman* was a tragic figure, since he was not a great man and was not so much brought down by a personal flaw but by a flaw in American society. As a democrat, I took the view that ordinary people could be tragic heroes, that is, victims. I devoured all that William Faulkner wrote about the 'truths of the heart' among those who not only endured but also prevailed in his fictional account of an all too real Yoknapatawpha County, Mississippi. For relief I read Chekhov, whom I much preferred to Dostoyevsky, for his observations about the human comedy.

I chose the history of drama as my special field. This meant reading the text of plays in translation across time and space, a wonderful exploration of themes, ideas and places. My supervisor, N. Bryllion Fagin, had seen the plays of George Bernard Shaw and Eugene O'Neill when they were new and was happy to guide me through what happened afterwards as well as so much that had come before in the development of drama across the centuries.

My encounter with political science was limited to seminars in American Constitutional Law and Jurisprudence. They were taught by Carl B. Swisher, who was a scholar puzzling over the upheavals that Franklin D. Roosevelt had created when Swisher was a special assistant to the U.S. Attorney-General in the 1930s. Swisher was a man of great wisdom; I once naively thought you had to be that wise to earn a PhD! We took Supreme Court cases seriously, for hot political issues about race and civil liberties had not yet been resolved by the courts. McCarthyism was especially important at Hopkins, for Alger Hiss had received an honorary Hopkins degree shortly before he was accused of being a Communist agent. Senator McCarthy attacked a China expert on the faculty, Owen Lattimore, as a Communist and Lattimore was indicted for perjury. The last story I wrote for the student newspaper was of the federal court quashing the indictment of Lattimore.

The Korean War was important, for I was of military service age, and thought I might end up in Korea instead of continuing studying at university. This did not happen because of a law giving students temporary draft deferment on the basis of a nationally administered test. There was no problem securing a high mark when most American college students were studying non-academic subjects. After the Korean War ended, my temporary military deferment was made permanent because of a knee injury I received when fouled playing high school football.

When not in the library I could pursue learning in the streets of Baltimore, a big city with a racial, religious and ethnic structure similar to St. Louis but a century older. By systematically trying all the newspaper offices in the phone book, the small Baltimore office of United Press made me a stringer, that is, a reporter they could call on when events required. I bought a trilby hat to make me look older and got a press card to go with it. This gave me experience in writing straightforward news stories as well as street experience. I covered my first murder trial at the age of 19. The trial taught me that just because the accused claimed that he had been mistreated by police feeding him only cheese sandwiches for breakfast it didn't mean he wasn't guilty. On election night 1952 I met my first Member of Congress, the newly elected Eddie Garmatz. I wanted to get a quote from him; he wanted me to join him in drinking from the bottle of bourbon.

Exploring the East Coast was an important part of my undergraduate education too. New York City was the big magnet, for it had theatre, opera, museums, and jazz. I would go there for a long weekend or when there was a break between semesters and see at least one play a day and on days with matinees, two. I bought standing room tickets to see operas such as Götterdämmerung and Boris Godunov at the old Metropolitan Opera. Washington attracted me because it was a one-industry town and its industry was politics.

I wrote two BA dissertations. One contrasted the meaning of time in the novels of Marcel Proust and Thomas Wolfe, as Proust wrote about *Le Temps Retrouvé*, whereas Wolfe saw time as a river always surging forward. Concern with time keeps cropping up in my later work (see e.g. Rose and Davies 1994). My second dissertation contrasted the evolution of the poetry of T. S. Eliot and of jazz music. In *Four Quartets* Eliot abandoned the youthful radicalism of *The Wasteland* for the integration of time past and time present and of this and another world. By contrast, New Orleans music initially expressed harmony in a fresh and original way, whereas bebop showed alienation from the world of conventional harmony.

After three semesters of undergraduate study I was given a three-hour viva for a degree. Having shown ignorance in reply to a question about a minor English literary figure, T. E. Hulme, I went to the library to read what he had written. The next day I went to the Writing Department chair, expecting to get an additional reading list. Instead I was told I would receive my BA at the end of my second year of study instead of the customary four. This created a challenge: What to do next? An obvious step was to take a master's degree at America's leading school for the postgraduate study of journalism at Columbia University. My accelerated undergraduate course raised the eyebrows of its Dean, and he asked me to come to New York for an interview. After being satisfied with my answers to his questions, the Dean explained that he wanted to make sure that I was not a still wet-behind-the-ears boy wonder. The interview was useful to me too. I decided that a school with a Dean like that would not advance my education.

The alternative option was to do a master's degree that might give me a head start in getting a good newspaper job. One of my drama teachers had spent a year working on his thesis in the British Museum and was very knowledgeable about the plays he had seen there. It made London sound even better than New York. I applied to the London School of Economics to do an MSc in international relations, thinking this might open up a career for me as a foreign correspondent. I had no knowledge of England nor had I ever read a book on international relations.

Exploring Europe

In September, 1953, I sailed for England, thinking I could speak English. My first encounter with a cockney taught me I was wrong. Just as Europeans tend to think of America in an undifferentiated way, I grew up thinking Europe was a single place and by going to London I was going to Europe. In the course of a year I learned I was only half right. England was then very un-American, but it was also separated from Europe by much more than the 20 miles of the English Channel.

The LSE appealed to me because a master's degree could be earned solely by writing a thesis. I knew that I could write and there was no requirement to attend classes or sit examinations. My thesis topic was the Labour Party and Anglo-American relations, with particular relevance to foreign policy. I thought this would give me a fresh view of the United States and of the cold war, as well as some insights into politics in England. Although the Labour Government of Clement Attlee and Ernest Bevin had been firm supporters of the creation of NATO four years earlier, there were still enough anti-Americans to provide material for a thesis. They were augmented by 'useful idiots' who thought that the Socialism of the USSR was the same as British socialism or even better. I adopted the standard research methodology of the day: I bought packets of index cards and started filling them with quotations extracted from books, political pamphlets and newspapers.

After Johns Hopkins the LSE was a shock. While many lecturers were keen teachers of undergraduates, those I met did not show the breadth and depth of scholarship that Hopkins had made me expect. The weekly lecture of the Professor of International Relations was a commentary on affairs of the week and broadcast talks reprinted in *The Listener*. We joked that if that weekly went on strike he would have had to cancel his lecture. I abandoned my first two supervisors. Fortunately, my third was Robert T. McKenzie, who was then working on his landmark book on *British Political Parties*. He was also worldly wise about politics and ran a seminar in which politicians were invited and cross-examined about their experiences.

I adopted the life style of an American student abroad. I went to the LSE almost every weekday to do a couple of hours reading in the library on topics ranging from the topic of my master's thesis to Hayek and Orwell. I attended the daily and almost always lively meetings featuring politicians of every hue. *What's On in London* was a better guide to my week than the School's lecture syllabus. In the evening I walked to a theatre, Covent Garden or the Royal Festival Hall. I took advantage of studying in a foreign country to talk to people I could not meet at home, and almost all my fellow students at the LSE at that time were in that category. I was impressed with how sharp-tongued Indians damned Britain's treatment of their country and quoted George Bernard Shaw at length. However, when they started telling me with equal force about my own country, I stopped taking their views on faith. One fellow student, a University of Chicago graduate, began introducing me to social science ideas and authors that were then beyond my horizon.

The legacy of war

The marks of war, whether of victory or defeat or both, were still evident everywhere in Europe. When I went around the City of London to view the dozens of churches built by Sir Christopher Wren after the Great Fire of London in 1666, many were only shells because they had been destroyed in the *Luftwaffe* blitz of 1940–41. Older monuments were to men of the parish who had died in Imperial campaigns and newer monuments catalogued the names of those who had died in the Great War, renamed the First World War when the dead of the Second World War were added.

Aerial bombardment and the mobilization of millions for military service and essential occupations meant that the Second World War was a total war in which the whole British population was involved. People who had never worn a uniform could thus say that they had fought in the war and take a quiet pride in the country's resistance to Germany. When the subject came up, Londoners described the shelters they had slept in while the blitz was on and the difference between attack by slow-moving V-1 rockets, which gave lots of warning, and speedy V-2 rockets that could deliver death without warning. Food had to be imported in convoys that cost lives and was rationed on a fair shares basis that led to the improvement of the health of the population during the war. Rationing continued for a decade afterwards. I was fortunate in having a landlady with a birdlike appetite, so I could have bacon for breakfast every morning.

Hearing experiences from people for whom war was an everyday experience for six years was different from reading about it in a book. These accounts, along with my experience of civil war in Northern Ireland, have provided me with a metric useful in assessing rhetorical claims about 'intolerable' conditions or denunciations of democratically elected politicians as 'fascist'. An RAF veteran and fellow academic, Peter Madgwick, once said to me, 'People should not make such judgments if they were not in the Second World War'.

My 1,300-page guide to travels was Sir Banister Fletcher's *A History of Architecture on the Comparative Method,* a late Victorian study that systematically compared and detailed architectural styles across time and space. From studying the tenth edition at Hopkins I had learned how to date and analyze the structure of buildings, a useful skill when walking the streets of European cities. I began applying this knowledge in the streets of London and environs, and then hitchhiked at weekends to see sights further afield and further back in history. By the end of my year at the LSE I had seen every medieval cathedral in England and lots of historic country houses and villages where the industrial revolution and automobiles had yet to leave much mark.

In the month-long Christmas break I went to Italy with a list of places to see that I had studiously abstracted from Bannister Fletcher. Travelling alone meant I was talking to Italians or not at all. For my first evening meal all I could do was point, since I knew no Italian and no one in the restaurant spoke English. It was a great incentive to start learning Italian. The architecture and mosaics of Ravenna opened my eyes to the world of which Constantinople is the capital and started my interest in what was at the further end of the Danube. I went south of Eboli to see the ruins of Greek temples at Paestum. These experiences gave me a perspective on European history very different from that taught in the Anglo-American tradition.

During the long Easter vacation I travelled around German-speaking lands before the *Wiederaufbau* had succeeded in restoring what war had destroyed. Besides missing roofs, there were men with missing arms and millions of missing men. In Vienna I could not go to the Staatsoper because it had no roof, but within an hour of arrival I found an opera house with a roof that was doing Richard Strauss's *Salome*. I saw my first Soviet troops there, as Vienna did not gain its freedom from four-power occupation until October, 1955. The reconstruction of Germany had only begun when I celebrated my 21st birthday in the only concert house in Munich with a roof on it. Since I had a standing room place, I could beat time against the wall while hearing for the first time Stravinsky's *Die Hochzeit*. I quickly learned not to have a large glass of Rhine wine in the interval of an opera if I wanted to stay awake to see the next act. Frequent trips to Germany subsequently have shown me the capacity of people to learn from their past political mistakes and rebuild from ground zero.

One evening in March, 1954 I interrupted a discussion with a fellow student in the LSE Postgraduate Common Room with a statement that reflected my ethical commitment to culture: 'I have to see Martha Graham'. I showed my readiness to keep our conversation going by asking, 'Would you like to come with me?' I knew nothing about Martha Graham, about dance, or about the girl I was talking to. I quickly became interested in all three, especially the third.

Coincidentally, the following month I learned that the subject of my MSc thesis was fully covered in what was Leon Epstein's first book (1954). I decided there was no point searching for another topic; if ever I wrote a thesis, it should be for a PhD and not at the LSE. As newspaper work was then my calling, the sensible thing was to abandon postgraduate study and go back to America to look for a job as a reporter. In September, 1954 I sailed back home, but I left my heart in England.

My Education as a Reporter

My priority on returning to St. Louis was to get a job and get married. I handed in my CV at the city's two daily newspapers. The editor of the *Post-Dispatch* gave me an interview. After scanning my impressively intellectual CV, he asked if I knew what I would be doing at first, I gave the correct answer: 'Writing louse

*The Vienna Staatsoper closed its summer, 1944 season with Richard
Wagner's Götterdämmerung. The picture showed what followed. The opera
house reopened with Beethoven's Fidelio in 1955*

items'. This was the term for two-paragraph stories about minor robberies or the
death of a wholesale butcher. The interview concluded with the statement that
there was no vacancy; they only turned up if someone quit or died. So I started
knocking on doors of advertising and public relations firms to see if I could get at
least a temporary job until something might turn up on the newspaper.

I wrote to the *Wall Street Journal* and it paid for me to come to Chicago for
an interview. It was then a boring business daily to which my father subscribed
for stock market news. As the interview progressed it became clear that this was
not my kind of paper. I took the opportunity to call on the Chicago News Bureau,
which was accustomed to covering what happened in the Chicago of Al Capone
and machine politicians. This interview likewise made clear that while a job there
would extend my education it would not make use of the education that I had
already had.

My first temporary job was lobbying on behalf of a proposed scenic Mississippi
River Road running more than 2,000 miles from the river's source in Minnesota to
the bayous of southern Louisiana. The river drained 20 senators and its tributaries
added 20 more. A civic-minded St. Louisan was behind the project. If plans were
made in advance, he foresaw a Great River Road being financed by public spending
when the next depression came. This strategy had been successful in promoting
the extraordinary Eero Saarinen arch on the St. Louis river front. I spent several

months travelling from one state capital to the other assessing potential interest among people in state government and civic groups. In the state capital building in Baton Rouge I was shown with pride the chips in the marble made by the dozens of bullets that Huey Long's bodyguards had fired to gun down the man who had just shot Governor Long. My canvass concluded that a regular job wasn't justified.

Since America has a multiplicity of elections, my next job was as part of a public relations team campaigning for a yes vote on raising the school tax. If it failed, the tax rate would have been disastrously cut, so I developed the theme SOS (Save Our Schools). It wasn't going to fail, since the unions of school employees were behind it, and so was the local Democratic Party machine and school principals who got their jobs with the help of political connections. When I gave a short campaign speech I had written to Edna Gellhorn, an early suffragette, she threw it away and extemporized a talk better than I or her sometime son-in-law, Ernest Hemingway, could have done. The publisher of a weekly black newspaper with minimal circulation sought me out for 'advertising'. When I explained we weren't buying any in weekly papers, he claimed that he could influence a lot of black votes. In the previous school tax ballot he had been paid $2,000, a lot of money in those days-especially for votes that he did not have the organization to deliver. The tax carried without him.

After six months of temporary jobs I achieved my lifelong ambition. The publisher of the *Post-Dispatch* died and I came in at the bottom as a general assignments reporter. My first story made page one: it was four paragraphs about what happened when a pig being taken to market escaped on a city street. When not sitting by a telephone waiting for something newsworthy to happen, I covered such beats as police headquarters and municipal courts. Picture-chasing was part of one's training, going out to get the picture of someone whose crime had become temporarily newsworthy. One memorable assignment was to go to a bar where five people had been shot on a Saturday night. By the time I got there the bar was back to normal. After I turned in my account, the editor decided that what happened was hardly news and gave the shooting only a single paragraph.

The work of a general assignments reporter is as far from being a journalist in the English style as Oxford is from Southwest Texas State Teachers College, which Lyndon Johnson attended. Each was educational, but in a different way. You can learn a lot from people you wouldn't meet in a University seminar. The chief inspector of police taught me about 'blame avoidance' long before Kent Weaver (1986) published his classic journal article on the subject. When asked off the record where he might go to search for the missing witness in a case involving payoffs by her brothel madam to the police, the inspector replied, 'I think I'll go to Vegas'. When asked why, he replied, 'I think she's in Arkansas but I sure do like Vegas'.

Whereas the traditional academic reads written sources, a reporter creates written sources. The Pulitzer tradition emphasized the importance of knowing how to find information. Two reporters were ex-FBI men, and ten had worked on Pulitzer prize stories. The basic rule is simple: figure out who should know the relevant facts and go straight to the source by telephone or a face-to-face meeting.

Once I was assigned to call a list of telephone numbers that had belonged to a hoodlum who was found dead in the boot of a car. I asked anyone who answered whether they knew the murdered man. One incautiously replied yes, but by the time a reporter reached the saloon where the phone was he had thought better and said he wasn't there. Verification was important. I once wrote a story about a man who carefully told me his first name was spelled Sam'l. So unusual was this that the editor told me to ring him back to double check whether he knew how to spell his own name. In pre-Google days one turned to printed sources; most of the books on the shelves nearest my keyboard continue to be reference works. The American approach to writing hard news had little place for literary flourishes or political judgments. The basic principle was the lawyer's maxim: *Res ipsa loquitur*, facts speak for themselves (www.profrose.eu/writings.php#america). I have since combined this with the English practice of arranging facts so that they point to a clear conclusion.

Working on a newspaper meant that you met a lot of interesting people and many were your fellow newspapermen. They were tough and worldly wise about the ways of politicians, police and much else. Senior reporters with whom I worked had won Pulitzer Prizes for investigative reporting that led to the conviction of leading politicians. The labour reporter wrote a profile of Dave Beck, the subsequently convicted leader of the Teamsters Union, with extensive quotations that showed him at his most grasping. When I inquired how he had got Beck to talk so freely, I was told, 'There isn't anybody, no matter how big a bum he is, who won't succumb to flattery'. Early one morning I accompanied a reporter to learn how to cover the local courts; he paused for a breakfast that included four whiskeys. When lunchtime came I begged off joining him for lunch with an excuse of needing to return a library book. When a reporter with whom I was sharing a press room at the court house found that the half bottle of whiskey he was carrying was nearly empty, he exclaimed, 'Christ, I can't write a boating column with only that' and abandoned his typewriter in search of a refill. The crime reporter killed a man.

I supplemented my union minimum wage by selling articles to the *Christian Science Monitor*, *The Reporter*, and *The Nation*. I contributed unpaid articles to *The New Leader*, a New York intellectual weekly that was radical with a difference, for it was founded by Menshevik refugees and Daniel Bell was a onetime editor. I also learned about producing television programmes by designing and scripting a series of programmes on civil liberties for the local educational television station, KETC, which was then briefly run by visionaries from the University of Chicago. The series applied principles locally, for example, about housing segregation in St. Louis. The Christmas programme was 'The Religious Threat to Civil Liberties'. The most ambitious programme was a play that I wrote about the martyrdom of Elijah Lovejoy, an abolitionist preacher who was killed by a mob across the river from St. Louis in 1837. It won a small cash prize that I spent to travel to Chicago for a weekend to see its stunning modern architecture.

High culture paperbacks were then coming on the market. I maintained my habit of reading voraciously and indiscriminately with standards imposed by a publisher that looked to Lionel Trilling for advice. Culture paperbacks were reprints of modern classics from Johan Huizinga's study of life in the Middle Ages to Erving Goffman's *The Presentation of Self in Everyday Life*. With unintended irony, in Jackson, Mississippi, the capital of a very segregated state, I began reading E. M. Forster's *Howards End*, an extraordinary novel about English class distinctions. On my day off newspaper work I tried my hand at more sustained writing. After one chapter I abandoned trying to write an autobiographical novel, but did write a four-act play about the dissociation of reality from the world of the advertising and television images. After sending it to Joan Littlewood at Theatre Workshop in London, I was not surprised that it was rejected.

I was offered the job of being the *Post-Dispatch* art critic, with opportunities to travel with the publisher, who had a formidable collection of French impressionists and post-Impressionists. I turned it down on the grounds that if I wanted to be an art critic I would go back to school and get a PhD in art history.[2] When a friend asked what chance I had to become an editor, I realised that I didn't want to succeed in the conventional sense of becoming the editor of a newspaper: I wanted to stick with writing.

In the evenings I would write letters back to Rosemary Kenny in England. With a proper job and a military deferment, in April 1956, I took an 18-hour propeller flight to England and we were married in Whitstable, Kent. My parents, my sister and I were the only Americans at the wedding. Our honeymoon was spent in Italy as Rosemary had never been there and I did not know when or whether I would ever see it again. I never met my father-in-law, who was in the British Army in the Boer War and at Gallipoli, and then ran a business in the City of London. He died relatively young in 1937. My mother-in-law, Clare Amberton Kenny, was a formidable widow who, like my parents, showed a stiff upper lip in seeing her only daughter enter into what was then unusual, a trans-Atlantic marriage and moving to America without any promise of seeing her daughter again.

In St. Louis we settled into an almost normal young married life; my wife taught school and I worked a 40 hour week. My mother-in-law kept us in touch with England by sending bundles from Britain with Typhoo Tea and copies of the London *Sunday Observer*. Finally we suggested it no longer made sense to send tea; notwithstanding all our efforts, St. Louis water made English tea taste different.

By 1957 I had a trade in my hands and had learned a lot about where to look for information, how to ask people questions, and how to verify facts. I also learned how to write in a style that would suit the paper's editor, if not always myself, and how to spot topics that could be written up with extra payment in the paper's Sunday culture section. The years I spent working on a newspaper were well invested, for it taught me how to evaluate as well as write newspaper stories. Subsequently, this has saved more than two years of my time, for I know how to

2. Our daughter Clare did just this and publishes on the history of clothing and textiles. See www.clarerosehistory.com.

skim a story to find what is fresh, what is not and what can be set aside until it is or is not validated by events.

Notwithstanding the achievement of my youthful ambition to be a newspaperman, I was dissatisfied. I had had too much education to enjoy day-to-day reporting and too little to be a scholar. I decided that I did not want to make a living simply by producing stories that were a good read in a weekly magazine, as A. J. Liebling then did for the *New Yorker*. Nor did I want to become an English journalist with a style that could make any subject interesting, however little the author knew about it. Least of all did I want to be trapped in the routine of a daily newspaper like Ted Thompson, a St. Louis reporter who wrote *Leg Man* (1943), a good book in the Hemingway style about the career that I might have had. My last day as a reporter he was himself the subject of a short news item, an obituary recording that he had died of cirrhosis of the liver at the age of 39.

Writing about the forthcoming demand for higher education from baby boomers in the 1960s I realized that I might be able to earn a living as a professor. But first I had to get a doctorate at the best university in order to find out what I could achieve academically. The choice in my mind was between Harvard and Oxford. The latter appealed more because all that was required was writing a book-length thesis. Oxford was also cheap, easy to get into and I felt more comfortable in old England than New England. In 1957 I quit my job on the *Post-Dispatch* and headed for Oxford, thinking I was leaving journalism.

Chapter 3

The Education of Amateur Political Scientists

The founding fathers of the discipline had to be amateurs, for there was no institution to train them and confer a credential as a political scientist. Aristotle was a good enough political scientist to inspire Marty Lipset, but he did not have a PhD. Nor could he be a member of the Greek Political Science Association, for it was only founded some 2,400 years later. Nineteenth-century authors such as Tocqueville and Bagehot were likewise amateurs, participant-observers of politics with a reflective and perceptive cast of mind. They were able to develop what today would be considered interdisciplinary points of view because there were no institutional pressures to think along the tramlines of a single discipline. The term political science was used in the plural to refer to all the social sciences at the launch of the Ecole Libre des Sciences Politiques (Sciences Po) in Paris in 1872.

Before the First World War Europe was a continent of cosmopolitan Empires rather than nation-states. Reading and travel made scholars aware that national responses to political problems differed and were intellectually significant for just that reason. Distances between national capitals within Europe were (and remain) less than distances between major cities in the United States. While not trained in political science, the founder generation was certainly educated by life to regard politics as important. The primacy of politics within Europe and the remoteness of American institutions meant that Europeans did not have to pay attention to political thinking across the Atlantic, nor was there much of it.

Being cosmopolitan was the mark of an educated person. Early American PhDs studied in Germany, not America. Talcott Parsons, a Heidelberg PhD, was the last in this line. By the 1890s there was a first generation of doctorates from Johns Hopkins University, including Woodrow Wilson, John Dewey and Thorstein Veblen; that work was followed up by the University of Chicago, founded in 1896. At that time American institutions, like their European counterparts, required a reading knowledge in one and often two foreign languages as a condition of securing a PhD.

The attractiveness of America for young European academics grew greatly following the Second World War. At that time the leading American social science departments combined the innovative ideas nurtured before the war at the University of Chicago with traditions of political sociology that were rooted in Europe and carried to the United States by refugees. European universities such as Oxford and Heidelberg maintained traditional approaches and had neither fresh ideas nor large resources. Thus, it was not an accident that the leaders of the Committee on Political Sociology, Stein Rokkan and Marty Lipset, met on American campuses in the 1950s. However, established professors in European political science departments were suspicious of the 'bin-tos', that is, young

Europeans who had studied in the United States as well as in their native country. Traditional English academics rejected, often with contempt, American writings using unfamiliar terms; there was no willingness to differentiate between words that were needless jargon and those that were fresh concepts (Daalder 1961; cf Rose 2013a).

This chapter describes the process by which political science started to become a professional discipline in Europe. Unlike histories based on archival material, I write about the subject from a personal perspective, and one different from my European contemporaries. I had all of my undergraduate education in the United States and all of my postgraduate study in England. Moreover, my Hopkins and *Post-Dispatch* training emphasized viewing Europe in a comparative context, disciplined reading and collecting evidence. By contrast, the undergraduate education of my English contemporaries emphasized writing essays drawing upon English history and institutions that were debated in tutorials in which skill in defending an argument took precedence over evidence.

Before the Transformation

England had very old universities but they were not universities in the sense of having a strong tradition of research, especially in the social sciences. Teaching undergraduates was emphasized, and politics departments were usually smaller in size than in American liberal arts colleges specializing in the teaching of undergraduates. As late as the 1970s the government's education minister, Sir Keith Joseph, an Oxford classicist, insisted on changing the name of the British Social Science Research Council, founded in 1965, to that of the Economic & Social Research Council on the grounds that the study of society was not a science. This revealed his ignorance of the original meaning of the term science — to inquire into the cause of things — and the impact that this approach had in late nineteenth century German universities, not only in physical sciences but also on what Joseph studied at Oxford, classical Greek and Latin.

The capacity of England's governors to maintain traditional institutions by slowly adapting to a changing environment encouraged a confident complacency in the political system. This was re-enforced by having avoided dictatorship and military defeat, the recent experience of many European neighbours. Those political systems tended to be viewed as literally incomparable because they were un-British. In the early 1960s the suggestion that the House of Commons establish committees to supervise Whitehall ministries was dismissed by a government minister with an economy of multilingual insult as an innovation *à la Americain*.

Attempts to promote a British approach to the study of politics have struck me as a retrograde attempt to homogenize the way in which approaches to the subject have differed and innovators have often been Australians, Canadians, Scots and others outside the Anglican tradition, such as Walter Bagehot, who pioneered behaviouralism in his 1867 book, *The English Constitution*. I declined to contribute a chapter to the British Academy's celebration of one hundred years of British political science on the grounds that what was British was not necessarily political science and what was political science was often un-British. My American background was not a disqualification from my publications being one of the most cited British (*sic*) authors, with references scattered across seven different topical chapters (Hayward *et al.* 2003: 503).

Two institutions — the London School of Economics and Oxford — were of foundational importance for the study of politics in England. They had the most undergraduates studying politics as part of a combined degree in social studies and history and the most teachers of the subject. Virtually all teachers were recruited as amateurs and many remained opposed to the very idea of politics as a subject for scientific study. The Political Studies Association (PSA), founded in 1951, was not a political science association because some leading members objected to the idea that the study of politics could be scientific. The Warden of Nuffield, D. N. Chester, vetoed calling the body the British PSA on the characteristically parochial grounds that 'We would always know who we were and any foreigners who didn't know were betraying their own ignorance'. As late as 1963 the PSA refused to allow a publisher to display its politics books at the PSA's annual conference (Grant 2010: 36; 22).

The London School of Economics

Shortly before they helped found the Labour Party, leading Fabian socialists such as Beatrice and Sidney Webb founded the London School of Economics (LSE) in 1895. They sought to promote knowledge that could be used to change society, a practice the Webbs had pioneered in studies of poverty supported by the substantial family income of Beatrice Webb. Fabians believed that society could be improved, and socialism offered the best guiding principles. Staff were recruited, such as the future Labour prime minister Clement Attlee, because they shared the Webbs' commitment to political change, not because of their knowledge of any academic literature. Attlee had passed his time reading poetry at Oxford and took the Oxford equivalent of Franklin D. Roosevelt's 'gentleman's C' at Harvard. The commitment to having a political impact was continued under William Beveridge, a pioneer of unemployment insurance policy, as director from 1919 to 1937.

The first professor of politics at the LSE, Graham Wallas, wrote an innovative book, *Human Nature and the Study of Politics,* but at the wrong time, 1908, and in the wrong place. Had he published it at the University of Chicago, Wallas would have been honoured as one of the founders of the behavioural approach to political science. As it was, four decades after publication in England an official report lamented that his work had been 'inadequately followed up' (quoted in Grant 2010: 15). Harold Laski's long tenure as professor from 1926 to 1950 was a dominant influence. Laski was a widely read Oxford graduate and popular lecturer on political theory, spicing what he said with anecdotes, mostly true, about his involvement with politicians. He was a propagandist for an increasingly Marxist definition of socialism and it was his year to hold the rotating chairmanship of the Labour Party when it won the 1945 election. When Laski started making statements about what the Labour government should do, Prime Minister Attlee sent him a laconic note saying, 'A period of silence on your part would be welcome'. Laski's politics had an impact; his extravagant left wing claims pushed into the Conservative Party a sceptical student who later became my wife.

Ironically, the best book written during Laski's tenure was R. O. Bassett's (1935) justification of British consensus politicians at a time when continental Europe was going fascist or Communist. Bassett was marginalized for saying this, since his position was in effect an endorsement of Ramsay Macdonald, who switched from being a Labour prime minister to a coalition prime minister in the crisis of 1931. When Laski died in 1950, the School's governors chose a conservative as his successor, Michael Oakeshott. His inaugural lecture defined political education in the classic English sense as learning what had been said and done in the past. It made him an inspiration for Conservatives who did not want to examine the premises of their position. Oakeshott rejected the idea of political science expressed in the LSE's motto, *rerum cognoscere causas* (to know the cause of things).

The LSE Department in which I enrolled to do research in 1953 had no research agenda. After hearing a good lunchtime talk by an LSE lecturer I immediately went into the library to read his books. All I could find was that his wife had written a book. Bob McKenzie was kept at arms length because he drew on such alien writers as Schumpeter and Michels for his classic study of British political parties (1955). When I mentioned at an LSE interview for a post-doctoral fellowship in 1960 that I was writing a paper for a conference organised by Stein Rokkan, Professor W. A. Robson remarked, 'The most boring person I ever met'. Fortunately, I did not get the job. A few years later, after getting a lectureship at Manchester, I was invited to give a seminar at the LSE. When I sent in my request for a train fare from Manchester, the department had no budget to reimburse visitors. The LSE lecturer who invited me reimbursed my train fare with his personal cheque. Being a poorly paid academic with three children to support, I cashed it.

When university expansion came, the LSE contributed many professors and staff to new departments. They were not among the pioneers in professionalizing political science in England. The first LSE professor who saw himself as a political scientist was not appointed until 1976. The first holder of the Sidney and Beatrice Webb professorship of public policy, appointed in 2001, is Ed Page, a Strathclyde PhD. The professionalizing of the School had costs. During his time as director Ralf Dahrendorf, a broadly educated political sociologist in the best German sense, unhappily saw its Economics Department abandon the requirement that economists needed to study any economic history in order to produce dynamic econometric models.[1]

---

1.   To see how the LSE has changed, go to www.lse.ac.uk/government/home.aspx.

Oxford

Oxford has always been an attractive setting for passing time; study was optional. In the late nineteenth century this was formalized in the distinction between taking a pass degree and an honours degree. For some people, matriculation at Oxford was sufficient. When I was there in the late 1950s two undergraduates dropped out because a sudden death required them to go into the family firm. The firm was a family-controlled seat in the House of Commons. What was learned to pass exams was a limited fraction of the education that Oxford offered.

When Oxford was under pressure to reform in the late nineteenth century there was a battle about what it should become. Mark Pattison wanted Oxford to become a centre of research on the German model. Benjamin Jowett wanted it to be a place to groom the best and the brightest to win the glittering prizes that London had to offer. The subject studied was less important than being good at it. T. B. Macaulay had declared that recruitment to the civil service on merit meant that if the test of merit was knowledge of the Cherokee language, then the pupils who were best at translating Cherokee would make the best civil servants (quoted in Rose 1964: 42). Jowett considered Latin and Greek sufficient, but without the commitment to serious scholarship that marked the study of the subject in Germany. The maxim — the unexamined life is the life not worth living — might have been familiar in classical Greek, but it was not deemed relevant to contemporary Oxford. The University was sufficiently open to talented young people whatever their family background to make it possible for youths from non-U families (a term referring to social class, not education) to use it as a stepping stone to Downing Street, as Harold Wilson and Edward Heath did. Sir Alec Douglas-Home had matriculated at Oxford and played cricket there.

The study of politics was introduced in 1920 as part of a degree in Philosophy, Politics and Economics (PPE). The degree was described as Modern Greats in an attempt to give it a bit of the cachet of the study of 'great' Greats, that is, the world of Greece and Rome. The classicists saw to it that there were two compulsory papers of sight unseen translations from French, German or Italian. There was no paper on political institutions, let alone comparative institutions. The term modern was relative: the two historical papers started in 1760. Each was taught in eight-week tutorial modules, in which an undergraduate read an essay on a set question for debate, and the tutor then commented. Argument, not evidence, came first. If an Oxford don was expected to listen to as many as 16 undergraduates reading essays aloud each week, any argument that would keep you awake would be welcome. When my grant ran out in 1960 I briefly took tutorials in the comparative political institutions of France, the Soviet Union and the United States. I set pupils the same essay topic — the power of the American presidency in the first and then in the eighth week of the term — in order to see how much they might have learned meanwhile.

There were two professors in politics at that time, one in political theory named after a fourteenth-century Archbishop and prosecutor of heretics, and the other named after the late nineteenth-century prime minister William Gladstone and normally held by a historian. The marginalization of contemporary political science continued up to the 1980s (www.profrose.eu/writings.php#studying; Stepan 2007). The dominant tradition was established by A. V. Dicey's dogma of the sovereignty of parliament, which narrowed the subject to a legalistic debate about how to interpret his *obiter dicta*. When I mentioned Dicey to W. J. M. Mackenzie, whose first hand knowledge of Oxford went back to the 1920s, he groaned and said, 'It all went wrong when Dicey was jobbed into a chair there in the 1880s'. Mackenzie left Oxford in 1949 to take a chair in Manchester, and another pioneer of political science, S. E. Finer, left in 1949 to become professor in the innovative University of Keele.

Most of the fellows teaching politics in Oxford were amateurs with no desire to become political scientists. In the 1930s an Oxford don noted, 'The subject is taught by a very few specialists and a large number of philosophers and historians who approach it with varying degrees of enthusiasm or disgust'. (R. B. McCallum quoted in Chester 1986: 48). John Redcliffe-Maud (1981: 21ff) was happy to become the first Oxford politics fellow because he reckoned his undergraduate examination results were not good enough to get him a fellowship teaching classical history and languages. Some dons spent a decade or two producing a single book, typically a work of history. Non-publication did not mean a lack of a good mind; there was simply no expectation that an Oxford don would do research. Being a don was a status rather than an activity. Even as recently as a decade ago the answer to a Princeton professor's question 'What are you working on?' was a puzzled look and the statement: 'I am an Official Fellow of X College'.

To enter Oxford you had to be admitted to one of two dozen male colleges. I wrote brief letters of inquiry from St. Louis to half a dozen colleges and promptly received back letters offering me a place and, as an addendum, asking me to complete a one-page admission form. In 1957 I matriculated at Lincoln College, founded in 1427 to fight the heresies of John, Wycliffe, who called for the translation of the Bible into English. The College entrance form asked for religion; I put down 'Protestant' and was not asked to read a lesson in the College chapel. It also asked my father's rank, profession or status. I put down merchant. University matriculation involved being marched in groups through the fifteenth-century Divinity School and a formula was muttered in Latin. This rite, not taking a degree, made you 'U', that is, accepted as a member of the Oxford community.[2]

Lincoln was then a typical undergraduate college and I spent three terms living in a college house with undergraduates. The effects of rationing were still visible. A friend would look at an orange very carefully before peeling it, as during the war an orange had been a Christmas treat. When I put potatoes in my soup at lunch to make it edible, a fellow student remarked: 'I haven't seen anyone eat like that since my uncle came back from the Japanese prisoner-of-war camp'. I spent one afternoon each weekend walking around a single college, studying its architecture and furnishings in detail. Typically they had been agglomerated over 400 or 500 years. Whenever I walked or bicycled between buildings I educated my eye on

---

2.   The Oxford of today has changed greatly from what I am describing; *see* www.politics.ox.ac.uk.

the townscape built up over 600 years (see Sharp 1952). It was an extraordinary education.

My grand tour of Europe was completed in the summer vacation of 1958 by spending five weeks with my wife and a friend driving from London to Istanbul and back, with a detour via Athens and Crete. As we drove from the old Habsburg Empire to that of the Ottomans we moved back centuries in time. In Yugoslavia we saw peasants, as in Biblical times, separating wheat from chaff by throwing it into the air. The places where petrol could be bought ranged from an old caravanserai to a military airport. At Edirne in Thrace we saw the first signs of the greatness of the Ottomans in the Selimye mosque of Sinan. At the Venice Biennale the Soviet Union's display of its art was closer to the kitschy covers of the *Saturday Evening Post* than to New York's Museum of Modern Art.

Following the advice of a few Oxford graduates I had met in America, I initially registered to do an undergraduate degree in PPE. After two tutorials I realised that this was a mistake and promptly re-registered to do a DPhil. The title emphasized the Oxford desire to distance itself from the German and American PhD (Simpson, 1983). It was only introduced at the end of the First World War to accommodate American scholars expecting Oxford to offer something higher than the Master's degree, which could not be earned but could be purchased by anyone who had an Oxford undergraduate degree. In 1946 Oxford introduced a BPhil. in politics, a two-year degree taught at a higher standard than the undergraduate degree but similarly emphasizing essays and argument. It was regarded as superior to the alien doctorate (Chester 1986: 164). At dinner dons preferred to wear an MA gown rather than that of a doctorate. I have seen Oxford fellows visibly wince when the uninitiated addressed them as 'Doctor'.

I was a second-class citizen because the lack of an Oxford BA meant that I was ineligible to buy an MA and could only wear a doctoral gown. When people ask me where I was trained, the answer is, 'I am untrained; I have an Oxford DPhil'. It was not awarded for a thesis in political science, a term damned by its foreign origins. It was awarded by the Faculty of Social Studies. Ironically, the lack of training left me open to read widely across disciplines without any sense of trespassing. It explains why I think of myself as a social scientist as well as a political scientist.

It was the heyday of linguistic philosophy during my time at Oxford. My contemporaries agonized with Wittgenstein and sought freshness with Ayer. This was a rigorous discipline in being careful about the use of words. Bob Putnam recalled that eight hours of tutorials about linguistic philosophy with Alasdair MacIntyre enabled him to coast through his first year of graduate study at Yale by translating jargon words into clear concepts that could be useful in empirical research. While I had no desire to spend all my life pondering imponderables, familiarity with this approach has enhanced my literary sensitivity to traps in the use of words as concepts and labels for quantitative indicators. However, I decided it was sterile to debate the meaning of meaning without simultaneously trying to engage with the meaning of what one could experience outside the seminar room.

At that time the only requirement to obtain an Oxford doctorate was to write and defend a thesis. This attracted me as I could write and had a topic to write about: the contradiction between principles of socialist foreign policy developed within the British Labour Party over two generations in opposition and what the Labour government of Clement Attlee did when in office from 1945 to 1951. It reflected my Pulitzer-trained scepticism about what politicians said compared to what they did. Labour's 1945 election manifesto promised a socialist foreign policy based on principles such as left talking to left and reliance on the United Nations. The one qualification to the leftwing bias of the manifesto was a sentence inserted by Hugh Dalton, who expected to be Foreign Secretary. He explained to me that while he couldn't outvote the fellow travellers on the party's manifesto committee, he could add a sentence that could be used to justify a Labour government standing up to the Soviet Union. Since the Attlee government's pro-NATO foreign policy produced recurring backbench revolts from the party's left, my thesis had a lot in it about domestic party politics.

The standard British working week was then 44 hours, so this was the time that I devoted to my thesis each week, and kept a daily count of the hours spent to make sure that this was done, as it took months to go through my primary sources. The starting points were paging through the Annual Conference Report of the Labour Party since 1900, that of the Trades Union Congress since 1894, and *The Times* and *The Manchester Guardian* daily from 1944 to 1952. I have thus been reading British daily papers for the past 70 years. I also read all the foreign affairs debates in the House of Commons' *Hansard*. Since Oxford is a copyright deposit library, almost every publication I wanted to consult was there. During the vacations I worked in the Library of the Labour Party at Transport House. Photocopying was not yet available so I took handwritten notes with an old fashioned ink pen and used hundreds of 3 x 5 file cards. I interviewed members and critics of the government from Clement Attlee to Konni Zilliacus, a fellow travelling rebel, and ended up an admirer of the Labour Foreign Secretary, Ernest Bevin.

My DPhil supervisor, Saul Rose of St. Antony's College, had been Denis Healey's successor as International Secretary of the Labour Party. He was chary of ideas and fastidious about the use of words, being literate in four alphabets plus Japanese. After a year, I was elected to a Studentship at Nuffield College; this included a grant that covered the cost of myself and my wife and our first child. Nuffield was, and remains, a College confined to postgraduate studies, which made it unusual in Oxford terms. However, the ethos had a lot in common with PPE; for example, there was no training of any sort. Quantitative studies took the form of the Warden asking, in response to a seminar paper on a legal dispute arising from building a wall to segregate middle-class from working-class housing in Oxford, 'What was Sir Stafford Cripps' fee?' In another seminar two Fellows of All Souls debated whether Lenin's statement that under Communism the urinals would be made with gold referred to the metal parts only or to the larger ceramic bowl as well. David Butler ran an excellent seminar in which he invited a politician up from London to answer questions prepared by a knowledgeable member of the College. This avoided the politician giving an empty speech, for the questions were pointed and British politicians were still trained to answer criticisms directly rather than evade them with the Blairite cry, 'Trust me'.

A team of Nuffield students using slide rules to calculate swing for the BBC election night programme, 1959. Richard Dimbleby and David Butler are in the background and I am in the centre with a pen in hand

Thanks to being able to type and wanting to earn a doctorate, I completed my DPhil in 24 months (Rose 1960).[3] It was the summer of 1959 and by coincidence a British general election was called that autumn. David Butler invited me to go along for the ride when he drove around constituencies to get the feel of the election. As preparation I read all the British and American voting studies that had then been written. The biggest impact was made by the appendix of Berelson, Lazarsfeld and McPhee (1954: 327–47); it listed propositions about voting derived from American surveys and in principle applicable to Britain. The 1959 election saw campaigning radically altered by the Conservatives introducing modern methods of political advertising and Labour introducing modern television techniques. As I was already familiar from my work in St. Louis with both advertising and television, I volunteered to write a chapter on public relations and ended up as the co-author of an innovative Nuffield election study, *The British General Election of 1959* (Butler and Rose 1960).

---

3.   Because my potential London publisher could not get a New York publisher to share the costs, the only publication from the thesis was an Op Ed article in the *Manchester Guardian* (www. profrose.eu/writings.php#england).

Interviewing politicians about how they sought votes revealed that they did not know any more about what made British voters tick than did David Butler and myself. So I went straight to source, two LSE PhDs in sociology who had founded survey research firms in the 1930s, Mark Abrams of Research Services Ltd, and Henry Durant, who had been given the franchise for the British Gallup Poll. They had evidence that could not be found in University libraries. Abrams invited me to contribute chapters to a Penguin special, *Must Labour Lose?* (Abrams and Rose 1960). My contribution built on a book that David Butler had given me because he did not have time to read it himself as he was going to America to observe the 1960 American election. The book was *The American Voter* (Campbell *et al.* 1960); it showed how carefully designed and analyzed surveys could provide an understanding of the behaviour of voters. This approach was different from the argument and speculation then prevailing in England; the use of evidence was also consistent with my Pulitzer training.

In 1960 Oxford appointed Norman Birnbaum, a leftwing American sociological theorist, as a fellow in sociology. In my last term there Birnbaum gave a small reading seminar that introduced the curious few to canonical works of sociology. When my proud father offered to buy me the red and blue silk gown of an Oxford DPhil at a cost of almost four weeks of an ordinary worker's wage, I asked instead for some Free Press books by Max Weber (1947), Robert Merton (1957), and a reader by Eulau, Eldersveld and Janowitz (1956). My mother airmailed me a copy of Marty Lipset's newly published *Political Man* (1960). One lucky day the Warden of Nuffield's secretary inquired if I would like to meet a visiting Norwegian who had asked about me: it was Stein Rokkan.

In autumn 1960, I had a doctorate, a wife and almost two children, but no job. David Butler told me that he did not think I was cut out for an academic career in England. By his standards, his judgment appeared correct; both Nuffield and LSE turned down my applications for post-doctoral fellowships. Since there were lots more universities in America than in England, I wrote 34 letters to American political science departments seeking employment. My Oxford doctorate had not prepared me for working in an American political science department. When asked at a job interview what I thought of Anthony Downs' *An Economic Theory of Democracy*, published three years earlier, I had to confess ignorance because no one in Oxford had talked about the book. This experience prompted me to join the American Political Science Association and start reading the *APSR* from cover to cover in an effort to reduce my ignorance. The only institution showing any interest was Michigan, but James K. Pollock turned down my application for an instructorship there. For too many months I scanned the British press for an advertisement of a job teaching politics. None appeared. Although I had succeeded in achieving two great youthful goals — I had a doctorate and had written a book — I was unemployed and perhaps unemployable in the British academic world.

Manchester Made Me

One morning in autumn 1960 I picked up my mail and found the offer of a job from W. J. M. Mackenzie in the Government Department at Manchester. This was a surprise, as I had not applied for a job there nor had one been advertised. I began to learn political science as an assistant lecturer in the Department of Government at the University of Manchester in 1961. It was Europe's closest equivalent to the social science faculty of the University of Chicago in the 1930s. Manchester attracted people who wanted to be professionals rather than amateurs and Manchester is a big city as different from Oxford as Chicago is from Princeton. Up to the beginning of the 1960s Manchester had a faculty rather than a departmental seminar with economists, anthropologists and political scientists scrutinizing whatever was presented in terms of both theory and practice (Chapman and Potter 1974).

The Government Department at Manchester was very stimulating, even though it then had less than a dozen members. When I arrived to meet my colleagues, Tony Birch challenged me by asking, 'Are they still doing elections in Oxford? We gave them up five years ago'. Unlike Oxford, Manchester colleagues talked about social science books and ideas, and I learned from following their lead. The books included Karl Polanyi's *Great Transformation,* a study of the Industrial Revolution, which began in Lancashire, and Bob Dahl's *Who Governs?*, a pioneering empirical study of power. I noticed that Dahl looked primarily at 'nice' issues rather than those that a Pulitzer-trained reporter would have examined, such as the police, race relations and who made lots of money from urban redevelopment.

The central influence in the Manchester Department was its sole professor, W. J. M. Mackenzie, a classical philologist by training, and a big man in every sense (www.profrose.eu/people.php). His idea of politics reflected wartime experience in Whitehall, when the battles about who to bomb were matters of life and death for the RAF as well as Germans. Even though Mackenzie had won many glittering Oxford prizes, he was a Scot who saw himself as an outsider. He once asked me: 'How old were you when you came to England, Richard? I was 19.'

Bill Mackenzie and I shared the first year undergraduate lectures, an introduction to British and American politics. My approach was simple: first define a familiar word such as elections conceptually; then spend most of the first lecture on Britain and the second on America, and at the end remind students what they had learned about the variability of electoral systems. Students were mostly proud North of Englanders for whom Manchester was their 'capital', just as Chicago is the big city for many American Midwesterners rather than New York. They included the current president of Iceland, Olafur Grimsson; Peter (now Lord) Levene, successful in business and in Whitehall; Dennis Kavanagh, who became author of the Nuffield election studies with David Butler in default of an Oxford student suited to that task; and Cabinet ministers, journalists, and Fellows of the British Academy.

Manchester students were bright, having won places in selective grammar (that is, secondary) schools, and their teachers were well educated and demanding, a contrast from what I had experienced in my youth. That system was changed by the abolition of grammar schools and the introduction of comprehensive secondary education. When I asked Tony Crosland, who introduced the measure, how he would evaluate the success of comprehensive education, he replied that he didn't want any young person to go to go to the sort of public school he went to.

My final-year class was in political behaviour, in which I translated many American concepts for application in England. It was an exciting time as disclosures about how British politicians actually behaved were beginning to appear in the press. I introduced what was probably the first analysis of survey data in British politics teaching, being given IBM cards by British Gallup and use of a counter-sorter by medical statisticians. I organised student volunteers to learn about public opinion by doing a proper survey. Many expressed surprise and even gratitude for the opportunity to find out how people lived and thought in circumstances very different from that in which they were raised.

Shortly after joining the department Allen Potter asked if I would like to write a book about England for a new comparative politics series being edited by Gabriel Almond. Potter did not want to do so for he was not sympathetic to Almond's approach. Before saying yes, I tried applying Almond's (1960) analytical framework to England. The result was a book outline better than the conventional Penguin textbook, so I happily signed a Little, Brown contract for *Politics in England* (Rose 1964). To write the book I had to read widely across the social sciences. Because there were very few journal articles or books with relevant data, I got some information by going directly to sources rather than to the library or a non-existent Internet. I was also asked to contribute a chapter on political culture in England to an American Social Science Research Council volume on *Political Culture and Political Development* (Rose 1965a). This led me to spend a summer in the Manchester library trying to figure out when England became modern. Depending on the definition of modern, the answer could be 'in the 1840s' or 'it isn't modern yet'.

Bill Mackenzie's marginal comments on *Politics in England* opened up new directions. He also warned me of pitfalls, for example: 'I never thought I would meet anyone who could write English, American and German-American; for god's sake, choose one language and stick to it'. After writing the first edition in American, I translated the book into English for the first London edition. This involved such things as extending the discussion of the nuances of class far beyond the grasp of American readers (cf. Rose 1964; 1965). By the 1970s this was no longer necessary. Gabriel Almond (1997; www.profrose.eu/people.php) added a particularly helpful piece of advice: 'Never use the word culture in the active voice'.

Shortly after my arrival in Manchester, Mackenzie mentioned that once celibacy was abolished at Oxford in the late nineteenth century, dons without a private income had turned to freelance journalism to finance a household with a wife and children. He added that I might find this useful too. As usual, he was right. Tim Raison, an old Etonian Conservative had the entrepreneurial insight to found *New Society* as a weekly that translated research by social scientists on a society in transformation into serious and informative articles rather than a newspaper op ed article or a radio interview. My first contribution was to its second issue. In addition to being paid a proper fee, I could later expand this contribution into a fully footnoted academic journal article. I wrote short, quirky comments on events and translated into English ideas expressed in articles written in German-American and appearing in the *American Sociological Review*. I also started making occasional appearances on Granada Television, which had its base in Manchester. *New Society* closed in 1988, as the Thatcher cutbacks in public sector jobs dried up the advertising revenue on which the paper depended for much of its revenue.

Out of the blue I was invited to become the bylined Election Correspondent of *The Times* in 1964. This brought me into contact with very shrewd lobby correspondents who had left school at 14 and were very experienced judges of human nature in politics (cf. Tunstall 1970). David Wood of *The Times* taught me how to 'decode' the political meaning of hints and allusions in which Cabinet ministers spoke in those days. Following retirement, Jimmy Margach went to the Public Record Office with his shorthand notebooks from 40 years earlier to read minutes of Cabinet meetings that showed which of his ministerial sources had given him a fair account and which had tried to mislead him. I also learned to lunch like a lobby correspondent on something better than Guinness. More than once I had lunches summarily ended at 4.30 pm when my host announced he had to get back to the office to sign letters.

The byline in *The Times* paid better than the paper itself.[4] It gave me visibility and by withholding the accolade of being 'Our Own Correspondent', it gave the paper deniability in case what I wrote was unsuited to its standards. Prominence in print led to me being invited to become the on-camera number cruncher for the election coverage of Independent Television News in 1970 and 1974 (www.profrose.eu/about.php). I was then replaced by a computer, but not before I had secured replacement of a one-dimensional swingometer by graphics that showed the ups and downs of what had become a multi-party system of competition.

Media exposure made it easy for me to expand political contacts and the money earned was critical in enabling me to pursue research on party politics in London and America. However, I kept to my resolve when leaving the *Post-Dispatch* to put scholarly writing first. When a literary agent asked if I would like to write a book about the press and politics I declined, because the book that the publisher wanted could not include the concepts and rigour appropriate to social science analysis.

The dramatic transformation of writing about British politics in the decade that followed is illustrated by changes between the first and third editions of a reader I edited, *Studies in British Politics* (Rose 1966; 1976). It brought together insightful articles not readily accessible in a pre-digital age. In the first edition, published in 1966, one-quarter of the contributors held British university posts; another quarter

---

4.   In response to the offer of a fee of 200 guineas plus a byline, I replied with the definition of a good newspaper job in the American depression: '$25 a week and all the bylines you can eat'.

held American university posts; and half were in the media, Parliament or public affairs. By the third edition a decade later, British academics had become the majority of authors of studies of British politics worth reprinting, less than one-fifth were American academics, and less than three in ten were from the media.

Committed Political Sociologists

The founders of European political science were schooled in the hard politics of Europe in the 1930s and the Second World War. All the founding fathers were caught on either the winning or the losing side, and some were occupiers and then occupied. Stein Rokkan left university to spend the war years out of sight in Northern Norway. In the Netherlands Hans Daalder stayed home from school the last year of the war because he did not want to risk being picked up on the street and sent to forced labour in Germany. Instead of enjoying views of Florence from his family's apartment, Giovanni Sartori spent a year of the war confined to a single room reading Hegel as a means of sharpening his formidable intelligence. Being a Finn, Erik Allardt was unfortunate enough to be caught up by his country's resistance to Soviet invasion and then experiencing Nazi occupation, an experience shared by Baltic peoples and Poles. Rudolf Wildenmann was 'lucky'; he was captured while serving in the *Afrika Korps* and sent to a prisoner of war camp in Canada, where he could study for a University entrance qualification, something he could not afford to do earlier. Karl Deutsch was more fortunate still, being able to reach America from his native Prague before war broke out. He spent the early part of the war teaching American history to US naval cadets. As Karl said, 'In war time we all make sacrifices'. The black flags that anarchists waved during the Paris demonstrations of May 1968, unsettled Mattei Dogan more than wartime Bucharest. As he explained, 'After Stalingrad it was easy; we knew who would win'.

The war and what went before meant that many people had a lot of catching up to do with their reading, and strong incentives to do so. In the summer of 1945 the Swedish government invited young scholars to come to Uppsala to read books that were not available in their country and that had been shipped from America. Stein Rokkan told me, 'We read until midnight'. In Germany the gap was greater. A friend who went to Frankfurt in 1954 to study the work of the founders of the Frankfurt school of sociology found that his University of Chicago library had a better collection of their books than was available there.

In Britain the situation was different: the great expansion of government services drafted into Whitehall the few who were teaching public administration, such as W. J. M. Mackenzie and Norman Chester; economists who could advise on the allocation of resources; and people like Mark Abrams who understood how ordinary Britons ate and thought, important subjects when total war required total commitment from people under bombardment and subject to tight food rationing. The war produced a number of insightful books and articles which were read in Manchester but not many other places. The broad effect was to re-enforce insularity and confidence that the British way was best and literally incomparable.

Avid students want to read what is new. Whereas classic books about politics in England were written before 1914 and in Germany before 1933 or in exile, American books were new and stimulating. Almond (1960) and Easton (1965) offered a radical break with the legalistic European emphasis on institutions of the state and Lipset (1960) and Campbell *et al.* (1960) offered empirical evidence challenging dogmas that reduced all politics to class politics. American foundations generously provided support for study in the United States. Stein Rokkan led the way as a Rockefeller Foundation fellow at Columbia and Chicago from 1948 to 1950. As outsiders, Europeans could pick places that reflected the books that they found interesting; Columbia, Chicago and Berkeley were the primary attractions for political sociology more than political science.

Nearly all the Europeans who went to America took a round-trip ticket. The object was to learn rather than emigrate and to build a new understanding of politics in Europe on the ruins of what they had experienced before.

European pioneers were not interested in American politics for its own sake; the priority was to study intensively ideas and method that could be applied in Europe, such as the Michigan approach to the study of voting behaviour, and ignoring books that could not, such as the literature on the American presidency. As an American who had learned to think as a European, I did not challenge this practice. Nonetheless, I continued to be stimulated by books by American political scientists about American politics. Many English academics have followed American politics through what was written by journalists while ignoring what was written by American political scientists. In 1961 the British Museum told a friend who wanted to consult the *American Political Science Review* there that it had been discontinued in 1939. This not only reflected limitations on shipping space in wartime convoys but also persisting limitations of scholarly interests. Inspired by reading American studies of the roles of legislators and by interviewing MPs for my doctoral thesis, I proposed doing a study of the roles of British MPs as the topic for a post-doctoral fellowship at Nuffield College. The idea was neither understood nor acceptable. It was only after becoming a Professor at Strathclyde that I could pursue this topic, encouraging a young lecturer, Bruce Headey (1974), to do a pioneering study of the roles of British Cabinet ministers.

Pursuing ideas across Europe

Individuals with similar ideas and interests in innovative social science developments were a category rather than members of a common institution. The first step toward the institutionalization of political science in Europe was the founding in 1959 of the Committee on Political Sociology (CPS) as a research committee of the International Sociological Association. The proposers of the Committee were Shmuel Eisenstadt, Morris Janowitz, Marty Lipset and Stein Rokkan. The two English members of the Committee were Bob McKenzie from Canada and Mark Abrams, the son of anarchist immigrants from Latvia and Lithuania. Marty Lipset was the first Chairman and Rokkan (1970) the organizing secretary. Its first meeting was held in Bergen in June, 1961. Sidney Verba and I were fortunate in being the youngest persons in the room. In 1970 I succeeded Stein as secretary and Juan Linz succeeded Marty as Chair.

The Committee on Political Sociology was a network of individual scholars sharing common interests defined conceptually rather than geographically (Kadushin and Rose 1974). Members were interested in party systems and elites generally; this sociological focus on institutions required much more contextual knowledge than the focus on individuals often found in studies of political behaviour. Comparative analysis required having a common conceptual framework that made it possible to relate one's own expert knowledge to that of experts from other countries. Of course, while you could take Rokkan out of Norway and Sartori out of Italy, you could never take Norway out of Stein or Italy out of Vanni. That was no bad thing, for it meant that whatever abstract concepts were being dealt with had to be applicable to societies as they actually are (for examples, *see* Dogan and Rose 1970).

The primary aim of the Committee was to advance comparative research by bringing together individual scholars in conferences that facilitated cross-national contacts and the publications of books. In its first decade and one half it amassed a substantial number of collaborative publications and provided conference and publication opportunities for then scarcely known political scientists such as Gerhard Lehmbruch and Philippe Schmitter. However, the Committee could not launch a systematic programme of research for two reasons: there was no European source of funding for such a programme and, as a committee of individuals rather than a formal legal institution, it could not receive or manage the funds required for comparative research.

The institutions that employed political sociologists were often not university departments. Stein Rokkan was originally appointed to a post in the Christian Michelsen Institute, Bergen; he did not become a professor at the University of Bergen until 1966. In many European countries survey research firms with political parties or the media as their clients offered jobs to people who had learned survey methods and had an interest in voting behaviour. The first book-length study of British voting behaviour was written by a journalist working in Fleet Street on the night shift and writing a thesis during the day with Gallup Poll surveys (Bonham 1954). The French *Centre National de la Recherche Scientifique* had positions in political sociology held by people such as Mattei Dogan and Michel Crozier. The German Max Planck Institute did not have an Institute for political sociology until 1985. A few people were able to pursue careers in business while undertaking serious writing on the side. Peter Nettl was an extreme case, for he made a fortune in the wool trade before taking a post in political science and then meeting an early death in a plane crash (Hanson 1972).

International associations sponsored by UNESCO, such as the International Political Science Association and the International Sociological Association, offered political sociologists a venue to meet and hold panels, but nothing more. Rokkan (1979: 17), a participant in UNESCO-related activities from its very early days, realized 'It did not take long to discover how little could in fact be achieved within the framework set up by the United Nations and UNESCO'. They were organizations of national associations rather than individual scholars. Being sponsored by UNESCO, any country that created a national association could be a member. This gave political science as practised in Brezhnev's Soviet Union, Ceausescu's Romania and Mugabe's Zimbabwe equal recognition with what was done in free societies. As late as the 1982 World Congress in Rio de Janeiro, IPSA gave representatives of totalitarian regimes prominent billing in the opening session. I was seated on the platform with Marty Lipset. As he had had a lot of experience of Communist manipulation of useful idiots, I watched to see what he would do. If Lipset had walked off in protest, I would have been the second to leave.

The Committee on Political Sociology was small because the number of Europeans interested in political sociology, and especially comparative political sociology, was small. Commitment of members arose from the fact that we, as individuals, were at that time very few in number. Even though there were members from more than a dozen countries, panels at international congresses attracted only 20 or 30 people. While sharing common intellectual interests, we also shared a lack of *Hausmacht*, for we were not professors or leading academic figures in national systems in which politics was subsumed as a branch of history, law or administration. We participated in the multinational Committee because our interests and the books we read and wrote had more in common with each other than with most academics in our own country.

Chapter 4

The Professionalization of Political Science

A professional is an individual who is trained to undertake an occupation according to recognized standards; possesses a certificate of competence such as a PhD; belongs to an appropriate professional association; and is employed in the practice of that profession. To become a professional requires institutions that provide training, credentials and an income. However, the institutional prerequisites of professional political science did not exist when I started out. This meant that I could feed my curiosity about society by reading as widely as I liked without being told that such fields as history and sociology were out of bounds to political scientists. The upshot is that my education is that of a social scientist who happens to publish in the field of political science.

The explosion in the demand for higher education in the 1960s created many new universities and transformed many older ones. This created the institutional structure that has led to the professionalization of political science across Europe. New institutions had none of the inbuilt opposition to change and both old and new institutions needed new staff to teach new student bodies. Many new, and a lesser proportion of expanded departments, defined their object as teaching new skills to students as well as offering commentaries on old texts. Established staff were expected to set an example in professionalization by doing research as well as teaching. The more ambitious departments encouraged bright postgraduate students to become professional political scientists and trained them in research methods and innovative foreign-language (that is, American) books of political science.

Professionalization has created distance between groups of people who nominally share an interest in politics. Political scientists are now divided from journalists, politicians and high-ranking civil servants by their professional training and institutional employment (*see* Chapter 11). In organizational terms, the subject matter of political science is whatever is taught and researched in university departments bearing that label. Within the groves of academe, contemporary political scientists tend to herd together in a single pasture rather than graze freely like a previous generation of amateur political scientists. The expansion of universities and of the political science profession now makes such demands on the priorities of political scientists that there is less time for pondering what is happening outside one's field of specialization.

The Expansion of Universities Nationally

The explosion of university education in the 1960s was a consequence of the post-1945 baby boom, the expansion of free secondary education, the higher aspirations of youths whose parents had never been to university, and the belief that the more graduates a country produced, the higher its rate of economic growth would be. The absolute shortage of academics already teaching politics meant that anyone who could show some sort of justification for being given a professorship could get a post and also some who couldn't got professorships. This opened up opportunities for people who were committed to political science to gain a secure position in a university; it also opened up opportunities for old guard professors to promote their proteges.

In Britain there were two primary sources of new professors. As Oxford dons usually did not want to leave the collegiate fellowships to which they were accustomed, lecturers from the anti-political science LSE could start new departments that perpetuated old syllabuses and ignored developments in political science in continental Europe and the United States. The prime sources of professors with new ideas were Manchester and Sammy Finer's department at the University of Keele. Jean Blondel and myself are examples. There was a similar pattern of uneven institutionalization of professional political science in the countries of continental Europe.

The explosion of departments of politics took place in three institutional contexts: new universities, upgraded institutions, and old universities. In the intellectual and political climate of the 1960s, new universities invariably established faculties of social science with provision for a department of political science, since there were no established traditionalists to oppose doing so. It was possible to establish innovative programmes of political and social sciences as in the University of Konstanz, or to make a fresh combination of traditional subjects, as happened with European studies at the University of Sussex.

Expansion also resulted in upgrading existing specialist institutions of tertiary education into universities by the addition of new departments, including departments of political science. Because of their history, these institutions often had less prestige and novelty but they were better positioned to accept more students more quickly. Mannheim is an example, for its origins date from a technical college created in 1907, while its political science department dates from the arrival of Rudolf Wildenmann as founder professor shortly before it became a university in 1967. Strathclyde is another example, for it was founded at the start of the Industrial Revolution to promote useful knowledge as an alternative to the education offered by Scotland's four medieval foundations. In 1913 it became the Royal College of Science and Technology, the Scottish equivalent of a German *Technische Hochschule*; it added a political science department when it was made a university in 1963.

Old universities of Europe usually had a lot of scope for expansion, because until the 1960s they were relatively small in student numbers. However, because they were committed to traditional outlooks in faculties such as law, the establishment of political science departments there was much more difficult than in new or upgraded institutions. As late as 1996, the Gladstone Professorship of Government was held by a historian, and many young historians appointed to teach politics in England during the 1960s expansion did not retire until after the year 2000. In the United States the Government Departments at Harvard and Columbia were conspicuous laggards in adapting to changes in political science.

By the end of the 1960s every professionally oriented political scientist was in an established chair with the institutional resources to promote a professional approach to the study of politics. Even though the German *Lehrstuhl* was not designed with Stein Rokkan's idea of collective research in mind, it was well suited to the promotion of political science. It gave holders of chairs who wanted to be professional leaders the resources required to shape a department. By contrast, the collegial character of an American department has tended to require its chair to balance diverse interests and outlooks within a large department of individuals, each of whom has his or her own interests and priorities.

The first asset of the founding chair in a new department is the power to determine its hiring policy. Talented young people who wanted to become professional political scientists could get jobs and so could some not so talented young people.[1] Since a professor could set the examination syllabus for a new department, this provided a means for training young people as political scientists and attracted students who wanted to make a break from the traditional subjects that they had studied at school. New departments could also train graduate students who spread this outlook to other universities that had not, could not, or would not train their own students in modern concepts and methods.

Secondly, the holder of a chair can promote a distinctive departmental profile through team research and raising the money to fund this work. Although many works of political science can be pursued by an individual sitting at a desk, some cannot. National election surveys are a prime example of a field requiring an infrastructure of skilled technicians and computing facilities, as well as statistically trained researchers. They also require large sums to collect survey data, which required national research councils to expand their scope from the physical sciences and medicine to include social science. Team research involving research assistants as well as a leader with ideas about what a team should do began to replace prize fellowships for talented individuals. The European Union now gives very substantial grants for pan-European teams to undertake comparative and collaborative research in political science.

Thirdly, an increased number of professional political scientists can publish a much greater volume of research. As of 1960 there was an absolute shortage of books written about national European political systems in the postwar period. By 1970, this vacuum was being filled and the median publication showed a degree of professionalism. When Mattei Dogan and I published *European Politics* in 1970, we had no difficulty in finding more than 40 articles to fill its 590 pages. The

---

1.   Jean Blondel's strategy in hiring at Essex meant that 'Almost all the first appointees of 1964 had
     left by 1970' (Budge 1994: 12).

political scientists and sociologists contributing were a mixture of social scientists based in European institutes and universities and those in American universities; many had a foot in both.

The importance of new and upgraded universities in developing professional political science in Europe is illustrated by the eight departments that founded the European Consortium for Political Research in 1970. Only Leiden, founded in the sixteenth century, was an old university, and Nuffield College, founded in 1937, was a new institution attached to a very old university. The Institute of Political Science, founded in Paris in 1872, was distinctive in being rooted in nineteenth-century ideas of the study of society. The University of Gothenburg was founded in 1907 and Bergen in 1946. Mannheim and Strathclyde were institutions upgraded to university status in the 1960s. Essex was the only completely new institution, being founded on a green field site in 1965.

Training Students: The Strathclyde Approach

In setting up a graduate programme at the University of Strathclyde in 1966, I had a clear idea of what I thought it would benefit students to learn: they should be able to understand political concepts and theories that purported to explain them, and be able to apply methods appropriate to collect evidence, and test how well or whether interesting ideas and theories stood up in the world of political practice. It was an advantage to be self-trained. Others could not follow the path that I had taken by instinct and accident, nor had I been trained to accept a particular syllabus that could then be laid down to students.

Many new politics departments sought to emulate American departments. As an American, I was particularly quick to see that many political science assumptions proposed as universal generalizations reflected the distinctive political system of the United States and, like American electrical goods, did not always work when plugged in elsewhere. My philosophy has always been that any political science concept developed in the United States that made sense when applied across national borders is useful and should be used. Hence, the study of politics at Strathclyde was designed to make students combine the critical evaluation of concepts with efforts to apply them in different national contexts. My lack of statistical training made me appreciate the value of having it in hand for use as and when appropriate. My concern with the meaning of words meant that a lot of emphasis was given to avoiding the confusion of words with the concepts that they were meant to indicate. Moreover, there was no tolerance for that convenient oxymoron beloved of rational choice narrators, stylized facts. Examples were drawn as appropriate from countries throughout the OECD world and from current affairs.

What Strathclyde offered

When chairs began proliferating in Britain there was no question of seeking promotion in Manchester: Bill Mackenzie was leaving to return to Scotland and the syllabus was not within my hands. The University of Strathclyde attracted me because it was the first department outside the United States to join the Michigan Interuniversity Consortium for Political Research. The departmental chair became vacant in 1965 when Jean Blondel, 'anxious to ward off possible challenges from elsewhere in Britain, pre-empted a possible threat from the behaviourally oriented department at Strathclyde by recruiting its founder, Allen Potter' (Budge 1994: 11). Potter told me that in Strathclyde the department head could devote 95 per cent of his time to the department and would not be bogged down in faculty and university committees. This appealed, because I saw doing research myself would be the best way to give leadership to a new department.

I was appointed Professor of Politics and head of department at Strathclyde in 1966. Strathclyde's predecessor institution was founded in the seventh year of the French Revolution to promote useful knowledge (Brown *et al.* 2004). The Principal who hired me, Sir Samuel Curran FRS, was a natural philosopher, that is, a theoretical physicist; his post-doctoral research involved applying his knowledge at Berkeley to the making of the atomic bomb. He had no use for things that didn't work. When I explained to him that the study of politics required both qualitative and quantitative skills, he replied, 'At last I know what the department is about'. He wanted the Politics Department to be one of the best four in Britain. I replied that this wasn't good enough; it should be a department with an international reputation. Curran told me, 'If you succeed, we will back you'. I knew that the other side of the coin said, 'If you fail you will be another second-rate academic up from England'.

As the sole professor in the department, I had a free hand to shape it as I thought best. Guiding ideas came from the humanities as well the social sciences. From my study of T. S. Eliot I interpreted the injunction — 'Make it new' — as not only requiring fresh thinking but also respect for 'it', that is, customs and traditions that were old but not necessarily to be dismissed as old hat. From E. M. Forster's *Howards End* I took the motto 'Only connect'. In that book Forster connected the world of the Wilcoxes, engaged in the bourgeois business of life, with the Schlegels, engaged in the world of ideas. While I am a Schlegel, there is enough of a Wilcox in my upbringing so that I have been able to see the connections between what could be learned in a library and outside books. My training as a reporter gave an emphasis to a very high standard of factual accuracy and care in ensuring that indicators were not only quantified but also meaningful.

My goal as head of department was to promote learning about politics by combining research and teaching. This meant that politics students had to be trained in research methods, which was then unheard of in Britain. They were also expected to apply the methods they learned to the world of politics. This was not typical of British politics departments at that time, and some claimed it to be impossible. I considered that the best way to reject such an opinion was by practical example rather than time-wasting academic debate. The Introduction to the brochure sent to potential graduate students described the department as follows:

> The Politics Department at Strathclyde specializes in studying substantively important political problems by sophisticated social science methods. Postgraduate study can best be advanced by combining formal instruction, individual research and informal contact between staff and students with

common interests. The size and style of the Department encourages discussion outside as well as in class. Concentrated training in substantive topics and in methodology permits students to go deeply into a few fields, while simultaneously gaining theoretical and practical knowledge. Special computing and data analysis facilities ensure that learning involves doing things as well as reading about what others do (www.profrose.eu/writings.php#studying).

To make the syllabus work required people who could teach with commitment and skill. Jack Brand introduced a Glasgow Area Survey modelled on the Detroit Area Survey then operating at the University of Michigan. This faced students with the challenge of designing a questionnaire and carrying out face to face interviews. William Miller applied for a post because, after taking a degree in mathematics and a doctorate in computer science, he wanted to apply his knowledge to problems in the real world. I hired him on the assumption that if he didn't like political science he could always get a job elsewhere. Miller became a politics Fellow of the British Academy. At the end of a late night after-dinner conversation in Oxford I offered Mark Franklin a job. He taught statistics and computer applications to data analysis and collaborated with Norman Nie in pioneering the development of SPSS before retiring as the Stein Rokkan Professor at the European University Institute, Florence. Derek Urwin taught comparative European politics and, when Derek went to Stein Rokkan's department in Bergen, Tom Mackie succeeded him.

To keep up with what others were thinking, time and money were invested in bringing visiting speakers for a day of informal discussions as well as a formal seminar. A number of leading American social scientists spending a year in England were happy to accept invitations to come up to Scotland. They included established American scholars such as the sociologist Jim Coleman, Sam Huntington and Mancur Olson and Europeans such as Giovanni Sartori, Erik Allardt, Hans Daalder and Henry Valen. Young researchers and graduate students such as Bob Putnam and Alberta Sbragia were also welcome. When Strathclyde faculty went on leave for a year in America, visiting staff were invited, such as Bill Mishler, who has since taught me a thing or two about statistics.

The one-year Strathclyde MSc syllabus offered what I thought people educated in politics needed to know and what the overwhelming number of students with an undergraduate politics degree did not know. It introduced students to new ideas and methods. The course did not ask students to write essays about books. Instead it asked students to apply the concepts and methods that they were taught to significant political questions. This went far beyond the practice of other universities at that time. Half the year was spent on writing a master's dissertation.

The first term concentrated on survey methods, statistics, and the use of computers, then a novelty for arts students. When a Sussex graduate in German and Politics said to me at the end of a first-term review that his mind had been completely changed, I replied: 'I'm glad you've learned something fresh but we are not a religious institution producing converts'. After a year I realised that something was missing; to fill the gap I created a class called 'From Methods to Reality'. Its course description said:

This Seminar is much more concerned with thinking than with reading. Students will be asked questions during each class to make sure, by working through examples, that they understand how to apply social science methods to analyse political realities. Each student is required to write a paper showing how a specific topic in the Butler and Stokes book on British voting can be treated better. This may involve showing why an election survey should add a new variable to the questionnaire; analysing in a fresh way a variable already included in the survey; or formulating a different hypothesis.

A key feature of the one-term 'Methods to Reality' class was that a student's paper was *not* expected to include any statistical analysis. That could only be done after conceptual issues and problems of fitting indicators to concepts had been dealt with. An outstanding example was an imaginative paper by Ofira Seliktar about how to study the political behaviour of Jews in Britain. She showed how to draw a representative sample of a population lacking a readily available sampling frame; questions to be added to the standard Butler and Stokes (1970) questionnaire; and how results could be analysed by applying Rokkan's model of class, ethnic, and religious cleavages to the party choice of British Jews. Where empirical data was available, students could write a master's dissertation testing their ideas. Several of these papers were later developed for publication in such places as the *British Political Science Journal* (Rallings 1975) and the *American Political Science Review* (Willetts 1972).

I set up the Social Statistics Laboratory (SSL) as a large space with computer terminals, technical staff to give help, and opportunities for students to educate or distract each other. Since a scientific university was accustomed to funding laboratories, it was well resourced. Moreover, the SSL had an accumulation of data sets that not only included what was available from the Michigan archive but also lots that I had obtained from British survey firms for my own research and surveys from across Western Europe analysed in *Electoral Behaviour* (Rose 1974). To calculate statistics students initially relied on a programmable Olivetti calculator costing the equivalent of a full year's professorial salary. When newly accepted students asked what they should read in the summer before starting the MSc course, the answer was simple — a book of instructions on touch typing — for at that time most British university graduates did not know how to type.

While Strathclyde was running an MSc course to train postgraduate students at an international standard, the British Social Science Research Council (now the ESRC) had a different view. When Michael Young, then the innovative chair of the SSRC, told me that the Council would give training grants, I asked him 'Will you define training?' The look on his face showed that he understood the point of my question: the academic politics of the Council meant that grants would be given without regard to what their recipients did or did not learn. This meant that Oxford and the LSE got lots of grants for students to pursue studies where the value added was the name of the institution rather than the content of the course. Jean Blondel showed ruthlessness in recruiting a dozen postgraduate studentships for Essex in the first year of ESRC funding. As Ian Budge (1994: 10) has proudly related, 'Most of the students failed, but budgetary inertia meant that the funding continued, thus providing the economic foundation for building a big postgraduate school'. My approach was different. While I took some gambles in admitting MSc students, I did so only if they had positive characteristics that I could defend to my colleagues who had to teach them.

Strathclyde's advantage was the combination of political substance and methods. Because it was different, it was not competing with LSE and Oxford. In the dozen years in which I led the Strathclyde MSc programme, I evaluated each applicant to see if he or she had something distinctive to offer, for example, having studied mathematics or foreign languages to a high level. When interviewing applicants in Glasgow or at the Reform Club in London, I looked for a spark of ingenuity or commitment that would not readily show up on paper. This could compensate for a lower-second class degree, as was demonstrated by Jay Gershuny, now a professor at Oxford, and Peter Bluff, who went on to become a producer of high quality television programmes on current affairs in London and New York. Our emphasis on comparison attracted students with languages to try their hand at a politics MSc. After doing this, Edwina Moreton went on to do a doctorate on Russia with Alec Nove at Glasgow University and ended up diplomatic editor of *The Economist*. My work on Northern Ireland attracted a number of very committed and courageous students.

Many Strathclyde MSc graduates went on to take a doctorate and gain a permanent university post. The best known include Ed Page, now a Professor at the LSE; Ian McAllister, now a distinguished professor at the Australian National University; and John Dryzek, who was taught by Bob Goodin, a temporary lecturer at Strathclyde, and followed him to Australia. An intention to pursue an academic career was not required. My view was that students could only make such a long-term commitment after they had undertaken a professional political science MSc. Thus, I do not consider that former MSc students who ran opinion polls for a prime minister or were an ambassador to the United Nations had 'failed'. Nor do I consider that ex-pupils who became members of a national parliament or the European Parliament thereby left the field of politics.

In those days a professor was the department head; my exposure to the German *Lehrstuhl* made me see that a professor could combine intellectual leadership and administrative responsibilities. The irrelevance of internal committees gave me time to devote to the department. Although I had never held an administrative post before, I had had a lot of experience in organising my time, and I made it a priority to do so at Strathclyde. There were days for being in the University, where I was readily accessible and was at my desk while others had gone home. There were also days for writing at home. Drawing on the experience of watching editors work, I learned to make some decisions very quickly and set others aside. Drawing on my experience as a reporter, I learned to read official papers quickly to see if their point was worth following up and how to do so. My skill in writing was used in writing internal University memos and research grant applications. In 48 years as a professor I have been supported by a succession of three long-term secretaries who found working for me a change from a normal Glasgow office job and whose abilities and loyalty I have valued highly.

Mrs. Margo McGlone at her retirement party. From 1967 to 1985 she was my secretary and shepherd to a generation of Strathclyde graduate students

While running the Strathclyde MSc programme was both congenial and rewarding, it was also a very time-consuming uphill struggle. In addition to being distant from London and South of England universities, Strathclyde's scientific inclination restricted the Politics Department to a size less than half that of big universities such as Manchester or new universities where politics could flourish quickly and cheaply without the need for costly engineering facilities. After securing fellowships for staff at Yale and Michigan, I decided it was time to do something for myself. By then I had become involved in public policy. I won a Guggenheim Fellowship and a Woodrow Wilson Centre fellowship to take 1974 off and spend six months in Washington D.C. in order to see how social science ideas were being applied in American government.

On my return from leave in 1975 I explored moving to a think tank in London, but was not attracted because they were too close to government or a particular party. They thus lacked the intellectual freedom to explore ideas over a long period of time. In 1976 I established the Centre for the Study of Public Policy (CSPP) within the Strathclyde Politics department (*see* Chapter 11). This led to an innovative five-year programme on the growth of government with funding from the British Economic and Social Research Council that included my salary. In 1981 I stopped doing two jobs and left the Politics Department to become the full-time head of the CSPP. My successor, Jeremy Richardson, was determined to put his own imprint on the department and he did.

Institutionalizing Professional Links Across Europe

By 1970 the first generation of professional political scientists had succeeded in establishing scholarly reputations and securing institutional bases in university departments in their own country, and professional ideas were beginning to spread to other universities in their country. Rokkan described this process as 'the development of national empiricism, in which political scientists won recognition in their national academy by conducting local and national studies, often at a high level of methodological sophistication'. However, institutionalization had consequences that Max Weber characterized as the demagification or disenchantment of the world. Rokkan called it 'a narrowing of perspectives, a concentration on the concrete, the local and the national, a rejection of universal comparisons'. It thus tended to produce publications with 'only incidental bearing on the central problems of a comparative sociology of politics' (quoted in Rose 1990: 590).

Within-nation institutionalization created the pre-conditions for institutionalizing multinational political science links. Within many European countries there were now several dozen individuals who saw themselves as professional political scientists, secure within their own national system and publishing studies that showed what they could do. Developments in communications and transportation — the jet airplane, wide-area electronic telephone systems and fax — were making it possible to network without regard to national boundaries. The jet airplane made it easier to get around Europe. At the time the ECPR was being established I once had breakfast at home in Scotland, lunch in London, dinner with Erwin Scheuch at his institute in Cologne, and was back in my office in Glasgow the next day.

Politics made the United States seem further away. On many American campuses the issues that aroused greatest interest — race relations, the Vietnam war, and Watergate — were uniquely American issues that did not address the scientific concerns of Europeans. In the United States comparative politics no longer meant the intensive study of a few European countries, of which England was sure to be one, but of major countries scattered across the globe. To support Americans who did have an interest in Britain, Stephen Blank, an early secretary of the American Council of European Studies, and I initiated the British Politics Group as a section within the American Political Science Association. I hired a room for drinks at the 1974 APSA convention to see who would turn up to discuss the idea. Anglo-American links produced an excellent turnout, including Austin Ranney, Don Stokes, Aaron Wildavsky and Sam Beer. The BPG was in business. I handled the organizational work and Steve Blank got Jorgen Rasmussen to take the critical role of unpaid Executive Secretary, which he performed with great success. The Group is now almost 40 years old and its activities have not only attracted hundreds of members in the United States but also many British members (*see* www.britishpoliticsgroup.org).

The ECPR

The European Consortium for Political Research was founded in New York in May, 1970. It was the result of pioneering efforts of Stein Rokkan and Jean Blondel, and a Ford Foundation executive, Peter de Janosi, a 1956 Hungarian refugee. The ECPR was a conscious attempt to advance professional political science wholesale. Its members are departments of political science rather than individual scholars, as had been the case in the Committee of Political Sociology. Nor are members national associations with all the national politics that is involved, as happens in IPSA (Newton and Boncourt 2010). The Ford Foundation grant of $272,500 to fund activities, including a head office at the University of Essex, was at that time equivalent to several million euros today. Since the subsidy was for only five years, it was also a stimulus to recruit more institutional members.

For the first three years the ECPR was an organization searching for ways to achieve its ambitious aims and offer services that would justify departments joining and paying dues. The first few business meetings of the founder members were unbusinesslike. I lobbied Norman Chester, a local government clerk before becoming Warden of Nuffield, to press for the preparation of an agenda and papers for each meeting and establish committees in which individuals would become responsible for creating ECPR activities.

The breakthrough came when Rudolf Wildenmann created the Joint Sessions of Workshops. He saw that the effort required to raise money for Joint Sessions for hundreds of people need not be that much greater than that for small ad hoc conferences. The first Joint Sessions were held at Mannheim in April, 1973, and have continued annually since. Because a week is spent in Workshops talking to people with similar interests but researching in other countries, they have been particularly valuable in socializing individuals into networks of European political scientists. Individuals whose interests may isolate them within their own institution can thus find likeminded colleagues and learn that a shared professional interest makes for better communication than a shared national passport. Moreover, massing hundreds of people in one place for Joint Sessions creates an awareness of a Europe-wide profession. By moving from place to place each year, Joint Sessions have introduced young professionals to institutions that are not alien to them, even though the universities organizing the Workshops are foreign.

The Essex Summer School quickly become a central training ground in methodological techniques. It was complemented for three years from 1972 by summer schools sponsored by the International Social Science Council and held successively at Cologne, Strathclyde and Amsterdam. These balanced discussion of substantive research issues and statistical methodology. Since then, training in transnational statistics has been dominant in summer schools and the attention given to theories and concepts and their substantive application in national contexts has suffered.

Initially the ECPR was strict about the E in its title: American institutions were not eligible to join. This was a practical recognition of the big difference then prevailing between a mature political science profession in the United States and a fledgling European profession. It avoided the former swamping the latter.

Moreover, American universities faced different circumstances. The founding meeting of the ECPR was held a few days after the Ohio National Guard had shot Kent State students demonstrating against the Vietnam war. At Yale, where we gathered before meeting at the Ford Foundation, there were signs of panic among some faculty who feared that, however justified, campus demonstrations could spiral out of control for reasons very different from those in Europe. While the Michigan-based ICPR supported summer schools in Europe and welcomed European pilgrims to Ann Arbor, the executive director of the APSA, Evron Kirkpatrick, was not inclined to cooperate. A onetime president of APSA explained to me, 'Ev has no interest in any organization that he cannot control'.

After six years as an active member of the ECPR's Executive Committee, I did not join a week-long Group at the 1976 Joint Sessions because there was nothing of interest. Naively, I turned up just before the triennial election and even signed the nomination paper for an additional UK candidate. When the votes were counted, I was no longer a member of the Executive Committee. Jean Blondel, who promoted the membership of the ECPR with evangelistic zeal and ferocious activity, stepped down as its founder-director in 1979. The institutional development of the ECPR since has shown the strength of its initial design. The collective efforts of two generations of political scientists has resulted in the ECPR growing from eight institutions in six countries to more than 350 institutions with member departments from 40 countries ranging from the United States to Japan (see www.ecpr.eu).

In place of the lone scholar in Oxford or Heidelberg, there are now hundreds of departments and thousands of professional political scientists networking across Europe from Trondheim to Catania and from Limerick to Tartu. Equally important, activities of the ECPR meet the needs of political scientists at different stages of their careers, ranging from summer school training for graduate students to subject-matter workshops mixing junior and senior academics and specialist pan-European research networks.

The European Union and political science

The European Union is a very different political institution from the ECPR, but its foundation in the 1950s was a political act that reflected experiences and values similar to those of the generation of amateur political sociologists. The purpose of the European Economic Community, as it was then called, was to replace the national divisions that had led to two destructive wars with institutions of transnational cooperation. Notwithstanding this, the founders of professional political science in Europe took no interest in Brussels in its early decades. From my first trip there when Britain joined in 1973, I understood its labyrinthine political system as a variant of politics inside the Washington Beltway. In the 1970s world recession I could study overloaded government in the conventional manner of applying a common framework to six national case studies (Rose and Peters 1978). As the EU's impact on national politics has grown, so too has my interest in the European Union. In the past four years I have spent more time in Brussels than in London, and this has taught me things about British politics that Britain's governors choose to ignore (Rose 2013).

The European University Institute (EUI) in Florence opened in 1976 to give PhDs in the social sciences to a cosmopolitan pan-European student body. The first Rector, Max Kohnstamm, was a committed European federalist who had survived German occupation in the Netherlands and worked closely with Jean Monnet in the creation of the EU. When the initial professor of political science, Giovanni Sartori, resigned in order to leave Italy for Stanford, I was asked to succeed him. While the offer was attractive, it was at just the wrong time to move schools for our three teenage children. The upshot was that I received a part-time appointment to carry out research on overloaded government. The EUI had a critical feature of a new University: it was initially a building site. You could find your electric typewriter go dead when a workman cut an electricity line by mistake.

The EUI now provides an institutional meeting place for political scientists from all over Europe to discuss substantive issues in the comparative study of politics (www.eui.eu). Its doctoral programme produces cadres of comparative political scientists in whom knowledge of languages and methods are well joined and for whom working across national boundaries is normal. Since this is what I have always believed in, it was a special pleasure to be awarded an honorary doctorate there in 2010.

The highly competitive EUI programme is complemented by the EU's Erasmus fellowships. Since 1987 this programme has enabled more than three million young Europeans to spend at least one term pursuing their studies in another European country. Each year thousands of political scientists benefit. The creation of the Eurobarometer in 1974 has also contributed to comparative political research. Although questions are necessarily tailored to the interests of its sponsor, the European Commission, the semi-annual survey does provide a data base for testing propositions about the influence of national context on political differences among individuals or whether they are much the same among citizens of 28 EU member states because of within-nation divisions of age, education and income common across Europe (Rose 2007). The EU has also become a large-scale funder of collaborative European research projects.

As an employer of political scientists I have benefited from the development of a generation of cosmopolitan political scientists. In the 1960s and 1970s it was difficult to find young PhDs to employ who could understand both differing national contexts and statistical methods. In job interviews in which I have been involved in the past five years there has been no shortage of qualified candidates coming from all over Europe. In two recent sets of interviews, the ten persons short-listed were of eight different nationalities and none had their PhD from an institution in their country of origin.

Unlike the European Union, the political science profession can accept diversity without imposing requirements of uniformity. The great majority of political scientists in Europe continue to focus their research on the politics of their own country. However, more and more researchers place their national case studies within a conceptual framework having hypotheses that in principle can be tested across national boundaries. There is also an expectation that the evidence to support generalizations, whether about institutions or public opinion, will be verifiable. The strength of European political science today is that it encourages testing ideas against the experience of more than one country, thereby raising a fundamental question of social science: Under what circumstances and to what extent are generalizations truly generalizable?

Paradoxically, a sign of a mature profession by comparison with the days when bookshelves had few books is that there are now more constraints on new fields of enquiry and on shifts in paradigms (cf. Kuhn 1962). Many professionals are refining what we know about politics by becoming more and more expert in an increasingly narrow field of study. A young professional submitting a journal article today will be expected to write about an established topic and review a mass of familiar literature before stating succinctly what she or he has to add. By contrast, the virtual vacuum facing the founder generation of political scientists permitted a wide-ranging search for ideas and evidence. While the insistence on professional standards raises the average level of performance, it can discourage tackling big and novel themes encapsulated in one of the principles guiding my research: Go for bears not budgerigars.

Part II

Experiencing History Forwards

When David Butler asked Isaiah Berlin what he should read before going to the United States as a graduate student in political science in 1948, he was told: 'Read history. The rest you can learn from newspapers and cocktail parties'. There is a lot in that remark, for if you don't know where you are coming from, it is hard to understand where you are or where you are going (cf. Neustadt and May 1986). History provides a narrative account of what has happened and an explicit or implicit explanation of why things have become what they are. Journalistic accounts of today's news are timely, but static. Fascination with the current popularity of a political leader ignores that what goes up can also go down.

Whereas history is backward-facing, social science can be forward-looking, offering propositions about future events that are more or less likely to happen. For example, the longer a politician such as Margaret Thatcher or Tony Blair stays in office, the closer she or he is to leaving. By explaining current circumstances in terms of the influence of variables, this implies that as and when these variables change, the future will be different from the present or the past. When pushed to evaluate President George H. W. Bush at the victorious completion of the Kuwait War, I carefully described him as at the crest of a wave (Rose 1991: 314). The implication of this became clear the following year, when the tide turned and Bush was drowned in defeat by Bill Clinton.

It is easy to emulate Dr. Heinz Zeit and make the retrospective claim that whatever changes occur are obvious and inevitable. When I began taking an interest in race relations in the 1940s it was not obvious that segregation would end in the American South with so little loss of life. Nor was it obvious in Northern Ireland in the mid 1960s that its Unionist government would end with so much loss of life. Anyone who had seen the stolid East German *Volkspolizei* ready to shoot to kill any person who attempted to get over the Berlin Wall could hardly expect the Wall to be breached overnight (www.profrose.eu/writings.php#europe). When one lives history forward, there is no certainty.

A memoir should convey the experience of what life was like when what is now past was part of the unknown future. I have always been careful to think about the cumulative effect of compounding small-scale changes and the direction in which striking events point. However, I have never planned my life on the assumption that I knew what the world would be like or what I would be doing two decades hence. My development as a British-based political scientist is easier to explain in retrospect than to have predicted when my ambition was to become a newspaper reporter in St. Louis.

The chapters that follow give practical examples of the motto 'Never say never in politics'. It is particularly apt when confronted with political institutions that appear both entrenched and objectionable, such as class discrimination in England, racial segregation in the United States, civil war in Northern Ireland, and the Soviet domination of half of Europe. People living in such environments do not expect quick fixes to their problems. What is required is ingenuity in exploiting opportunities for change as and when they unexpectedly occur. Meanwhile, patience is needed — and the classical root for the word patience is suffering (Rose 1997).

Chapter 5

England Then and Now

My first impression of England from the deck of a ship at Southampton in 1953 was how small everything was. The wagons that trains used to carry goods appeared to resemble the wagons of the toy train set that I had as a child rather than the American trains I knew that pulled one hundred or more freight cars across a continent. The second impression was how old buildings were. In St. Louis any building that had been standing for more than 100 years, and there were not that many, was defined as old. In America pre-Civil War buildings dated from the 1850s or earlier; in England they dated from the 1630s or earlier. While the opportunity to experience old buildings met my interest in architecture, the absence of central heating did not. A third reaction was how early everything closed. At the end of my first day in London, at 10 pm I left the theatre where I had seen T. S. Eliot's latest play and realised that I hadn't eaten since breakfast. I looked for a place to eat; it was hard to find one that was still open.

My first challenge was to find somewhere to live. I was fortunate in getting a bed-sitter room in a rent-controlled flat in Mayfair near Bond Street tube station. This enabled me to learn the city by walking back late at night from the theatre or from a meal in a late-night Greek taverna in Soho. My landlady, a widow, took me under her wing and gave me insights into her life in England before 1914 and of bombing, which started with a Zeppelin raid in the First World War. Having run a late-night bridge club in the 1930s for people who played cards for high stakes, she made shrewd comments about what one could see on the streets of London. However, I did not agree with her view of my Australian friends at the LSE: 'You know who their ancestors were', that is, convicts transported from England.

My second task was to learn English. English as spoken was not the same as the English I had read in books and certainly different than the way it was spoken by everyone I had ever known. My desire to learn was not driven by an idea of becoming English but because I wanted to fit in, a useful attribute for a foreign newspaper correspondent or a student of comparative politics. The first time I found myself saying 'hahf' rather than my native 'haaf' I laughed out loud at my new voice. Within three months I could use the cricketing term 'sticky wicket' as a metaphor, although I was clueless about the rules of cricket. In six months I was sometimes mistaken for a Canadian by English people who didn't know how Canadians spoke.

Living in England meant that I needed to understand how English people lived. This had a practical side. If you didn't learn about things such as early closing day and how to do sums in pounds, shillings and pence, everyday activities would be full of frustrations. There was also an intellectual side: the whole point of living in a foreign country was to learn how foreigners differed from the America I knew.

To do so I cast a much wider net than attending lectures and reading textbooks on politics and sociology. I listened to stories that all kinds of people whom I met told me. This gave me a fund of knowledge that I could later use in interpreting the evidence produced by sample surveys of the British population. It also meant that I knew a much greater variety of people than English people who kept to their own place and class.

Learning About Class

Hitchhiking around England to see cathedrals gave me my first experience of interviewing; I talked with motorists and lorry drivers who gave me lifts. While they were hardly a scientific sample, it was a larger and more varied collection of people than in the typical focus group. When drivers learned that I was an American, they were happy to tell me about how they lived. These conversations were my introduction to the English class system. This was an eye-opener to someone who had grown up in a community in which the key divisions were race and religion. If an English person aggressively challenged me about the treatment of black people in America, I learned to reply, 'I can't get over the way you treat white people'. That ended our discussion.

Although political sociologists usually define class by occupation, the people I talked to invariably discussed class distinctions in terms of such markers of status as how you spoke or dressed. A Cockney told me that if ever he won a fortune gambling on the football pools he would take elocution lessons in order to spend his wealth without being patronised for his social origins as soon as he opened his mouth. Manual workers wore cloth caps, lower-middle class clerks and barely middle-class people wore felt trilby hats, and bowler hats were the preserve of officers and gentlemen. Since sumptuary laws had stopped being enforced in seventeenth century England, people could change their class by changing their attire. Thus, Labour politicians of working-class origin such as Herbert Morrison and the youthful Roy Jenkins would wear striped trousers and black cutaway double-breasted jackets to signify the rank they had achieved. When army officers wearing civilian clothes complained that they were not saluted by Horse Guard soldiers in Whitehall, a *Daily Mirror* journalist who had spent his military service washing dishes was photographed receiving a military salute because he wore a bowler hat when walking by a Horse Guards' soldier. A leading Labour MP drew a different distinction for me between his colleagues who wanted to sleep with titled women and those who were egalitarian like himself.

Up to a point the LSE was classless for few students came from high-status families and many were the first person in their family to attend university. The inclusion of sociology as a compulsory subject ensured that all undergraduates were given a conventional Marxist-influenced introduction to theories of class. I did not go to such lectures. Walking around London showed me the big differences between five-story houses that, until the Second World War, required a number of servants, and small two-story terraced houses with two rooms up and two rooms down and a toilet out the back.

In Oxford a don could unselfconsciously describe England's three classes as the upper class, the middle class, and the lower class, before correcting himself in the realization that such language was not appropriate after the Second World War. Status distinctions were finely drawn between students according to the type of secondary school they had attended and to their Oxford college. As an American who had spent several years working before coming to Oxford, I found it easy to make friends with students from Ruskin College, established for people who had left school for work at age 14 or 15 before pursuing further education as an adult. Ruskin students had been educated by life as well as by books.

College servants educated me in what different classes should and should not do. After being elected to Nuffield College, I invited a servant of Lincoln College to tea there, since her husband was a worker in Lord Nuffield's factory. She accepted but without explanation did not show up; she left me to figure out the reason why. When I received my doctoral degree I invited everyone at Nuffield from the Warden to the head porter to a drinks party. The Warden came but the head porter did not. A decade later Bill Clinton spent more time at Oxford chatting with the head porter of his college than writing tutorial essays. The head porter was the only person from the college Clinton invited to his presidential inauguration.

Moving to Manchester in 1961 made me conscious of the social divide between the North and South of England. My previous knowledge of Northern England was almost entirely limited to cathedral towns. From an Oxford perspective, Manchester appeared un-English, because it was a city of industry and commerce. It was also non-U, in the sense of lacking a public-school middle class and businessmen who wore bowler hats. In Manchester class tended to be measured by money not voice or headgear. The traditional motto was, 'Where there's muck, there's brass', that is, where there is industrial pollution there is money. The lack of smoke coming out of factory chimneys was considered bad news, a sign of unemployment due to factories being shut down.

In Manchester consumption goods were valued rather than social status. People who had never owned a car or refrigerator or had central heating rightly believed that having enough money to buy these goods made life more comfortable. I agreed. Whereas my parents had given me books when I got my doctorate, when we moved into a new home in Manchester with small children they gave us our first English refrigerator and washing machine, goods that I could not afford to buy on the salary of a university lecturer. The materialism of people in the North of England had many similarities with the American Midwest. When the political debate focussed on differences between the North and South of England, I did the North of England thing of making some money by selling an article to *The Economist* called 'A Yankee Lancashire' (www.profrose.eu/writings. php#england).

After half a dozen years in England I learned how to get one up on people who tried to place me below themselves in their status order. When a person realized I wasn't English, a standard gambit was to ask: 'How long have you been here?' My factual answer was to the point, 'Since rationing'. If I didn't like the tone of voice in which the question was asked, I added, 'When Winston Churchill was prime minister', a pointed reminder that England was not what it used to be. If people challenged my ability as a foreigner to understand English politics, I explained how I got my work permit: 'My professor had to swear to the Home Office that I should receive a work permit because there was no Englishman competent to teach my subject. My subject is British government. My professor is a Scotsman'.

Class Parties?

The British party system that I started studying in the 1950s was a two-party system: the Conservative and Labour parties together won up to 97 per cent of the popular vote and 99 per cent of the seats in the House of Commons. They saw themselves as the representatives of collective classes — albeit their definitions of class were oversimplified in different ways. The Labour Party declared it was a socialist party for workers by hand and brain, thus excluding only the few who had enough wealth to live without working. The party was financed by the biggest trade unions, whose members were male manual workers, such as coal miners, engineers and railwaymen. The four women on the party's National Executive Committee were elected by the bloc votes of big unions. The leadership was heavily public school and Oxford-educated, drawn to Labour by a mixture of motives, including an intellectual belief in Socialist principles, confidence in the ability of Whitehall to manage society, and a sense of obligation to help people who were economically far worse off than they were. Clement Attlee and Hugh Gaitskell were exemplars of this commitment.

The Conservative Party declared that it represented all classes in a society loyal to God, Queen and country. Different classes were recognised as having different roles in an organic society. The outlook was epitomized by an eighteenth-century funeral monument to a Christ Church Oxford servant 'who, by an exemplary life and behaviour, and an honest attention to the duties of his station, deserved and obtained the approbation and esteem of the whole society'. The Conservative dismissal of reasoning about politics and the interwar diplomacy of Conservative governments were consistent with its description as the stupid party. Some Conservative intellectuals gloried in this label. Lord Hailsham proclaimed the party's rejection of what it considered too clever by half socialists by proclaiming, 'Thank God we are not from the LSE'. His rhetoric was stronger than his facts, for the first LSE graduate to become a Cabinet minister was one of Hailsham's Conservative colleagues.

Given my experience of seeing society divided by race, religion and ethnicity, I tended to see class divisions as a default position arising from the absence of these cleavages. As I knew nothing about the history of British party competition, I had to look up facts, just as I would when writing a newspaper article. Two facts particularly struck me. The two-party system of Conservative and Labour was the outcome of three-party competition that had also involved a Liberal Party and before that Irish Nationalists. Although the working class then constituted two-thirds of the electorate, since the introduction of universal suffrage the Conservatives had won more elections than Labour.

The failure of class to equal party made me sceptical of the assumptions common in most writing about British party politics at that time. I was also sceptical of Tony Crosland's claim in his 1956 book, *The Future of Socialism,* that a classless society could be promoted by policies financed by what he assumed would be a steady 2.5 per cent annual rate of growth. In the review of the book that I wrote at the time, I wondered whether Crosland would remain so optimistic if he were the Chancellor of the Exchequer. The Conservative ignorance of the condition of the English working class made me sceptical of their claims to be a party of all the people. When I was an expert member of a panel that included Enoch Powell and he asked rhetorically — 'What is the value of having many youths go to university?' — I shot back 'To my Manchester students it is £200 a year', a sum that today is equal to thousands of pounds.

The 1959 British general election was not only a turning point in how British parties understood class politics but also transformed me from being a casual observer of the subject into being an expert. Conservative advertising appealed for votes across class lines. In a full-frontal example of sociological pornography, the party ran half-page ads in the popular press with a photograph of a cloth-capped worker captioned: 'You're looking at a Conservative' (Butler and Rose 1960: 136). Old-style Labour as well as Conservative politicians disliked appeals to mass tastes using the techniques of commercial television. A BBC executive explained his opposition to advertising on the grounds 'A man will always prefer a prostitute to his wife'. After the Conservatives won the election, a post-election cartoon showed the Prime Minister seated at the Cabinet table saying, 'Well, gentlemen, I think we all fought a good fight'. Seated around the table were a refrigerator, a black-and-white television set, a washing machine and small car, which were then symbols of affluence. Drawing on my St. Louis experience, I wrote the relevant chapters for the Nuffield election study about the use of mass advertising to appeal to a mass electorate. Having no Fabian objections to people enjoying the fruits of affluence, I wrote without patronizing those who did so.

To avoid being trapped by the subject of my doctoral thesis into limiting my research in party politics to the Labour Party, following the 1959 election I did a study of the Bow Group, young Conservative Oxbridge graduates who were seeking to broaden the appeal of the party's programme and to become MPs (Rose 1961). A young Conservative parliamentary aspirant explained to me that someone like himself, who was only 'first generation public school as well as Oxbridge', could now seek a safe seat in Parliament in competition with those born into politics, like Winston Churchill's grandson or those who married into the aristocracy, like Harold Macmillan. However, this was not easy. The first seat that he held was a marginal seat and he lost it. After further searching, he was adopted as a candidate in a safe seat and ended up a senior Cabinet minister.

A younger generation of party politicians wanted to appeal for votes on grounds of competence rather than class. The Labour Party campaigned successfully in the 1964 election with the slogan, 'Let's Go with Labour'; it avoided any indication of the direction in which it would head. When I asked Tony Crosland a few months before the election what difference he thought a Labour government would make

'Well, gentlemen, I think we all fought a good fight . . .'

A Spectator cartoon that epitomised the 'Never had it so good' election victory of the Conservative Party, led by Prime Minister Harold Macmillan

he told me: 'Not much. But you only have to look at the government front benches to see how bereft of ideas and incompetent they are. We're bound to be better than that lot'.

Party leadership was passing into the hands of meritocrats, typically, first-generation university graduates of demonstrated political ability. As one of my confident Manchester undergraduates, Dennis Kavanagh, explained to me, 'We all slept with a copy of Michael Young's *The Rise of the Meritocracy* under the pillow'. Harold Wilson, the Labour leader chosen to succeed Hugh Gaitskell was an early example; he had been to a state school, won a scholarship to Oxford, and was buying his house on a mortgage.

Standing outside traditional partisan and class alignments made me rely on systematic evidence rather than personal experience to understand class structure. I found that ideological stereotypes of manual workers as Labour voters, trade union members, low in education and lacking home-ownership did not fit empirical evidence. At the 1964 election only one-quarter of manual workers matched the ideal-type specification of a Labour voter. The median manual worker had two working-class characteristics and two middle-class characteristics. The article was accepted for publication in *Sociology*, the official journal of the British Sociological Association. The journal required a brief biography that included the name of one's secondary school, a marker of social class. I reported it as 'City

Streets School, St. Louis' (Rose 1968: 158). I never learned whether the editor was taken in by this or printed it after abandoning the attempt to write a letter asking whether I was trying to mock British sociology's obsession with class.

My understanding of advertising and of voters, combined with freelance journalism, gave me access to political campaigners on both sides of the partisan divide. Over cordial and leisurely meals and drinks, campaigners were ready to describe what they did, often acting in ways very different from the conventional textbook model of vote-maximizing politicians. David Butler and Tony King encouraged me to write an account of political campaigning in the style of a Nuffield election study. I had read enough books on campaigning to know that such studies were ephemeral. Sometimes they were misleading, such as Theodore White's claim that John F. Kennedy's bid for the presidency reflected the transformation of American society, ignoring the fact that Kennedy won less than half the vote.

To show the contrast between what campaigners did and abstract theories, I developed a detailed model of what a rational campaign would look like. This paradigm was used to guide interviews with campaigners and, since campaigns are public events, to analyse the outputs of campaign organizations. The resulting book was called *Influencing Voters: a Study of Campaign Rationality*. Applying Robert Merton's theory of latent functions to the systematic analysis of advertisements and expenditure, I demonstrated the extent to which campaigners behaved in seemingly irrational ways (Rose 1967: 23ff, 186ff). A theoretically oriented American reviewer found this surprising. Knowing party organizations at first hand, I wasn't surprised.

By 1975 the Conservatives had a meritocratic leader whose father was a lower middle class shopkeeper. Margaret Thatcher felt more comfortable with the six Jews in her Cabinet than with the smaller number of Etonians, because their religious background, like her class background, meant they needed merit to succeed.[1] Among politicians of my experience, Thatcher was outstanding in articulating convictions that were clear though not consensual. She used the powers inherent in the British system of government to push through policies regardless of controversy. At press conferences during election campaigns I used to watch her advisers tensely afraid that her unbridled enthusiasm for freeing citizens from dependence on the state would lead her to go over the top with a remark that would lose millions of votes. She never did, but she could have. The longer she was in office the more attention she paid to her political id than to her super-ego. The result of pushing Thatcherite policies too far was the loss of support in opinion polls and in 1990 rejection by her own MPs.

---

1.   When asked in the early 1980s by Jim Alt, a shrewd political scientist who moved from England to the United States, what was new in Britain, I noted that there were now six Jews in the Conservative Cabinet. He immediately queried, 'Why aren't they doing better?'

Personality in place of party programmes

The openness of parties to researchers, party members and ordinary voters was qualitatively different in the 1950s and 1960s than it is today (Rose 1996a). There were no barriers imposed by go-fers, chiefs of staff or armed security police. In the 1950 election Clement Attlee went campaigning in a family car driven by his wife and without any entourage. Politicians did not read from tele-prompters but spoke directly to their audience and were judged by their ability to handle hecklers. Sometimes they couldn't. When a pro-capital punishment MP told a student audience that some murderers had spent less time in prison than he had spent in the House of Commons, a student cried out, 'That's right; they should have hung you!'

I could easily get a press pass to go to party conferences, and did so for a quarter of a century. I heard Aneurin Bevan skillfully use the microphone to override the storm of left-wing protest occasioned by his U-turn to endorse nuclear weapons at the 1957 Labour Party conference. At the 1962 Labour conference I saw the despondent look on the faces of pro-European Labour friends when Hugh Gaitskell passionately rejected joining the European Union as it would mean the end of a thousand (*sic*) years of British history. At a special Labour Party conference in January, 1981, friends of mine from Oxford who had become Labour MPs mingled together only to go their separate ways immediately afterwards, some joining the breakaway Social Democratic Party while others held to the belief that there was no political future outside the Labour Party.

When I started research, British parties were organizations with hundreds of career staff and a formal structure in which decisions were made collectively. In *The Problem of Party Government* I documented the multiple institutions of a party (Rose 1974a). When there was no information available in print, I could ring up or go see friends working in party headquarters to ask for information. Since that book was published, parties have become focussed on a leader who is surrounded by advisors and courtiers who protect him or her from other personalities who are seen as challengers. Leaders either ignore party institutions or treat them as their personal belonging to do with as they wish.

The fascination of the media with personality is understandable, since names make news and political journalists are much better in writing about people rather than difficult problems of government. The fixation of careerist MPs on their party leader is understandable too, since party leaders control party patronage. Up to a point the media has been correct in describing each victorious party leader as a charismatic figure, since the term's root meaning is a person who destroys existing institutions and substitutes his or her own personality. Just as Colonel Parker had marketed Elvis Presley as a white boy who could sing black, so Peter Mandelson had the insight and determination to promote Tony Blair as the Labour leader who looked blue but could produce a red victory. Unlike Thatcherites, who were defined by *what* they believed in, Blairites have been defined by *who* they believed in.

Instead of focussing on personalities, interesting as they often are, I initiated the comparative study of presidents and prime ministers (*see* Rose and Suleiman 1980). Cross-national differences in national institutions are more important than within-nation differences in personalities. Big structural changes in the political environment have altered the role of leadership from the time of Roosevelt and Truman to that of Reagan and Bush and from Churchill and Attlee to Thatcher and Blair (Rose 1991, 2001). Changes have included the introduction of television, inter-generational change in the recruitment of legislators, alterations in procedures for choosing party leaders, and the increasing influence on their actions of what happens in the rest of the world. British prime ministers have been cut down to size because winning a vote in the House of Commons is not the same as winning a vote in the European Union. American presidents have found that global engagement brings with it vulnerability to failed states and armed non-states.

The dominance of personality over policy was brought home to me when trying to interest a BBC producer in a programme about my book on *The Prime Minister in a Shrinking World*. Changes since 1945 could easily be visualised by cross-cutting between black-and-white film clips of staid prime ministers born in the Victorian era and colour film of contemporary incumbents showing how 'with it' they are. The response confirmed the problem my book highlighted. The BBC was only interested in programmes that viewed politics through the prism of personalities.

When editors changed at *The Times* after the 1974 elections, I moved to the *Daily Telegraph* to write about elections. There it was a pleasure to work with Bill Deedes, whose wisdom was garnered in war and in observing Westminster life as a journalist and backbench Conservative MP. As the golfing partner of Dennis Thatcher, Bill was the nominal recipient of the fictitious letters of the prime minister's spouse, satirized in 'Dear Bill'. These connections made me acceptable in Westminster during the years of Margaret Thatcher's eminence. A change in ownership brought new brooms to the *Telegraph*, and in 1988 I was among the many swept out. Changes in the media meant that it was no longer possible to ride both academic and journalistic horses at the same time. This turned out to my great advantage, for I was beginning to spend a lot of time in Berlin researching lesson-drawing. Once the Berlin Wall fell, my mind was focussed far to the east of Fleet Street. I spent the 1992 election night at home cleaning the files of what has since become the first of 20 New Russia Barometer surveys (*see* Chapter 8).

From England to Scotland

Not being English, I had to learn what the difference was between England and Britain and did so slowly. Like most people I knew at the time, I thought the South of England was England until I moved to Manchester. Only after moving to the University of Strathclyde in Glasgow did I learn that there were differences between England and Britain and they depended on states of mind as well as the boundaries of states. England can refer to the football team that is a member of FIFA and competes in the World Cup or it can include Wales if it refers to many Acts of Parliament in which the Principality of Wales is subsumed as a region. A territory can be described as Britain when it includes Scotland and Wales or as the United Kingdom if Northern Ireland is added. The BBC is actually the UKBC

(United Kingdom Broadcasting Company). Admiral Nelson's call to his seamen at Trafalgar — 'England expects that every man will do his duty' — was addressed to crews that were more multinational than a NATO force would be today.

Until devolution brought home the fact that the United Kingdom was more than England, the two terms were often used interchangeably. Bob McKenzie, a Canadian by birth but a Londoner by assimilation, liked to joke that the only reason that England called itself the United Kingdom in international affairs was to avoid sitting next to Egypt at meetings of the United Nations. In 1981 Louis Heren, a Cockney-born *Times* journalist, thought there was nothing odd in authoring a book entitled *Alas, Alas for England: What Went Wrong for Britain*. The concept of the Crown as a territory of indefinite domain made it possible to accommodate accordion-like changes in the scope of British government due to marriage, inheritance, military conquest, exploration and colonisation (*see* Rose 1982: chapter 1).

My first sight of Glasgow was in 1962, driving through East End tenements with three children under the age of three in search of the airport with an Air Icelandic propeller flight ready to take us to the United States. Its grimy stone face was the urban shock equivalent to my first sight of sharecropper shacks in rural Mississippi. The advertisement of the politics chair at Strathclyde made me investigate more fully. I found Glasgow a big city with big attractions as well as big social problems. As an American, I was accustomed to both. The University is in the city centre, across the street from a magnificent Victorian City Hall building and in those days a short walk from newspaper offices, a television studio and an opera house.

Whereas Dover Street, where my Manchester department was located, had once been the home of Karl Marx's collaborator, Friedrich Engels, when writing *The Wealth of Nations* Adam Smith drew examples from Glasgow's High Street, just down the street from my Strathclyde office. The High Street also offered a striking example of the integration of medieval social services. At the top of the High Street there is a Cathedral, a hospital and a cemetery, and at the bottom the Gallowgate. The city's architecture is European not English. Flats like those in which Freud lived and worked in Vienna can be found in the West End of Glasgow; the house in which Freud died in London could not be found in either Glasgow or Vienna.

The Valley of the Clyde offers a wide choice of places to live. We chose to settle in Helensburgh, a town of 10,000 where the Highlands come down to the sea. It is 40 minutes by train to Strathclyde, long enough to read a journal article and then some, and 35 minutes from Glasgow Airport. To the west the nearest proper airports are in Iceland and then Alaska. In 47 years we have lived in three different counties — Dunbarton, Strathclyde and Argyll — without moving house, thanks to the penchant of politicians to re-organise local government boundaries. We bought half a house that was then one hundred years old and designed by a Scottish vernacular architect on enlightenment principles, unlike the Gothic revival houses built in North Oxford at the same time. Its rooms and 12-foot ceilings can accommodate the thousands of books accumulated in pursuit of varied interests over the years. Although I have never worn a kilt, in winter I do wear knee-length wool kilt socks to keep warm while writing in my study. Looking after a large garden has taught me the wisdom of the remark of Denis Healey, a former Chancellor of the Exchequer, that managing the economy is more like patiently cultivating a garden than like writing a computer programme.

Moving to Glasgow from Manchester meant going from a city that London deemed provincial to a place that was simply different. People do not have the hang-dog attitude of provincials; they are proud of being Glaswegians, Scots and British. This produces a triple identity that is easily worn and altered with circumstances. Travelling abroad you could explain where you are from by invoking football, whisky, the Highlands or in Italy, Verdi's *Macbetto*, which concludes with a coded reference to Italian independence, a hymn to *Repubblica Scozia*. I quickly learned that Scotland is also a league of city-states. When Donald Dewar was first minister of the Scottish government, he welcomed a European conference to his native city of Glasgow without ever mentioning Scotland. In American terms, Glasgow is like Chicago and Edinburgh is like Boston; they are as close as Berkeley is to Stanford and just as different from each other.

As an American from a border state, it is easy to handle multiple identities. I called the first edition of my United Kingdom book *Politics in England* because England not only has five-sixths of the UK's population but also because politicians from Scotland, Wales and Northern Ireland must work within a political system dominated by Englishmen (Rose 1965: 26). In 2000 James Naughtie, a Scottish-born London-based journalist, taxed me with using that title when presenting my award for a lifetime of achievement in studying UK politics. I quoted the foregoing passage and noted that four leading Cabinet ministers at the time — the Prime Minister, the Foreign Secretary, the Chancellor of the Exchequer and the Lord Chancellor of England — as well as generations of successful London media personalities, himself included, went to London to seek what Lord Birkenhead had called the glittering prizes of Empire.

No sooner had I arrived in Scotland than a small question mark was raised over the substantial facade of government in Westminster. The Scottish National Party (SNP) won an upset by-election victory from Labour. The Prime Minister, Harold Wilson, appointed a Royal Commission on the Constitution in an attempt to stifle the Nationalist challenge. The Chair of the Commission not only sat on the issue but even fell asleep in the chair next to me in a weekend devolution seminar in Oxford. When the SNP failed to defend its by-election victory at the 1970 general election, the cloud appeared to have passed. Differences of opinion in the Commission's Report had an additional soporific effect. However, the SNP's success in winning victory in seven seats at the February, 1974 British general election could not be ignored, for it meant that Labour had to govern without a working parliamentary majority. When a privately conducted opinion poll was interpreted as showing that devolving powers to Scotland could help Labour gain a majority, Wilson promised to bring in devolution. The default of the Conservatives in England gave Labour an absolute majority to govern, and Wilson was stuck with a commitment to devolution.

Having seen Westminster's authority undermined in Northern Ireland (Chapter 7), I could not ignore a second and non-violent challenge on my doorstep. While Harold Wilson had, in Walter Bagehot's phrase, 'broken the cake of custom', it was unclear what sort of a meal he would or could make of devolution. In discussions with British ministers I soon realized they were out of their depth. One minister thought devolving taxing powers on cigarettes, a common practice in the United States, would cause people like himself to stock up on potentially cheaper cigarettes in Scotland. I suggested he look at the cost of a train fare before calculating savings. Another thought that devolving spending powers to Scotland would satisfy Scots because they could decide what to spend more on and what to spend less money on. He did not appreciate that the SNP was using the prospect of North Sea oil revenues to promise to spend more on everything!

Many enthusiasts for devolution missed the point too; they assumed that whatever preferences were shown by public opinion surveys would decide what the UK government would do. While Scots were divided about what they wanted, London was united in wanting to devolve less. When I took a public finance expert to explain American fiscal federalism to Joel Barnett, the Chief Secretary of the Treasury, he listened and then said it wouldn't work. Assuming that Treasury officials had been feeding him administrative objections, I expressed mock surprise that British officials lacked the ability of collectors of revenue in my native Missouri. Joel explained that administrative issues weren't the problem; the point was that the Treasury and the Cabinet wouldn't wear a transfer of fiscal powers.

Instead of explaining what had yet to happen, my research programme concentrated on understanding what was in place, namely, a highly centralized United Kingdom government of a multinational state. In order to examine the diversity of ways in which centralized authority varied in different parts of the United Kingdom, I created a Work Group on the Territorial Dimension in United Kingdom Politics, which met annually to make comparisons between political institutions and politics in different parts of the UK. Panels were organised by subject matter, such as local government or voting behaviour, rather than by nation (Madgwick and Rose 1982). We welcomed all concerned with these issues, including Canadians, a few English eccentrics, and an Ulster loyalist leader who listened carefully and was later killed by a car bomb planted by other loyalists. With Ian McAllister I produced a reference book, *United Kingdom Facts* (1982); its motto was, 'All the facts that *British (sic) Political Facts* leaves out'. Drawing on the experience of Ireland since the 1920s, I co-authored an article on the political as well as economic consequences of independence. They were substantial, such as Ireland remaining neutral in the Second World War and rejecting the introduction of a national health service afterwards (Rose and Garvin 1983).

Events justified the strategy of focussing on how the United Kingdom operated, anomalies and all, for in 1979 devolution failed to secure endorsement in a Scottish referendum. The Conservative victory at the 1979 British general election put the Mace, a mute but heavyweight symbol of Westminster's authority, firmly in Unionist hands. An unintended consequence was a pro-devolution backlash in Scotland. After Labour regained office in 1997, a new devolution act authorized the first Scottish parliament in almost 300 years. In recognition of the need for students of government in Westminster to understand non-English political practices, I altered the title of my textbook to *Politics in Britain*.

The sponsors of devolution assumed that what Westminster enacted would get rid of pressure from Scotland for further changes. They were wrong. The victory of the SNP at the 2007 Scottish election enabled it to form a minority government. To counter the SNP, the Labour government appointed Sir Kenneth Calman to chair a committee to recommend 'new and improved' devolution measures acceptable to the British government. I sent Calman a copy of my earlier book, and he seized upon a table giving alternative explanations of the demand for independence, each implying a different response from Westminster (Rose 1982: 188). Calman was inclined to diagnose the demand as reflecting economic problems that could be resolved by higher British economic growth. I suggested that instead it could reflect a popular loss of confidence in Britain's governors that could only be met by restoring confidence in Westminster. In the British general election that followed in 2010, only two in three English voters expressed confidence in either the Conservative or Labour parties and in Scotland even fewer. The collapse of Labour across Britain at that election helped the SNP to win an absolute majority in the Scottish Parliament the following year and call a referendum on independence in autumn, 2014.

To my mind the alternatives of independence and devolution are inadequate; the key concept is interdependence. The United Kingdom institutionalizes interdependence in a multinational Westminster Parliament in which Scotland has some seats but England has more. What happens in Brussels or Beijing can have more impact on all parts of the United Kingdom than what happens in Westminster. The cross-national interdependencies arising from globalization diminish England's claim to be a big fish by increasing the size of the pond. In the words of a former Belgian prime minister, 'There are two kinds of countries in the world today: those that are small and know it and those that are small and don't' (www.profrose.eu/writings.php#england).

The choice facing Scots today is between alternative forms of interdependence. The SNP leader Alex Salmond thinks Scotland would be better off independent. When an Aberdeen student challenged him to give an example of what difference independence would make, Salmond took my breath away by giving a straight answer: 'We wouldn't have had troops in Iraq'. By contrast when I asked two Glasgow-born Foreign Office diplomats where they would recommend a young Scot to go today in search of glittering prizes — London, Brussels or New York — I was struck by their silence.

The challenge facing Britain's governors is how to maintain the commitment of a big majority of Scots to the United Kingdom. Instead of trying to build confidence in Britain, the campaign against independence has been based on the maxim in a poem by Hilaire Belloc: 'Hold on to nurse for fear of something worse'. Emphasizing the uncertainties of independence may see off the threat of a Scottish majority endorsing independence in the September, 2014 referendum. However, it does not address the problem of what to do about the decline in confidence in government in England. Nor does it address the challenge posed by former American Secretary of State Dean Acheson in 1962: 'Britain has lost an Empire but has yet to find a role'.

Chapter 6

America Then and Now

All my European friends read books by American political scientists, but it is very rare for any to show an interest in comparing and contrasting the American and European political systems. Students of American politics have likewise taken no interest in European politics. As late as the 1980s a president of the American Political Science Association could be a well known and respected scholar yet never have had a passport. Instead of making comparisons with what happens in other countries, American academics usually make comparisons with abstract models that lack 'legs', that is, they do not travel to the many countries that are governed through a parliament elected by proportional representation. Likewise, the outlook of Rhodes Scholars who have studied at Oxford but made their career in American politics rarely show any sign of the effects of years of studying abroad. Keeping quiet about having done so can even be electorally prudent.

Without comparison there is no evidence of the extent to which America is exceptional or sets an example that other countries should or could follow. Yet it is unclear which countries the United States is most appropriately compared with. Editing a book on *The Welfare State East and West* with a Japanese colleague (Rose and Shiratori 1986) made me very conscious of the ambiguous position of a country geographically between Europe and Asia. When I asked Nathan Glazer, who contributed the chapter on the United States, whether he was part of the East or West, he responded as a person for whom New York was the world: 'Neither; I'm from the Bronx'. In practice, American public expenditure on welfare has more in common with Japan than Sweden and the most populous state, California, faces Asia.

At times I have benefitted intellectually from importing American ideas to Europe and exporting ideas in the other direction. A quintessentially American book that is little read in Europe, Dick Neustadt's *Presidential Power*, has provided me with insights useful in studying the power of British prime ministers. In a complementary manner, I have drawn on European perspectives to write about how the power of the President is limited by engagement in the world far beyond the Washington beltway and to show empirically under what circumstances and to what extent American public policy is exceptional (Rose 1991 1991a). Being from a border state, I am especially sensitive to the fact that there is more than one way to portray American society. In 1964 Sam Beer asked me how I thought he should begin a Harvard course about America that mixed Europeans and Americans. I suggested he start by asking: 'Is a Mississippian an American?' Being a patriotic Yankee, Sam did not take up my offer.

I am doubly deviant in being a Europeanist with a deep and abiding interest in the United States and in being an American with a continuing interest in placing American politics in a comparative framework. From time to time people ask me why I have not made my career in an American university or why I live in Europe without being born here. Fifty years ago I told a journalist writing a profile of Americans living in England, 'I want to have the best of both worlds. And I'm American enough to think it can be done' (www.profrose.eu/writings.php#england). I haven't changed my mind since.

The America in which I grew up during and after the Second World War is another country from America today. The population has doubled from 150 million to more than 300 million and changed greatly in its composition and politics while doing so. The bulk of America's population no longer faces east toward Europe but west toward Asia or south toward Latin America. I have kept in touch with the United States for both professional and personal reasons. Hunting for a job while at Oxford led me to join the American Political Science Association in 1958. In the days when the *APSR* was readable, I read it almost cover to cover until my research interest turned from American political science to American politics as practised by presidents. I have criss-crossed the Atlantic by everything from slow boat and uncomfortable propeller aeroplane to a comfortable seat in a jet. I have also spent days and nights crossing the continental United States by car, Greyhound bus, train, and in jet flights that are similar in length to a flight from Scotland to New England.

Free at Last

An interest in jazz made me aware that even though the Civil War had led to the abolition of slavery it had not ended many forms of racial discrimination. While the virtues of the Southern cause and white supremacy were not taught in my school, all Missouri schools were segregated by law. Racial covenants in housing deeds precluded the sale of a house in a white neighbourhood to a black person. After being declared unenforceable by the Supreme Court, housing segregation was informally enforced by real estate firms.

In those days racial discrimination was attacked through the courts. The lead was taken by the Legal Defence Team of the National Association for the Advancement of Colored People (NAACP). I began following their patient pursuit of justice through the courts while still in secondary school. At the age of 16 I was asked to become a dues-paying member of my parents' Southern (and segregated) Presbyterian Church. As a convinced secularist, I refused to do so. When my parents said a small contribution was all that was required to show allegiance, I replied by saying that the issue was one of principle. To emphasize the point, I offered to contribute the dues that the church wanted to the NAACP. No more was said.

When I was a student in Baltimore it was a segregated city; Johns Hopkins had an integrated student body in terms of religion and ethnicity but not race. It also had a faculty that knew the South from their upbringing as well as their research. Between semesters in January 1953 I took a 2,400-mile tour of the South on Greyhound buses. I met the Jim Crow system at first hand when the bus passed into Virginia from Washington D.C. In a New Orleans that had not yet become tourist infected, I heard lots of jazz, including Alphonse Picou playing his classic clarinet solo on *High Society*. I also went to Charleston, a beautiful backwater, albeit also the city of a tragic novel and opera, *Porgy and Bess*. In Richmond, Virginia, I went through the Museum of the Confederacy. The trip gave me a better feel of the Deep South, which previously I had only read about. It felt like it read.

A large black population meant that Baltimore also had jazz. When Louis Armstrong went on tour with Benny Goodman in a battle of the bands, I got my first sight of him there. The show closed with Armstrong and his band marching up to the stage from the back of the auditorium. We all turned our heads away from the on-stage Goodman band to welcome Armstrong back. The tour soon broke up, for Goodman couldn't take playing second fiddle, as it were, to Armstrong. Musicians then less well known also played in the city. One Monday night I heard Dave Brubeck play in a nearly empty black bar and chatted with him between sets; there was no one else there to talk to besides the bartender.

In a constitutional law class at Hopkins I read with fascination the way in which civil rights lawyers slowly chipped away at the edifice of segregation that the Supreme Court had legitimated in 1896. Instead of flamboyance, care was taken to show that the doctrine of 'separate but equal' was violated when a state provided inferior funding and worse trained teachers for black schools. At this time, the landmark desegregation case, Brown vs. Board of Education, was pending in the Supreme Court. The acceptance of segregation was shown by John W. Davis, a former US ambassador to England and Democratic candidate for President in 1924, being the attorney for the segregation side. One Monday morning in spring 1953, I was a youthful spectator of Supreme Court justices delivering decisions and wondered what the well dressed black lawyers in attendance were looking for. A year later, Chief Justice Earl Warren achieved his goal of a unanimous decision declaring segregation unconstitutional and the black lawyers got what they had long waited for, justice. This has given me an appreciation of law as a tool for creating change and made me sceptical of assertions that cultural change requires many generations.

When I returned to St. Louis from England in 1954, there were hardly any signs of the Supreme Court ruling having an effect. As a side line I produced a television series on civil liberties on the local educational television station. It was difficult to get black people to appear on television to discuss discrimination. The first schools to be desegregated were Catholic schools. When irate parishioners threatened to sue the Archbishop about this action, they were reminded that whatever the civil courts decided he had the power to excommunicate them. The only union that was integrated was a Teamsters local; it brought in a heavyweight 'enforcer' from Chicago to lean on white cab drivers who protested.

The outcome of the bus boycott that Martin Luther King Jr. and colleagues organised in Montgomery, Alabama was in no sense inevitable. In 1957 I met Rosa Parks, the woman who started it all by refusing to move to the back of a bus. What struck me most was her appearance. Instead of being a striking personality, she looked ordinary, like any domestic servant I might see on the bus that ran near

The memorial in Montgomery Alabama to the 40 people killed in the Deep South because they sought civil rights. The quote from Martin Luther King Jr. echoes the Old Testament prophet Amos at 5,24

my parents' home. This told me that the protest in Alabama for which she was the spark had the potential to become a broad movement to overcome white Southern resistance to the enforcement of Supreme Court decisions.

Before returning to England in August, 1957, I took my wife on a motoring holiday across the South. In rural Arkansas the only sign of integration was that the houses of white sharecroppers were just as ramshackle and poor as those of black field workers. For better as well as worse, New Orleans hadn't changed. In Montgomery, Alabama, a local newspaper reporter told me that reports of trouble had been exaggerated by publicity stirred up by Jews and Communists who had come down from New York. At Tuskegee Institute, founded by Booker T. Washington in Alabama to train the sons and daughters of slaves, progress meant that it was launching a liberal arts course to complement vocational programmes in subjects such as building and tailoring. When I asked the Dean, Charles Gomillion, whether he thought his daughter would ever go to college in Alabama, he replied, 'Mr. Rose, there isn't a college in Alabama good enough for my daughter; I've been a student at the University of Chicago'. He didn't mention that the month before he had put his life on the line by calling a meeting to take steps to secure free and fair elections in his black-majority county. Gomillion's motto was 'Keep everlastingly at it'. After 30 years of patient pushing, he finally secured a Supreme Court decision mandating what he sought.

The election of John F. Kennedy did not change the *laissez-faire* attitude of the White House toward enforcing the Supreme Court desegregation decision.

When I challenged Dick Neustadt in early 1962 about Kennedy's policy of benign neglect of desegregation, he replied that the President's great responsibilities for foreign policy required him to keep Southern Democrats on board in order to maintain backing for what Kennedy wanted to do abroad. This reflected the fact that the Deep South, where discrimination in voter registration was still rampant, had contributed the electoral college votes that Kennedy had needed to win the White House. My reaction was that looking after the rights of Americans was more important than looking after the rest of the world. Dick's point was made that autumn when Kennedy was confronted with the Cuban missile crisis. My point was made in September 1963, when the bombing of a church in Birmingham, Alabama was a call to act that no President could ignore.

Race relations problems were emerging in England. To meet a labour shortage created by full employment, London Transport recruited West Indians to work as bus conductors, the lower-ranked job on buses manned by two persons. There was opposition from unions, for example, trying to keep Sikhs from employment because the religious requirement to wear a turban meant they couldn't wear a bus conductor's cap (*see* Beetham 1970, drawing on a dissertation he wrote under my supervision in Manchester). By 1964 England had as large a black population as St. Louis. The Home Office anxiously recruited two veterans of wartime counter-espionage to conduct a survey of race relations. I received a grant from it to study race relations in my native St. Louis.

In the long, hot summer of 1964 there were civil rights demonstrations all over the South, some triggering murderous responses. Non-violent protests in St. Louis were met by non-violent foot-dragging and gradual concessions. I put on my best English accent and interviewed people on both sides. White officials told how federal pressures were making them adapt traditional practices in police, housing and employment. A black activist and later a 16-term Member of Congress from St. Louis, Bill Clay, was campaigning to get blacks promoted from being a truck driver's assistant to a driver by threatening a beer boycott. When the beer company, Anheuser-Busch, raised questions of differences in educational qualification, he told them, 'Shit, you don't need an education to drive a beer truck. The only difference between the driver and his assistant is 20 cents an hour and the colour of their skin'. The company took his point. My report carefully documented the institutions, the laws and the number of officials that would be needed to create a set of anti-discrimination measures in Britain like those then prevailing in America (www.profrose.eu/writings.php#america).

By the time my report on race relations was delivered in London, a racist Conservative candidate had won an upset victory against a leading Labour politician in the 1964 British general election. The new Labour government was in a panic about a prospective white backlash if it enacted any laws that would effectively protect non-white immigrants against discrimination. It claimed that using the law to enforce rights was inconsistent with British practice, an argument subsequently used and abandoned in Northern Ireland. Trade unions were opposed, since the beneficiaries of job discrimination tended to be their existing white members. When I was sounded out about becoming the research director of a new programme on British race relations, I politely refused. Simultaneously, in the United States the 1965 Voting Rights Act promoted by Lyndon Johnson meant the start of an era in race relations different from what I had grown up with.

The shooting of Martin Luther King Jr. in 1968 was much more significant to me than the killing of President Kennedy five years earlier. I have always found it difficult to believe that James Earl Ray, the uneducated convict from St. Louis who was arrested in London for killing King, could have secured the resources to flee that far without help from co-conspirators. I suggested half in jest to Andrew Greeley, a priest-professor from Chicago, that we should try to fund Irish research by writing a best seller with the title 'Who Really Killed Martin Luther King?' Greeley made the intriguing comment that, while there were a lot of FBI men in his parish, this was the one topic that none of them would ever talk about. In Europe the Pope gave an unobtrusive sign that religion remained stronger than race. He broadcast a statement in which he grieved for Martin King and for Luther King; the full name of Martin Luther King did not pass his lips.

In 1976 I attended the Democratic Party convention in New York City that nominated Jimmy Carter. Ignorant Northerners assumed that any white person who spoke with such a strong Southern accent must be a sympathiser of the Ku Klux Klan. That was certainly true of his father. Carter's mother was the opposite, a nurse whose inclusive view of Christianity led her to regard blacks as well as whites as people. The most populous place in Sumter County, Georgia, where Carter grew up, was Andersonville National Cemetery (www.profrose.eu/writings.php#america). It held the bodies of 13,000 Northern troops who died while imprisoned there in the Civil War. Outside the gates of the federal property the local chapter of the United Daughters of the Confederacy erected a monument paying tribute to the Swiss-born commandant of the camp who, after refusing to implicate President Jefferson Davis in the mass deaths there, was hanged in Washington in November, 1865.

Even more alienating to New Yorkers than Carter's Southern accent was that he talked about his religious beliefs as a born-again Southern Baptist. In my guise as a BBC reporter, I rang the office of the Anti-Defamation League (ADL), the chief Jewish organization campaigning against racial discrimination, and asked for a statement about attacks on Carter because of his religion. An ADL official with the accent of a German refugee refused to denounce the attacks. If Carter knew what was happening, it didn't affect his behaviour. The concluding benediction was not, as politics would have dictated, given by the Catholic Archbishop of New York City and a rabbi. Instead, he called up to the platform the Rev Martin Luther King Sr., who let fly with the full force of a black preacher. This was a manner of speech as alien to New Yorkers as it was familiar to Carter. The message was: 'Free at last. Free at last. Thank God Almighty, we are free at last'. The 'we' included Jimmy Carter as well as all for whom the Kings spoke.

Washington: A Small Town Now Global in Impact

Visiting Washington

At the end of my first month as a student at Johns Hopkins, I paid my first visit to Washington; Harry Truman was President. I have been back for short and longer visits under 11 presidents since. Over more than 60 years, both Washington and I have changed a lot.

Washington was not a cosmopolitan city when I first knew it (Gutheim and Washburn 1976). In pre-air conditioning days, its heat and humidity made the British Foreign Office classify it as a tropical posting. Its Southern character made it unappealing to New Yorkers and New Englanders. You didn't have to cross the Potomac River to Virginia to know you were in the South; the city's schools and housing were completely segregated. It was more than 24 hours by train from Truman's home and more than three days distant by train from California. Washington had a small town feel that made it a comfortable place to live for Members of Congress. For people such as Cordell Hull, a Congressman turned Secretary of State throughout the Second World War, it had a big city feel, for Hull was born in a log cabin in the mountains of Tennessee.

After getting off the train from Baltimore I would start walking from the Capitol Building to the Lincoln Memorial or the Jefferson Memorial. The home of the Department of Agriculture was a marble temple built to honour farmers like my mother's family. To get to a shellfish dinner along the river I would walk through the old South West, a neighbourhood of frame and often shabby houses that were home to many black residents; houses and people were later cleared by urban renewal programmes. On my first visit to the White House I was the object of special attention. Having checked out of my hotel, I joined a tour while carrying a small suitcase. Halfway through the tour, two presidential security guards grabbed my arms and demanded my bag. When they opened it, my pyjamas and toothbrush fell out.

Although long settled in Europe, I have kept my hand in American politics. An Oxford degree has provided a useful network of contacts. When I went to see Congressman John Brademas, an Oxford DPhil from the college next to mine, I was wearing a Lincoln College tie because its blue colour matched my summer jacket; his chief staff assistant was wearing a Lincoln tie too. The small town experience of bumping into friends on the street is also common. When a Washington friend invited me to dinner to meet some interesting people, with one exception they were old friends, former students or both.

I covered presidential conventions as a freelance journalist from 1964 through 1976. When the Republicans nominated Barry Goldwater in 1964, his political views appeared extreme, even to party managers. Hence, free drinks were offered in the press room rather than a press conference where he could be questioned. In response to my request for a gin and lemon, the bartender filled a large tumbler with lots of gin and a slice of lemon; fortunately, it also had some ice. At the 1964 Democratic National Convention in Atlantic City I attached myself to the third and last Alabama delegation. The first two delegations were lilywhite but split between pro- and anti-George Wallace factions. The group I followed had both black and white delegates; they gained media recognition but were not seated. Afterwards, the Alabama delegates and their supporters made the boardwalk outside the convention hall shake with camp-meeting shouts.

At the 1968 Democratic Convention there was no division on racial lines; the step-by-step strategy of the Gomillions had won that victory. Instead, the Vietnam war split the convention. The music was different too. The anti-war Eugene McCarthy group were entertained by Peter, Paul and Mary singing 'Puff the Magic Dragon'. The backers of Hubert Humphrey were in no mood to sing, for he was a liberal whose heart was not in the war. However, as Lyndon Johnson's Vice President he was tied to it. As Humphrey once said, 'I love Lyndon dearly, but I wish he wouldn't ask me to open my veins and write it in my own blood *twice* a day'.

When anti-war protesters massed along Lake Michigan opposite the convention hotels, I mingled with them for a while and then moved to mingle with the Chicago police, who were massing to keep the demonstrators from advancing toward the hotel (www.profrose.eu/writings.php#america). About 6 pm the Chicago police unintentionally demonstrated the truth of the adage: 'Every country must have a political police; what it can't afford is a stupid political police'. Unprovoked, the police threw teargas at the demonstrators. Since the teargas was thrown into the wind coming off the lake, it drifted back over the police and me too. I ran for the sanctuary of the Hilton Hotel. The actions of the Chicago police were prime-time news. When news reached the Convention Hall, there was an uproar. The anti-war delegates showed greater self-control than the police. They shouted and demonstrated, but did not resort to the physical force that would have caused the suspension of the Convention before it nominated Humphrey as its presidential candidate. After midnight the anti-war demonstrators made a candlelight procession along Michigan Avenue singing 'America, the Beautiful'. The scars remained. In the bus I took out to the airport at the end of the week, the conversation turned to the actions of the Chicago police. We changed seats to split into pro and anti-police groups; I was among the antis. In November Richard Nixon was elected president by a margin of less than one per cent over Hubert Humphrey.

In 1972 the Democratic Convention in Miami Beach that nominated George McGovern saw the party united. Race was no longer an issue, since the party was now fully integrated. Since whites were a majority in the population of Southern states, Nixon was sure to win the South. Winning wasn't an issue for the Democrats. In the words of Willie Brown, a leading black politician from California, 'We are the party of all the minorities'. The election result confirmed this claim: Nixon won by as big a majority of the popular vote as Lyndon Johnson had secured for the Democrats eight years earlier. There were already whispers that victory was not secure. Herb Alexander, the national expert on party finance, told me in a hotel lobby that there was more to be heard about a little-reported break-in at the Watergate Hotel that summer.

Working Washington

By 1972 my growing interest in public policy research (Chapter 11) led me to start a twenty-year programme of Washington-based research. The social indicators movement had brought together a number of first-rate academics to show the usefulness of social science knowledge by applying it to problems of public policy. Pat Moynihan got President Nixon to appoint Mancur Olson and Raymond Bauer to government jobs with the task of producing a volume of social indicators. This appealed to me as I had been trying to identify quantitative indicators that could be used to test comparatively what disadvantages Ulster people had suffered because of having a partially legitimate regime (Rose 1971: chapter 15; 1989). I had assembled statistical yearbooks from 18 countries in search of data. I applied for and received a fellowship to spend six months at the Woodrow Wilson Centre in Washington to work on the application of social science methods to public policy in the summer and autumn of 1974.

No sooner had I arrived in Washington than it became evident that everyone knew what Herb Alexander had been talking about two years earlier. The Watergate scandal meant that the indicators that most people were talking about were those that would show President Nixon was lying. There were a few exceptions, such as Pat Buchanan, who thought that the only evidence that mattered was that Nixon had won the election.[1] My sympathies were not with Nixon, but as a believer in the rule of law and a Pulitzer-trained reporter I was disappointed to see how many Democrats were looking for blood not evidence. The evidence that came out showed that while Nixon had not approved the Watergate break in, he did participate in the cover up of incompetent conspirators.

On the night President Nixon resigned, my wife and I went out for a big steak dinner to celebrate. The restaurant was closing early so everyone could get home to watch his final television speech. Instead of offering an apology, Nixon offered his resignation. When mingling afterwards with a happy throng in front of the White House, I bought buttons for my children with the motto: 'Nixon inoperative'. The vendor said I could pay whatever I liked as a contribution to the cause. When told that the cause was the Socialist Workers' Party, I gave him a dollar and said, 'That's what you get under capitalism'. The next morning we watched the helicopter take off from the South Lawn carrying Nixon into his premature retirement. No one in the crowd gave the Southern farewell, 'Y'all come back'.

My research project was about Management by Objectives (MbO), a business technique that a clutch of Harvard MBAs had introduced in hopes of increasing the efficiency of federal spending. The President's signature appeared on a letter to each department head asking him or her to send a list of presidential objectives. Staff in the Office of Management and Budget were assigned to develop milestones to monitor progress toward achieving these objectives. The MbO programme was headed by Fred Malek, a deputy to John Ehrlichman and

---

1. A similar White House claim was later made when President Clinton was denying that he had had a relationship with Monica Lewinsky.

H. R. Haldeman, the so-called Prussians, who sought to exercise tight control of domestic policy. Departmental heads couldn't ignore this request. However, the idea that the President had to ask rather than tell his Cabinet what his objectives were indicated to me the President had little interest in most policies enacted in his name.[2] Management specialists describe ignoring most activities in an organization as management by exception. This raises the question: How are normal policy issues dealt with?

I interviewed officials in OMB who were monitoring agency objectives and then interviewed officials in the agencies who were being monitored. The result was an excellent education for myself in Washington politics; friendships among career staff in the federal government; and a book in which the first chapter was entitled 'In search of political objectives' (Rose 1976). The last chapter was called 'Does the President have objectives?' The attempt to introduce this business practice into government showed that the business that matters in Washington is politics not profit. Moreover, survival in Washington politics means that you often had to go into business for yourself rather than be a dutiful cog in a hierarchical organization chart. The MbO programme was an education for Malek, a West Point graduate with experience in Vietnam before he gained his Harvard MBA. Malek told me that the first thing he learned working for the President was that 'Washington is a place where the shit hits the fan every morning before 9 am'.

Even though the MbO programme was never fully implemented, I argued that the analytic approach it introduced had not disappeared but evaporated, that is, it had become part of the climate of opinion and could thereby have a long-term effect (Rose 1977). However, it did not have a short-term effect. In September, 1977, I met President Carter's director of management. He courteously sat me down by the marble fire place in his massive office and, instead of telling me his plans, started quizzing me about how his Republican predecessors had done his job. After telling him what I knew, I staggered up Connecticut Avenue and met Allan Schick, a public administration expert. I said, 'My God, X doesn't know what he is doing. Why can't he learn from history?' With the wisdom of the millennia, Allan told me, 'History is a record of failures. Since you have just won the election, you cannot fail'. I immediately thought of Shelley's poem about Ozymandias, king of kings, whose ruined statue could only be looked on with despair.

By this time I had a bad case of Potomac fever, that is, a desire to keep my hand in Washington politics. The cure was a good idea: edit the first comparative study of presidents and prime ministers. At that time the Brookings Institution, which was inclined to the Democrats, would only publish books by fulltime staff members. The American Enterprise Institute (AEI), a pro-Republican think tank, had the free market idea that it would have more choice of ideas if it published books by anyone with something worth saying. Austin Ranney and Howard

---

2. Fearing defeat in his race for the California governorship in 1962, Nixon told a former Hopkins classmate of mine that his consolation was he wouldn't have to deal with dog shit topics like drug control.

Penniman, lifelong Democrats, were then on the AEI staff commissioning books about elections around the world. They arranged for AEI to fund me to edit a book comparing presidents and prime ministers (Rose and Suleiman 1980). Having already been a visiting fellow at Brookings, spending time at AEI helped me build contacts on both sides of the political street. Friends who were Democrats were surprised that anyone they knew would work with a pro-Republican think tank. They were even more surprised when I said that AEI was prepared to sponsor research of all kinds because it was confident that in the market place of ideas its ideas would win. It took two election victories by Ronald Reagan and three by Margaret Thatcher for American liberals to realise that a two-party choice of think tanks was in keeping with the views of the electorate (cf. Rose 1993: 473ff).

By the 1980s Washington was no longer a small Southern town. It was a big city with lots of bright people, both foreign and European. When Marty Lipset, a native New Yorker and onetime Harvard professor, decided to move back to the East Coast from Stanford, he chose to be at a university in the Washington area, George Mason, because more stimulating political conversation could be had in Washington than in New York. A sojourn as a visiting scholar at the International Monetary Fund working on taxation and the growth of government and a period as a World Bank consultant following the fall of the Berlin Wall extended my split-screen vision of Washington politics, one-half being the view of an American and the other that of a European.

Washington is now a city with a global impact. I have described this through a three-stage model of the post-modern presidency (Rose 1991). First came postage-stamp presidents, for whom doing little was enough and foreign entanglements were to be avoided. Franklin D. Roosevelt created the activist modern presidency, which is the dominant model. I see a third stage, the post-modern presidency. In order to manage the American economy and defend the country in an increasingly open world, the president must continuously engage with it. While the United States has a big displacement in the world, a consequence of interdependence is that other countries in the international system can now affect the United States. To deny this is to pursue a foreign policy without foreigners. Yet many members of the Washington policy community continue to do so. In the days when international phone calls were made through an operator, I asked the operator placing my call to Rome whether she spoke Italian. Her proud Southern answer was: 'No, suh. This is Washington D.C. Ah speak American'.

Originally I wanted to call my book *The World Closes In on the White House*. However, the publisher, Ed Artinian of Chatham House, vetoed this on the grounds that potential readers would ignore the book on the assumption that it was about foreign policy. When the first edition of *The Post-Modern President* was published in 1988, the prime example of the effect of interdependence was the Japanese economy. This is no longer so; today the prime example is the People's Republic of China. Non-state actors such as al Qaeda and rogue states such as Iraq and Afghanistan have also added force to the argument at the cost of many American lives. Yet when the Annenberg Foundation commissioned a massive review of the presidency literature by leading American scholars, there were no chapters on two key institutions on which the White House depends for dealing with international relations, the National Security Council and the Federal Reserve Board. There would not even have been a chapter comparing presidents and prime ministers if I hadn't accidently met the co-editor, Joel Aberbach and he generously invited me to contribute a chapter (Rose 2005).

To paraphrase Andy Warhol, any country can be famous in Washington for 15 minutes. The European side of my mind saw that getting the sustained attention of American decision makers is a particular challenge for foreign embassies. Pressure group theories suggest that the logical thing for embassies to do is to lobby officials who can influence decisions that are of interest to them. The openness of issue networks and the extent of transnational policy links involving everything from agriculture to aircraft makes this feasible. As a British Ambassador explained to me, he would work with Senators from Washington state and the Air Force side of the Pentagon to promote the purchase of Boeing bombers with Rolls-Royce engines.

I put a research proposal to the MacArthur Foundation in Chicago to study how the British and German embassies advance their policies in Washington in the absence of what many American political scientists assume is the sovereign coin of influence, votes. My proposed strategy was to interview select staff in the embassies to find out which bits of the federal government they sought to influence and then, putting on my best St. Louis accent, interview their American counterparts to see whether they discussed issues with foreign representatives in terms of differing national interests or common transnational interests. Since upwards of half the staff of a big embassy in Washington are not diplomats but seconded from departments such as finance, defence and trade, this indicates that many departments of national governments have interests that they need to promote abroad as well as at home.

You can't win them all. The proposal was rejected by the MacArthur Foundation on the advice of American political scientists who felt it was too 'foreign' to provide any insights into how America's government is affected by its engagement with other countries. By the time the letter of rejection arrived, it was not a set back. The unexpected fall of the Berlin Wall had catapulted me into research on a new set of countries. I listened to news of the 1992 election of Bill Clinton with Czech politicians in the American Embassy in Prague and watched his inauguration ceremony on a hotel television set in Vienna.

Chapter 7

Northern Ireland: Nothing Civil About Civil War

Unlike many people who write about Irish politics, I have no family connections with Ireland, North or South. At Johns Hopkins I had read the plays of Synge, O'Casey and Yeats with interest, and the writings of James Joyce. My only contact on the ground was hitchhiking around Ireland in the very quiet summer of 1954 with my LSE theatre-going companion. The Abbey Theatre was then, as my Hopkins professors had told me, in the hands of didactic bigots. We walked out in the middle of a play. One afternoon an older Irishman in a German car gave us an adventurous ride across unmarked paths in the hills of Wexford where he had been out in the 1920s. 'Out' was a code word for having been in one or another Republican army. Near Sligo a Catholic priest stopped to show us William Butler Yeats' grave. Under bare Ben Bulben's head it had the epitaph: 'Cast a cold eye on life, on death; horseman, pass by'. The moral the priest drew about this Nobel prize-winning Protestant was: 'Poor man, he had nothing'. In a youth hostel near Galway a Jesuit novitiate told me with pride how his uncle had fought for Franco in the Spanish Civil War and why it was a good thing that James Joyce's *Ulysses* was banned in Ireland. I learned how the law was enforced in the West of Ireland when a member of the *Garda* (the police force) expressed regret that we hadn't tasted the local pride, *po'teen*, that is, illegally distilled whisky. Northern Ireland was only seen in transit back to a ferry heading for Britain.

Writing *Politics in England* made me conscious of the need to qualify a number of generalizations with the statement 'except for Ireland'. This was particularly true for the chapter about legality and legitimacy; it was weak both theoretically and empirically. I had absorbed enough of Wittgenstein to conclude that there was no point in debating what words 'really' meant. However, I could research legitimacy empirically in what was then a totally neglected part of the United Kingdom, Northern Ireland. My goal was to explain why political institutions that were fully legitimate in England were only partially legitimate in Northern Ireland.

The whole of the island of Ireland had been part of the United Kingdom until 1921. However, the predominantly Catholic population rejected the legitimacy of British rule while the Protestant population, which was in the majority in the North of Ireland, was committed to maintaining the Union with Britain. Both sides appealed to arms. The Fenians, founded in Ireland and the United States in 1858, had the avowed purpose of achieving Irish independence by force. In response Unionists adopted the motto suggested by Winston Churchill's politician father in 1886, 'Ulster will fight and Ulster will be right'. In 1916 Irish Republicans launched an armed insurrection against British rule. Five years of fighting followed between the British Army, Irish Republicans, and Ulster Unionists. In 1921 the island was partitioned between 26 overwhelmingly Catholic counties that now form the independent Republic of Ireland and 6 predominantly Protestant counties of the Province of Ulster in Northern Ireland, which remain part of the United Kingdom. Republicans then had their own civil war between those who accepted independence for 26/32nds of the island and those who would not recognise the legitimacy of a Dublin-based government that accepted this political division.

In an effort to erect a barrier between political problems in Ireland and Britain, the Westminster Parliament authorized a Government of Northern Ireland based at Stormont, a suburb of Belfast. Its Parliament was elected on the same principle as the British Parliament. Since Protestants were two-thirds of the population, the Unionist Party always won a parliamentary majority. In constituencies with a majority of Catholics, moderate Catholic politicians loyal to the Irish tri-colour flag[1] were elected as a hardly loyal opposition. Republican winners of elections refused to take their seat on the grounds that the system was illegitimate. Intermittently such groups took up arms in unsuccessful attempts to gain a united Ireland by force. The Unionist government enjoyed unchecked powers similar to those of its British counterpart, including control of the police. Whitehall pushed oversight of Northern Ireland to the furthest and lowest reaches of the Home Office. When internationally publicized demonstrations for civil rights began in 1968, the official nominally acting as overseer saw his duty as looking the other way. This was consistent with the Labour government's desire to avoid entanglement with any form of the Irish question. The terms of reference for the review of Northern Ireland local government it authorized in 1969 excluded any consideration of changes in the electoral system, even though blatant gerrymandering was used to prevent Catholic majorities controlling local councils in symbolically important places such as Londonderry.[2]

When interviewed for a chair at Strathclyde in 1966 I naively said that moving there should help me carry out research on Northern Ireland, as Glasgow was as close as one could get and still remain neutral. After moving there, I quickly learned how strong religious divisions were in Glasgow, starting with schools segregated between Catholics and non-Catholics by laws strongly supported by the Catholic hierarchy. Children learned the words of the national anthem of the Irish Republic, *The Soldier's Song* or alternatively Protestant marching songs such as *The Sash* or *Croppies Lie Down*. On the walls of Strathclyde University, political balance was shown by different handwritings inscribing the acronyms FTP and FKB. Occasionally I met Scottish neighbours who had childhood memories of going to bed to the sound of gunfire in Belfast or Dublin in the early 1920s.

1. The flag of the Irish Republic unites green, the symbol of the Gaelic tradition; orange, the tradition of William of Orange, whose followers belong to the Protestant Orange Order; and white, the aspiration for peace between green and orange.
2. The original Gaelic name is Doire. The prefix of London was added after livery companies of the City of London made it a plantation in the early seventeenth century by similar procedures to those used to establish plantations in Virginia at the same time.

A Warm Welcome From All Sides

When I started my Northern Ireland research in 1965, both social scientists and governments in Belfast and Dublin were promoting theories of positive change. The failure of the 1956–62 Irish Republican Army (IRA) campaign to mobilize popular Catholic support and kill many Protestant defenders of the state was interpreted as the last gasp of violent republicans. Economic growth and increased education were expected to replace historic cleavages with democratic political divisions along class and economic lines familiar in England. The Unionist prime minister of the devolved Northern Ireland government, Terence O'Neill, endorsed this view, seeking new industries to stimulate economic growth. His strategy was consistent with the social science theories of modernization that expected economic change to make religious divisions irrelevant. In a frank moment O'Neill explained:

> The basic fear of the Protestants in Northern Ireland is that they will be outbred by the Roman Catholics. It is as simple as that. It is frightfully hard to explain to a Protestant that if you give Roman Catholics a good job and a good house, they will live like Protestants, because they will see neighbours with cars and television sets. (Quoted in Rose 1971: 301)

Fitting theories to life on the ground

When I got off the boat in Belfast in July, 1965, I said that I wanted to look at election results and understood Northern Ireland had some interesting ones. This prompted a laugh and a flood of anecdotes. For example, there was the story of the 1951 UK election in which the West Belfast seat was won by a Republican candidate by 25 votes. When an English academic at Queen's University Belfast said to an Ulster friend, 'Think how exciting it would have been to be one of the 25', the reply was, 'Think how exciting it would be to have been all of them!'. When I repeated the anecdote to a Belfast MP he recalled, 'Yes, I remember there was a wee Protestant at the count banging his fist on the table and saying "If only I'd voted another 26 times"'.

I was welcomed with great hospitality by many people who in spite, or because, of involvement in Ulster politics had never met a political scientist, especially one who would listen to them talk at length about how their political system operated. Most Unionist politicians were optimistic about the future, notwithstanding signs of opposition being mobilized by Dr. Ian Paisley, a fundamentalist Protestant clergyman. Ulster Catholics noted that the hand of friendship extended by Terence O'Neill to the Irish government in Dublin was not extended to them. When I met John Hume in 1966, he was organising a credit union to help Catholics in Derry get loans cheaply rather than go to the gombeen men, Catholic loan sharks. He put me on the spot by asking what to do about the situation there, with Catholics a substantial majority of the population but gerrymandering giving most of the local council seats to Protestants. I suggested that before attacking Protestants Hume should win the Stormont seat held by the Catholic who went along with the system that he wanted to change. Three years later Hume won the seat and then much more. In 1988 he received the Nobel Peace Prize jointly with the Unionist leader David Trimble; both sought to resolve differences by bargaining rather than bullets.

A grant from the American Social Science Research Council enabled me to get perspective on Northern Ireland by going to Stanford for three months in January 1967. Our small children wondered whether they were in America, which to them was represented by their grandparents' home in St. Louis. The contrast between the Midwest and California in winter made me wonder too. The children went to Disneyland and I sat in my office at Stanford trying to connect modernization theories with what I was reading in the Belfast *Telegraph* newspaper. What I learned was summarized in an article for *World Politics* about dynamic tendencies in the authority of regimes (Rose 1969). It set out a two-dimensional typology differentiating regimes in terms of a democratic criterion, popular support, and an effectiveness criterion, securing compliance with basic political laws. On this basis the Northern Ireland system of government was partially legitimate, for Protestant Unionists supported and complied with it, while Catholics did not support it and did not comply with political laws such as the ban on the public display of the flag of the Republic of Ireland.

Once a British ESRC grant to finance a survey came through, I designed a questionnaire that was meaningful at the conceptual level and on the ground in Northern Ireland. There was no difficulty in asking about support for a constitution that for generations had been the object of controversy and violence. While each side approved breaking laws to achieve their political aims, they did so in different ways. Protestants showed a readiness to endorse the use of any measures (that is, force) to keep Ulster British. The Catholic minority favoured illegal actions that were symbolic, because they feared that resort to force would result in a bloody defeat.

Questions about the use of violence for political ends were not so much hypothetical as contingent. Piloting of the questionnaire started in summer 1967, shortly after three Catholics had been killed by people representing the ultra-loyalist Ulster Volunteer Force. A few months before, celebrations of the fiftieth anniversary of the Easter Rising against the British crown had been held in the Republic. Less than eight weeks after the final interviews were completed in August, 1968, the first civil rights marches started. This was the start of a long hot autumn of protests that followed the strategy of parades by the Orange Order through Catholic neighbourhoods, namely, assertive non-violence. One of the organisers was Michael Farrell, a Strathclyde student from Ulster who had suggested the wording of a question about violating government bans on demonstrations. I was struck by Irish voices singing the American civil rights song *We Shall Overcome*. Farrell explained that demonstrators were bound to sing something and since he didn't want traditional Republican songs to be sung, he handed out song sheets used by black American protesters.

Demonstrations were called off in January, 1969, when Catholic marchers were the object of a police riot in Londonderry. A snap general election followed.

Journalists flew in from London and pathetically tried to understand what was going on by learning the names of parties and assimilating what they were told to an English context. After four years imbibing Ulster politics, I did not make that mistake. Like their counterparts in America's Deep South, Ulster men and women voted as their ancestors had shot.

The election revealed splits in the Unionist ranks. For the first time in almost a quarter of a century, Terence O'Neill faced a contest in his constituency. He won a plurality but not a majority, because that vote was split between Dr. Ian Paisley and Michael Farrell. John Hume won the Catholic seat in Derry for the Social Democratic & Labour Party (SDLP), newly formed in rejection of the Republican label that Unionists used to justify excluding disloyal Catholics from political influence.

My contacts with SDLP members at Stormont encouraged me to believe in the wee people, a colloquial term for leprechauns. I would meet a group of Stormont MPs around tea time in the members' bar. The standard rite was that each person would buy a round of double whiskys and a pint of Guinness as a chaser. From experience interviewing in the House of Commons, I had learned to sink the pints but could not handle the whisky. After a few rounds I became anxious that the whisky in my glasses would make me appear unsociable. When I looked down, they were empty. To this day I don't know whether I was saved from embarrassment by wee Paddy O'Hanlon or wee Paddy Devlin.

Guns Come Out

I booked a visit to Londonderry a month in advance of the Bogside Rising of 12 August 1969. That was the day when the Royal Black Preceptories, the local equivalent of the Orange Order, marched, for very different reasons than my high school band. The Blacks, as they were known, marched to commemorate the breaking of the Catholic blockade of the city in 1690, an important event in the war that put paid for centuries to Irish rebellions against the English Crown.

When I arrived in Derry the etiquette of the Bogside Rising had been established. Catholics had built symbolic barricades a few feet high around the streets leading into the Bogside to prevent the incursion of Protestant marchers. The Royal Ulster Constabulary (RUC) and the B Special Reserves posted themselves a short distance away to prevent the incursion of Catholic demonstrators into the city centre. The Catholics were armed with heavy hurley sticks used to hit the ball in Gaelic football. They batted stones at the RUC, bouncing them on the ground first so that it would be harder for the police to anticipate which way the stones would bounce. The RUC defended themselves with riot shields. As the afternoon wore on, younger boys were drafted to fill bottles with petrol that could be turned into fire bombs that were thrown at RUC cars.

I put on my best American accent to talk with demonstrators and with the RUC. Although the term 'rising' has overtones of a violent insurrection, Catholic participants claimed that their immediate purpose was defensive. Twice in the past year the police had beaten civil rights demonstrators and they feared a Loyalist march might lead to this happening again. The sight of a blue and white flag flying from the top of one of the new high-rise flats in the Bogside made me wonder what a United Nations flag was doing there. On second look, I realised that the flag had the plough and the stars of James Connally's Irish Citizen Army, a forerunner of the IRA.

I started conversations with RUC men by asking what time they had come on duty. Many had started their day as early as 6 am, being brought from a distance to reinforce the local RUC contingent. By evening there was clearly a stalemate. Because Catholics could go home for tea or to the pub for a pint, they could have gone on all night. I wondered what tired RUC men would do. After dark they began throwing teargas in an attempt to disperse the demonstrators. By comparison with the teargas of the Chicago police, British teargas is milder; however, Irish stones are more dangerous threats to bones and eyes. When the RUC began to disperse, the demonstrators did likewise, and the warm, sunny evening ended quietly without the sound of gunshots or ambulances.

The next morning I went into the bookshop of the Association for Promoting Christian Knowledge in search of knowledge that would help me understand what I had witnessed. An answer was offered by a paperback about the Fenians. Before going to Belfast Airport I drove the streets of West Belfast looking for signs of a Fenian rising or of Ulster Volunteers in action. I was a day early. Confrontations in West Belfast went over the top the following night. Eight people were shot and killed, six Catholics and two Protestants.

When I returned to Belfast the following month the British Army rather than the RUC was patrolling West Belfast and all appeared peaceful. However, the marks of trouble were everywhere. I was shown the holes in concrete posts on the Catholic Falls Road created by tracer bullets fired by the police. Over lunch the parish priest of a Falls Road church told me there had been two men with handguns on the roof of the parish hall trying to hold off a Protestant mob for hours until heavier firepower could be brought up from the South of Ireland. Elsewhere in the city guns pressed into use by Catholic defenders were so rusty that the ammunition clips could only be inserted with difficulty. The bottom line was, 'Never again'. The priest intimated that men met in the parish hall one night a week to engage in military drill, while he made house calls. I went to lunch at Stormont with Terence O'Neill's political secretary, Kenneth Bloomfield. He introduced me to Phelim O'Neill, a liberal Unionist cousin of Terence O'Neill, as someone who was researching the Northern Ireland problem. In his best Oxford manner, O'Neill said, 'I hope you have a treble first' (that is, an extraordinarily good degree).

Although I could see events moving toward civil war when finishing *Governing without Consensus* in the winter of 1970, it was unclear when, how or even whether a civil war would break out. I therefore selected photographs that spoke for themselves. The front cover showed the British army in battle dress in a Catholic part of West Belfast. Inside the book the first page of photos was divided between aerial photographs of the Stormont Parliament in its parkland setting in East Belfast and houses that had been burnt out in Catholic West Belfast. The next two pages showed the handwriting on the wall. Slogans read 'Up the IRA' and the

Protestant equivalents, 'UVF' and 'No Surrender Forever'. The last photo was of the morning after in West Belfast: a man sweeping up rubble in front of terrace houses flying black flags of mourning.

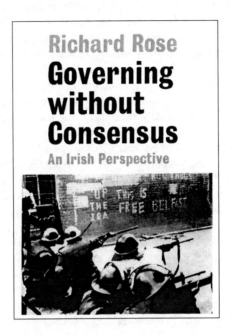

In August, 1971, the British Army arrested and interned indefinitely without trial more than 300 Catholic men who were sometimes rightly and sometimes wrongly suspected of association with the IRA. This boosted IRA recruitment and its military activity. When my book came out a month later, more black flags were on display, and there were thousands more deaths to come.

Theories of the Troubles

When the Troubles broke out, the most comfortable explanation was to reduce the problem to economics. That offered a far easier solution than my own diagnosis of a political conflict involving irreconcilable territorial demands justified by nationality and religion. The Labour government that put British troops into Ulster was much readier to boost public expenditure there than to introduce effective anti-discrimination measures. It whistled past graveyards full of bodies from the past and with room for more. Its Conservative successor likewise preferred an economic analysis. One of its Northern Ireland ministers, David Howell, asked what I thought of the idea that most Ulster people were moderates with only a small number at each extreme. I replied that my survey evidence showed a U-shaped distribution of opinion, with most people at the extremes and very few in the middle. Howell changed the subject.

Northern Ireland politicians had repeatedly tried to turn politics into an economic debate uniting the interests of badly housed and poorly paid Protestants and Catholics. Paddy Devlin, interned in his youth because of Republican activities, vehemently rejected nationalism, telling a Republican critic, 'F*** off back to the 14th century'. However, he ended up in the non-violent but still Catholic SDLP. The Northern Ireland Labour Party's commitment to the British Constitution made it unacceptable to Catholic socialists, who were green as well as red.

The Communist Party of Northern Ireland was so committed to economic determinism that it opposed civil rights demonstrations on the grounds that they distracted attention from the class struggle. At a meeting it called with V. K. Krishna Menon, an internationally prominent left wing Indian, I met a printer who told me he voted Communist. When I asked whether it was true that there were two Communist Parties in Northern Ireland, one for Protestants and one for Catholics, his answer was, 'I wouldn't know; I'm from East Belfast' (that is, I am a Protestant). When I left the Communist meeting with lawyer friends to go drinking at a Republican shebeen in West Belfast, one muttered, 'Bloody Protestants'. Not long after I met a trade union official from East Belfast who looked to Moscow for a different reason: guns. He reckoned that the Kremlin was the only certain source of opposition to the Vatican. When he told me that Ulster loyalists needed anti-tank guns, I said, 'Oh my god, you mean the Catholics have tanks', and made an excuse to end our conversation.

In December 1971, I was invited to give the Workers Educational Association annual Christmas lecture to Glasgow school leavers. Since it was designed to interest young Glaswegians in studying social science at University, I proposed a talk reviewing theories of the Northern Ireland Troubles, ranging from the psychological to the theological. The Labour-controlled Glasgow City Council banned pupils from attending. A Labour MP, Norman Buchan, explained to me that the Labour councillor who chaired the Education Committee was a Hib bigot, that is, an old-fashioned Irish Nationalist. The Hib bigot did me a favour. The lecture hall was packed with pupils from other school districts and I published my talk in the *Glasgow Herald*, making it accessible to everyone (www.profrose.eu/writings.php#northern_ireland).

At an after-dinner talk that I gave at Harvard in March, 1972, Daniel Bell, Sam Beer, Karl Deutsch and Marty Lipset argued that Northern Ireland's problems were due to belated modernization and that economic development should end the strife. My retort was that it all depended on what you meant by modernization (Rose and McAllister 1983). If the definition was economic, then England was the first modern country and Marx was its first serious theorist. However, if modernization was about cultural transformation, then Enlightenment France was the first modern country and Voltaire was its exponent. In a footnote to *Governing without Consensus* (1971: 511n), I suggested that, to paraphrase words often used to endorse religion, the only problem with Voltaire's modest proposal for modernization was that it had never been tried in Northern Ireland.

At the all-party Conference at Darlington later in 1972, William Whitelaw, the British government Secretary for Northern Ireland, referred to the difficulties of finding a final solution, a phrase that he quickly withdrew when he realized what it meant in a German context. He corrected himself and he spoke about finding 'ingredients of a solution' to the Northern Ireland problem. When I asked Whitelaw to say in his own words what the problem was, he smiled and remained silent. We both knew that the problem was that there was no solution, at least none in a form that would be normal in a Westminster-style system of government.

Governing Without the Rule of Law

Throughout the Troubles Northern Ireland courts were open, but their doors were closed to civil rights cases. I committed an act of barratry, that is, inciting a law suit, by getting the Joseph Rowntree Trust Ltd to commission an Ulster lawyer to see if closed doors could be opened. His opinion concluded that the only legal route to challenge the status quo was through the European Court for Human Rights in Strasbourg. This was consistent with what soldiers sometimes said after reading the conditions of internment to a person held on suspicion of IRA associations: 'You have no rights'.

The IRA refused to recognise the authority of courts maintained by what it deemed an illegal British occupying force. A young man who joined a group I was drinking with in a cosmopolitan Belfast hotel suggested one exception to the doctrine of non-recognition: Shooting judges. The youth was the son of Maire Drumm, the firebrand orator of Republican violence. She reaped what she had sown, being shot dead in her bed at the Mater Hospital by Protestant paramilitaries posing as laboratory assistants (McKittrick *et al.* 1999: 84). Sometimes the aim was not so good. The IRA man who tried to shoot the Chief Justice of Northern Ireland missed him as he was entering a building at Queen's University Belfast and instead hit an aide standing next to him. I might have been in that position, because I was then acting as an advisor to the Chief Justice in his capacity as chair of the abortive Northern Ireland Constitutional Convention of 1975.

The Protestant position was clear: the Northern Ireland government was part of the United Kingdom and Protestants were prepared to defend it through their control of the police or through paramilitary organizations. A local Ulster history of what Edmund Burke would have called a little platoon described the approach as: 'Each Sub-District remains and rightly so, more or less of a private army, proud of its own particular way of doing things' (Clark 1967; cf. Farrell 1983). In an effort to integrate the security forces across religions, the British government insisted on disbanding the Ulster B Specials and recruiting both Catholics and Protestants in an Ulster Defence Regiment. The civil servant who sent each B Special an invitation to join the new official force explained to me that if he hadn't done so they might join an illegal Protestant force. His fears were soon realized. When Britain suspended the Stormont government in March, 1972, the following Saturday 10,000 men marched down Royal Avenue in Belfast in an intimidating protest. William Craig, a Stormont MP on the stand reviewing the marchers, told me afterwards that a public and disciplined parade was a better alternative than leaving thousands of disaffected Protestant loyalists to decide in private how they could express their frustration and anger.

Both Labour and Conservative governments offered palliatives that often backfired. To address housing discrimination that had triggered the first civil rights march, the Northern Ireland Housing Association was established. I lobbied the representative of Downing Street in the Province to appoint Mrs. Conn McCluskey to its board, as she was behind the first civil rights march to protest against discrimination in housing. Instead, the person appointed from her town was a Castle Catholic, that is, someone who would go along with the Unionists. Mrs. McCluskey later told me that she had written to the British government saying that if they came out for justice she would back them, but if they didn't, 'then the lads will start it up all over again' — and when the British government did not, the lads did.

Successive inquiries into violence, starting with that led by a liberal English judge, Leslie Scarman (1972), were 'too little, too late' attempts to come to terms with the situation. When I told Scarman that the protection of civil rights in Northern Ireland compared unfavourably with Mississippi (Rose 1976a), he responded, 'Surely, Richard, you can't mean that'. I replied, 'How about the suspension of *habeas corpus*?' That stopped the conversation, since *habeas corpus* had been suspended in Northern Ireland for most of the past century to permit indefinite internment without trial of suspected Republicans.

While many Ulster police and British soldiers sacrificed their lives, a few public officials did more: they sacrificed their honour. When I heard the radio report that 13 people had been shot dead by British soldiers during a demonstration in the Bogside in January, 1972, I wondered how many women and children had been killed. When I learned that all the dead were men, I knew it wasn't an accident. The British government promptly claimed that the soldiers had fired in self-defence. This did not dispose of the witness problem: 10,000 people had been at what became known as the Bloody Sunday demonstration. A priest-professor at University College, Dublin, said to me a few months later, 'After we burnt the British Embassy, things calmed down'. An inquiry under Lord Justice Widgery was set up in the colloquial sense of the word. It took decades more of deaths and another inquiry costing several hundred million pounds in legal expenses before a British prime minister, David Cameron, would admit that the killings were without justification.

To participate in electoral politics in Ulster required civil courage far beyond that needed in Britain and America. The cover I chose for my second book, *Northern Ireland: Time of Choice* (Rose 1976b) gave graphic evidence of the alternatives, the bullet or the ballot. A Dublin interviewer interpreted the drawings as offering a choice between a gun or a coffin. One day when I casually asked John Hume 'What's new?', he replied, 'They'll be shooting politicians next'. 'Their own side or the other side?', I inquired. Hume replied, 'They always shoot their own side'. Another SDLP politician, Austin Currie, told me he reckoned a Republican who had been at primary school with him would be his murderer. When Currie asked the local police what he should do, they recommended a Smith & Wesson .38 as fitting neatly in a shoulder holster. Gerry Fitt, the first leader of the SDLP, told me that when a Republican mob came to stomp him to death as he

was getting ready for bed and he pulled a gun on them, they called him 'a f******
coward'. The IRA targeted British politicians, and almost succeeded in killing
Prime Minister Margaret Thatcher with a bomb planted at the 1984 Conservative
Party Conference. The IRA did not target Ulster Protestant leaders such as Dr. Ian
Paisley for fear of the reaction that such an action would set off.

Having controlled the government continuously since 1921, Protestants had
little experience of organizing illegal paramilitary formations that could function
like an underground army. The Orange Order marched proudly wearing bowler
hats and silk sashes rather than following the IRA dress code of combat berets
and sometimes balaclavas to hide faces from being photographed by British
intelligence. The lack of a disciplined central organization meant that Protestant
paramilitaries included people who joined in search of money or used violence
sadistically rather than strategically. John McMichael, an Ulster paramilitary
leader in search of a political solution, several times came to talks that I gave.
He was killed by a car bomb, probably planted by a Protestant paramilitary who
doubled in racketeering and providing information to the IRA (McKittrick et al.
1999: 1103f).

The contrast in organizations is illustrated by the way Belfast children responded
to a projective test thought up by a PhD student of mine, James Russell. Protestant
children were asked what would happen if Bernadette Devlin was driving down
the Shankill Road, her car got a flat tyre, and she was recognised. They said that
a crowd would gather and she would be lynched and her baby too. By contrast,
when Catholic children were asked about Dr Ian Paisley being recognised in the
Falls Road, they replied that someone would send for the Army (that is, the IRA)

and it would take him away. Something like this subsequently happened to two undercover British agents. When recognised in the Falls Road area, the IRA took them away for interrogation and they were, to use its parlance, executed.

Anyone living in Northern Ireland cannot escape from ties to the community from which he or she comes. Thus, along with civil courage a person must tolerate a degree of moral ambiguity for the actions of their own side. When I asked a Belfast priest one Saturday night whether he expected to see murderers at the communion rail the next morning, his answer was, 'I hope so'. He did not want his church to be separated from its people. A Methodist bishop friend, Eric Gallaher, was asked to officiate at the funeral of a young Protestant man who had met a violent end. After making enquiries indicating that the deceased was not a paramilitary, he accepted. However, when the coffin was taken from the home, Gallaher found it met by a paramilitary guard of honour. As a working-class socialist, Gerry Fitt sought to engage with Protestant constituents as well as Catholics. But when many priests walked in the cortege of Bobby Sands, who was the first IRA convicted prisoner to kill himself on a hunger strike, Fitt bemoaned, 'How can I tell my Protestant neighbours that all Catholics aren't murderers?'

The deadly conflict in Northern Ireland taught me the limits of the law. I developed a fourfold model of the legal process with two types of justice culpable people being punished and innocent being acquitted and two types of injustice, innocent people being punished and gunmen going free. Northern Ireland produced ample examples of injustice as well as justice. With William Miller, a Strathclyde politics colleague expert in system dynamics programming, we developed a computer simulation that showed how alterations in the law could alter the odds on justice and injustice. For example, internment without trial increased the number of innocent Catholics incarcerated, whereas the use of the Republic as a safe haven enabled IRA gunmen to escape trial and punishment for their deeds. We learned that this mode of thinking was outside the ken of lawyers and even a Yale Law School seminar where I presented the talk had trouble facing up to this way of accounting for what was happening in Northern Ireland.

What an Outsider Did

Governing without Consensus was published to the accompaniment of dissensus expressed with bullets and bombs. I had the choice between leaving the subject or staying with troubled people. Without hesitation, I stayed. While having no illusions about what an academic outsider could do, I felt an obligation to do something, however small, to further understanding of what was euphemistically called 'the situation'. I gave priority to telling people who had the power to take decisions that dealt with the Troubles to look in the right places to understand it rather than look where it suited their convenience.

Consistently I argued the need to reject the Westminster model of government by majority rule in favour of a power-sharing government established by rules that Westminster could set but only Ulster politicians could put into practice. The Westminster model had already been breached by direct rule from London, which suspended first-past-the-post elections. I recommended a government in which posts in Cabinet would be assigned in proportion to each party's share of the vote and parties could take turns in choosing which departments they would head. This would allow a Unionist party, if it finished first, to choose between the key security post of Home Affairs and Finance, and a Catholic party that finished second to choose the other department and so on. Although the idea was then dismissed as too clever by half, the power-sharing agreement that was eventually adopted more than a quarter-century later similarly required all parties to the conflict to share out offices between them.

A solution that appeared logical to those ignorant of the situation on the ground was to separate warring groups through a new partition. Areas of Ulster that were predominantly Catholic would become part of the Republic and Northern Ireland would then be the home of Protestants. This idea ignored the fact that the two communities were not neatly segregated geographically. The largest concentration of Catholics was in Belfast, but were a minority there. Thus, partitioning land by religion would have condemned more than three-fifths of Catholics to live under permanent Protestant control and a tenth of Protestants to have a complementary fate. An analysis of re-partition published in *The Irish Times* produced a qualitatively different response than anything else I wrote on the Troubles (www. profrose.eu/writings.php#northern_ireland). When I was rung up to elaborate on the article, the voices of my interviewers suggested that their faces were almost grey with the thought of the consequences of re-partition. At least half a dozen times I went to bed in Scotland wondering whether the morning would reveal that the British army could no longer keep a lid on violence and Ulster families were fleeing in opposite directions for protection among their own kind.

The British government's suspension of the Northern Ireland Parliament in 1972 made a Westminster Cabinet minister directly responsible for what was called 'temporary direct rule' in Northern Ireland. This gave impetus to Britain's search for a political exit. It authorized an Assembly election that was meant to lead to a power-sharing executive set up on terms dictated by Whitehall. I went on record pointing out that majorities could not be coerced. In May, 1974, the Ulster Workers' Council combined trade union and Irish tactics by calling a general strike against power-sharing. To encourage observance, shipyard workers were told that any cars on the yard's car park would be burnt at 3 pm if they had not been removed. It was the first successful general strike in Europe for generations.

After the success of the Ulster Workers' Council strike in 1974, I wrote a set of recommendations along the lines outlined above and sent them to an ex-Nuffield student, Bernard Donoughue, then working in Downing Street, with a request to forward them to the Northern Ireland Secretary, Merlyn Rees. When he did not reply, I rang to ask what was happening. Given the thrust of my letter, Bernard said there was no point in passing it on to Merlyn as my ideas were 'Not on'. In the words of W. J. M. Mackenzie, who had seen much that made him uncomfortable during the Second World War, I could explain but not justify Donoughue's response. I signed the occasional note to the Permanent Secretary responsible for Northern Ireland, 'Yours Cassandraically'.

The only contact I sought in Washington was with Senator Edward Kennedy, who initially issued statements that were much more influenced by IRA supporters in Boston than by realities on the ground. I felt that of all people Kennedy should try to keep the gun out of politics. Through Dick Neustadt I secured a meeting with one of his senior staff and advised that the Senator should look to the SDLP for guidance, as it was pro-Catholic but anti-gunmen. Kennedy was eating lunch alone at his desk that day and when his staffer introduced me to him, Kennedy grilled me for an hour. His questioning was to the point: What can I do? At that time, there wasn't much except press for the extension of civil rights and oppose the use of violence. Immediately after Bloody Sunday I suggested to Kevin Boyle, who was responsible for organising the follow up demonstration in his native Newry the next Saturday, that he invite Kennedy to be in the front line of the march as a shield against another round of gunfire. It didn't surprise me that the Senator's office said that because of a previous engagement, Kennedy could not attend.

When in Belfast I became accustomed to hearing the occasional sound of bombs and slept like a fireman, ready to jump into my clothes immediately if there was a bomb scare or worse at my hotel. Ironically, the only bomb scare I experienced was at the Reform Club in London; it turned out to be a false alarm. Only once was I nervous when the person I was expecting to meet me at the airport didn't turn up but two burly Ulstermen did, saying they were acting on his behalf. Before getting in the car I rang the friend and got no answer. I decided it unlikely that anyone who wasn't a friend of a friend would know my movements that morning, so I followed them into their car and they delivered me safely. My students were not immune from risks. When James Russell got out of the back door of a bus in the Falls Road to carry out interviews with school children, a young man came in the front door with a gun to hijack the bus. Paddy Devlin started an interview with Ian McAllister by placing the gun in his shoulder holster on the table between them and asking Ian what he wanted to know.[3]

After internment began I never took my Ulster address book with me when I went to Northern Ireland. A Yale student I was helping with a dissertation about what was then the novel institution of the Ombudsman did take a list of addresses of councillors to interview in County Fermanagh in the middle of winter. He did not realise that having such a list was grounds for a prison sentence since it could be used to plan political assassinations. After checking into a bed-and-breakfast, he went out to fill up his hire car with petrol. While he was out, the landlady went through the luggage of her strange guest and, having found the list of councillors, met him on his return with his bag and told him there was no longer a bed for him there. He drove back to Belfast airport fast and slept in my house in Scotland that night.

Because you can't work all sides where gunmen are concerned, I dropped a particularly interesting contact with a former British civil servant who had been

---

3.   Ian did not waver from concentration on asking questions relevant to his thesis, and cannot recall whether the revolver was a .9 Browning or a Smith and Wesson Leeson Street Special, one of a suitcase-full brought to Belfast by a committed Irish-American.

stationed in the Middle East to advise sheikhs and soldiers there on the political use of force. He was sent to the British Army headquarters in Northern Ireland after the Army's imposition of a curfew on West Belfast Catholics in 1970 backfired and boosted recruitment for the IRA. I knew journalists and historians with privileged access, such as J. Bowyer Bell, author of, among other things, 'The Role of the Thompson Submachine Gun in Ireland, 1921' and published in 1967 in *The Irish Sword*. These guns, smuggled in from America, were still in use at the start of the Troubles in 1969. They were soon replaced by Armalites smuggled in from the United States, which in turn were superseded by Russian AK47s shipped via Libya. A Strathclyde graduate student, Sarah Nelson (1984), showed both courage and tenacity in writing a thesis about how and why Protestants formed paramilitary organizations. A thesis by Bob Purdie (1990) about the role of Republicans in the civil rights movement was informed by his earlier activities as an international Marxist in Britain and Ireland. An unbookish looking man in his late 20s came to see me about doing a Strathclyde PhD on the IRA, and gave an assurance that he would have no trouble getting access to information. I erected a pedantic barrier about a thesis requiring academic theories and acknowledgment of sources. Fortunately, he never came back.

In retrospect I believe that I was once interviewed on behalf of the CIA by an American professor who came to my Strathclyde office to discuss our mutual academic interest in nationalism. After he left I realized that the man accompanying him and introduced as a student was a bit mature and, complete with a trench coat, he looked more like a spook than a student. Republicans also appeared to be watching me. Early in the Troubles over a drink at the Crown Bar in Belfast a well connected Sinn Fein activist asked me whether I thought the Irish tradition of shooting British soldiers would make the British government pull out. I said I didn't think it would work. It didn't, but not for lack of IRA effort.

I talked to elected representatives on both sides, because I had established a reputation for having informed and independent views and respecting confidences. This respect was tested once after I had lunch with the Secretary of the Catholic SDLP and the Secretary of the Ulster Unionist Party was eating at the same restaurant. On meeting the Unionist in his office after lunch, he casually asked what the SDLP view was on a current issue. I prefaced my reply by saying, 'From what I read in the paper...' and gave my views without reference to anything that was not already public knowledge. Occasionally I went out of my way to emphasize I was talking to both sides. Over lunch in the dining room at Stormont, a senior Unionist civil servant explained to me the government's plans for economic development, which strongly favoured a Protestant part of the Province close to British markets. After we got up from the table I conspicuously crossed the room to say hello to John Hume, whose Derry constituency was omitted from the development plan.

There were some comical misunderstandings. Once the British Army entered the Province following the Bogside Rising, Downing Street sent in a senior civil servant, to act as its eyes and ears. Sir Ronald Burroughs wrote apologising for neglecting to reply to a letter because he had misplaced it in a sporting coat that he only wore when out shooting. My secretary handed it to me with the wry comment,

'Birds, I hope'. My imagined activities as an advisor to the Speaker of the abortive 1975 Constitutional Convention were attacked in Stormont by an independent Protestant MP who had a strong claim to being the most eccentric member of the Convention (Northern Ireland Convention, 1976). The Reverend Martin Smyth, head of the Imperial Orange Order and subsequently a British MP, assumed from my American background and ambiguous surname that I was Jewish. He told me proudly of the Orange Order having Jewish members in North Belfast as well as black members in Nigeria.

When I massaged the back of my collar because of pressure from an ill-fitting shirt, Harold McCusker, a Unionist MP, thought I was giving him a Masonic sign. Our talk then turned serious. In reply to an open-ended question about what he was doing, he said, 'Going to funerals'. Several Protestant farmers and part-time members of the Ulster Defence Regiment had recently been killed by IRA groups in his Armagh constituency. When I asked what his constituents thought of the biblical injunction that it was more blessed to give than to receive, for such was the elliptical way one spoke about tit-for-tat killings, he replied with firm dignity, 'We are the people who pay the rent'. Before the end of the Troubles, more than one hundred of his Armagh Protestant constituents in the police or Ulster Defence Regiment had paid the rent, that is, they had been killed by the IRA (McKittrick et al. 1999: 1489).

I knew casually some people who were killed in the Troubles and in a society with a total population of 1.5 million I often met people with relatives, friends and/or neighbours who were victims. The point of terrorism was that it combined targeted political assassinations with the semi-random planting of bombs in public places. For example, a friend with whom I am still able to exchange Christmas cards unexpectedly had to work a Saturday morning hospital shift in Belfast. Had she followed her usual practice of meeting friends in the Abercorn cafe that morning, she would have been there when an IRA bomb went off, injuring, mutilating or killing 130 people.

I made the most of Fleet Street contacts to publicize my views in London. My sources were different from carefully calculated leaks from Whitehall. When I offered an alternative interpretation of events to a television producer, he replied, 'Who told you that? The Northern Ireland Secretary is my source'. I explained that my remarks drew on what was known by the million and one-half people living in Northern Ireland. When I heard on the lunchtime news in 1975 that Eamon de Valera had died, I rang The Times and offered a piece about de Valera's turn from intransigence to acceptance of a divided Ireland that could be an example to Dr Ian Paisley. I was told that if I could write an Op Ed piece in an hour and a half it would be printed the next day. I did and it was. A few years later in a television hospitality lounge Paisley showed me that he was capable of changing his mind. He lifted his glass of whisky and said, 'I once signed the pledge not to drink'. IRA leaders were less ready to change their minds.

After the 1982 Northern Ireland Assembly election it became clear that temporary direct rule was likely to continue for decades. I had nothing fresh to offer and it was time to focus my research on the simpler subject of the growth of government (*see* Chapter 11). The Troubles continued for decades longer, eventually surpassing the duration of the Thirty Years War in Germany. The death toll rose above 3,500. Taking into account differences in population, the number of politically motivated deaths in Northern Ireland has been the equivalent of more than 140,000 in the United Kingdom and 700,000 in the United States.

The most relevant line in Irish literature about the Troubles does not come from a posturing William Butler Yeats but from Sean O'Casey's *The Plough and the Stars*: 'Take away this murdering hate'. The more I knew of Ulster the more it met Aristotle's definition of tragedy, requiring mercy to achieve release from what in classical Greek is called *miasma*, the stain of spilled blood. The problem has not been unique to Northern Ireland. In primary school I had learned the words of Abraham Lincoln's Second Inaugural Address, spoken a month before the end of America's Civil War and his own assassination. I quoted them at the end of *Governing without Consensus*: 'With malice toward none; with charity for all: with firmness in the right as God gives us to see the right, let us strive on to finish the work we are in; to bind up the nation's wounds; to care for him who shall have borne the battle, and for his widow, and his orphan'.

Chapter 8

Fallout From the Berlin Wall

Given my St. Louis upbringing it was not an accident that I was interested in Central Europe. The first grade in school was called kindergarten not primary one; friends had German names such as Burgheim, Goldwasser, Markus, Schweich and Zimmerman. On a holiday forty years later, I drove through Spessart and Franconia and saw place names familiar from my school class lists. I did not have a friend with a British surname until I was 17 nor a friend with an English surname until I came to England. The lands of the Prussian, Habsburg and Tsarist empires were familiar to me as the birthplace of the grandparents or parents of many of my friends. The bakery shops sold *stollen* and *streusel* rather than tea cakes and crumpets. Virtually all the classical music on the local radio was by German composers and most of the war news involved Nazi Germany. I knew enough modern German history, backwards, current and forwards, to know that if you can't come to grips with Germany, you can't understand Europe.

I never thought that I would write a book about Russia and now I have written four. Nor did I ever think I would write a book about Central or Eastern Europe, and it too has been the subject of four books. In primary school I had learned that the Soviet Union did not have a people-friendly government. At Hopkins I had the good fortune to be exposed to the European culture of pre-revolutionary Russia. The lecturer in music history was a White Russian woman who wore a tocque appropriate to a pre-1914 Diaghilev premiere in Paris. My London ballet companion led me to Covent Garden, where I could beat time to Tchaikovsky and strike hard accents with pleasure at the rhythms of Stravinsky. Reading as well as writing for the *New Leader* in New York in the mid-1950s introduced me to an alternative version of the Russian revolution. When the Moscow Arts Theatre visited London in 1958, I went to four Chekhov plays in order to see how they presented these great plays in keeping with the great tradition on which they were based. It was like watching opera, and the audience of White Russians who had settled in London were noteworthy too. I knew the texts well enough to catch how Soviet censors had twisted the end of *Three Sisters*.

By the time I had become a social scientist, the empires and countries that I had learned about in my stamp collecting days had disappeared. Fortunately, we had a copy of my mother-in-law's pre-1914 school atlas. Too many of their peoples had disappeared too. Only the Soviet Union, in its triumphalist Stalinist form, had survived. Moreover, it had expanded greatly as the result of being forced to fight Nazi Germany when Hitler reneged on the Molotov-Ribbentrop pact of August, 1939.

The Reality Behind the Wall

My first experience of the Cold War was in the summer of 1954, when the LSE Students' Union was offered visas for a group tour of the Soviet Union, then a closed society. I eagerly signed up to see what it looked like. However, as an American citizen I also had to have an American visa. In the heyday of McCarthyism, this was not forthcoming. As the deadline for departure drew near, I explained to a foreign service officer that the purpose of my visit was to do the American thing of making money by selling stories to the press about what I saw there. He replied by suggesting that I might instead enjoy a Mediterranean holiday. By withholding any decision, the official avoided having his signature on my visa application. The Embassy's refusal was a turning point in my life. Instead of going to the Soviet Union, I hitchhiked around Ireland with my English ballet companion, who a year and one-half later became my wife.

A Committee on Political Sociology conference in West Berlin in 1968 provided my first encounter with the Berlin Wall. I went to East Berlin with Juan Linz to see what had been the core of the Kaiser's city (Linz 2000). Juan was an interesting guide, as his previous visit to Berlin had been in 1936. In one of the great museums there was a display of Socialist-realist art; Juan's revulsion was almost physical. Another day I went to East Berlin with Mattei Dogan, a Romanian-born French sociologist. He led the way to the unmarked location of the bunker in which Hitler died. We found it as it was growing dark. We stood together in silence and Mattei then spat vigorously. A subsequent visit in 1981 was to take our art-historian daughter to Dresden following a conference in West Berlin. The way the regime had Sovietized what was once called the Florence of the North was a crime against culture. Vladimir Putin (2000) reacted differently. When posted to Dresden a few years later, he saw it as a city with an enviable standard of living.

As a byproduct of the Committee on Political Sociology being attached to UNESCO-based international associations, I attended a number of meetings in the Communist bloc. At the 1970 International Sociological Congress in Bulgaria a woman who looked like Mrs. Khrushchev asked to give a presentation at a panel that I chaired. Her paean to Marxist-Leninist social science was delivered so vigorously that it deserved being accompanied by the banging of a shoe. Afterwards, I smiled and thanked her for giving us such a good insight into the quality of Soviet social science. To see what Bulgaria was like outside a tourist resort for foreigners, I went on a day-trip to view old churches. In the course of driving through largely agricultural areas I saw only one tractor. The entertainments on the beach were a mixture: there were camel rides invoking Ottoman days and a clarinetist whose tone was more like that of Benny Goodman than of Mozart.

In 1974 Jerzy Wiatr, an IPSA go-between with the Communist bloc, arranged a Committee meeting in Warsaw that Russians could attend. We stayed and ate standard Communist cuisine in the refitted stables of Jablonna Palace. One evening when a minister came to speak, we ate in the Palace dining room and enjoyed food fit for a high-ranking member of the *nomenklatura*. At a multilingual table Polish sociologists preferred speaking German to Russian. I met there a distinguished Polish methodologist, Stefan Nowak, who had fallen afoul of the authorities. To keep out of trouble, he volunteered to study Italian Renaissance musicology.

As a side trip from a 1975 conference in Vienna, we drove to Prague. In a hotel reserved for Western tourists, my wife enjoyed the attention of a waiter with white gloves who called her *gnädige Frau* while a string trio played music in the best pre-1914 style. As a consequence of detouring to have a lunchtime beer in České Budějovice (formerly, Budweis) we crossed the border travelling along a back road through what had once been the woods of Bohemia. Every few kilometres our car was stopped by armed soldiers who searched the boot and undercarriage to see if we were trying to help someone escape. I acted dumb and smiled. We were not about to deviate from the road, for trees had been cleared 50 yards on each side to give soldiers a free-fire zone. There were also high fences strung with barbed wire in an unusual way. The next day I realized that the barbed wire at the Czech border was strung just like that in concentration camp photographs in a museum in the Prague ghetto.

My first trip to the Soviet Union was in September, 1976, to give talks on the forthcoming American presidential election. It was sponsored by the United States Information Agency, which gave me privileged status. I saw the CIA files on my audience; I wonder what my KGB file looked like. At Andropov's Institute of North American Affairs I spoke to an audience that was up to Washington standards in the questions asked. At the central library of the Soviet Union I was told proudly that a researcher anywhere in the Soviet Union could request a book from its vast depository. I thought how convenient it was for the KGB that it did not have to collate information from libraries in 15 republics in order to keep its eye on what people wanted to read. At a talk in Leningrad an *agitprop apparatchik* gave me the full Nikita Khrushchev treatment in order to make sure that the audience knew the 'correct' story. When he vigorously proclaimed that Americans had a mindless existence like that in Huxley's *Brave New World*, I politely suggested that a more appropriate book for the times was Orwell's *1984*.

Before going to the Soviet Union I had taken the market economy for granted; only after experiencing its absence did I understand what it is. In Moscow I went into the National Hotel, where Lenin had stayed, and patiently transliterated the menu. After three attempts to order were rejected because what was on the menu was not in the kitchen, the waiter helpfully pointed out the few items in both places. In an Uzbek restaurant the staff were afraid to serve a foreigner; I sat for an hour at a table without being approached. Fortunately, I then discovered a Georgian restaurant that would take money from anybody. In both Moscow and Leningrad I had ballet tickets. After seeing a vast surplus of food at the buffet of the Moscow theatre I assumed the same would be available in Leningrad. Unfortunately, that was not in the State Plan. After a splendid ballet I went to the dining room of my hotel; it refused to serve me as a dinner there had not been scheduled in my travel arrangements. I reckoned there might be something sold at the railway station to people boarding the night sleeper to Moscow. My hypothesis was confirmed. Thanks to an enterprising push cart vendor there, I dined in the street on cups of tea and Russian pelmeni.

For my second trip to Moscow for the August, 1979, IPSA World Congress I was well prepared. I took with me dried apricots, oat cakes, chocolate bars and a half bottle of whisky. This made a better breakfast than what was on the table where I stayed at Moscow State University. As an IPSA committee member I was invited to receptions where the quality of the vodka and food served varied with the position in the *nomenklatura* of the Soviet host. At one reception we enjoyed the rank of generals and at another that of lieutenant-colonels. When I went with a Russian-speaking American academic to the same hotel a third time, we could only be taken care of (that is, ripped off) in its bar for American tourists. One evening I went for dinner with a group of quantitative American political scientists. Unfortunately, their lack of familiarity with how numbers can be manipulated meant that the bill was five times what it should have been.

I stayed away from the opening ceremony of IPSA in Moscow in 1979 because I did not want to be part of a charade granting respect to that system. Later I learned that other political scientists were content to be on show in the very chamber in which Stalin's trials of imagined enemies was held in the late 1930s. During the IPSA Congress a Russian specializing in British political parties asked to interview me. I timed the meeting so that he could help me get to a reception at the American Embassy. We took a bus to a main boulevard where he flagged a black (that is, illegal) taxi. When the driver reached the very well marked American Embassy he drove past in order to stop clear of the wide-angle lens the KGB kept pointed at the building. The driver did not want to try explaining to its KGB monitors that he wasn't conspiring with American intelligence but just an ordinary Russian trying to make an illegal buck. My academic colleague politely walked me a few steps toward the Embassy and then quickly bolted. Even though he had been cleared to talk to a British academic expert, he had not been cleared to meet Americans.

Social scientists educated in the Communist bloc had a very different reading list than Western social scientists. Given its critical content, the Party approved translation of my book on Northern Ireland into Russian. However, if anyone wanted to read my views about England as a stable democracy, it was only available in *samizdat,* carbon copy versions produced by a furtive typist. The opacity of Soviet writings encouraged people to think hard if they wanted to get at the reality that a Marxist education masked. After Janos Kornai was found to have lost his faith in Communism, he was punished by being assigned a low-level job. But with obscurity came the freedom to think about the socialist system by testing what he read against reasoning from first principles and against what he observed in factories and in the streets (www.profrose.eu/people.php).

Free to Choose

In early 1988 I was offered a permanent post as a research director at the *Wissenschaftszentrum Berlin* (WZB), the largest free-standing social science research institute in Europe. Had the timing been different, I would have been tempted to accept. Instead, I became a visiting professor comparing vocational training in Germany and Britain as a case study for work I was then starting on lesson-drawing (*see* Chapter 11). My three-year term began in divided Berlin in autumn, 1988. This gave me an improved understanding of German institutions,

Crosses between the Reichstag and the Brandenburg Gate commemorating people who lost their lives trying to flee over the Wall

for better, e.g. giving youths a useful skill, and for worse, e.g. laws keeping shops from being open when working-class women and academics wanted to shop. My wife solved that problem by going on the weekend to a nearby Esso station to get milk and sundries, since it was legally able to sell groceries to customers classified as travellers.

As East Berlin included the core of the Kaiser's capital, it was full of museums and opera, and this was a big attraction to my wife and myself. It was also full of stark reminders of the harshness of the so-called German Democratic Republic. When we passed through the gates at the station where West and East Berlin residents had to part, we saw brother and sister say good bye to each other. The curator of a major East Berlin museum could travel to Romania to carry out research but not to his counterpart museum in West Berlin. Near the Brandenburg Gate in West Berlin there were crosses to commemorate those who were shot while trying to escape from the country with the highest standard of living in the Communist bloc. Rather than spend the East Marks we had been forced to buy as the price of admission to the East German workers' paradise, we preferred to eat in freedom in West Berlin, where the truth of the old German proverb *Stadt macht frei* (Cities make for freedom) was very evident.

From the start of our second Berlin stay in autumn, 1989, it was obvious that something was happening. Gorbachev had propounded the Sinatra doctrine, which told East Germans that it was up to them to control any protests rather than rely on Soviet troops to suppress Germans. However, as is always the case with history forwards, it was unclear what would happen next. The Saturday before the Wall fell there was a massive demonstration in East Berlin. I thought of attending but decided that, because I had a cold and a research grant application to write, I would be better spending the afternoon in the office. Besides, I did not know how to run and shelter there overnight if the demonstration got out of control. Within a week, that problem had disappeared and a new *wiederaufbau* began in far better conditions than those of 1945 (Rose and Haerpfer 1997). The Wall became a tourist attraction and my wife worked hard to gather souvenirs of this once in a lifetime event.

Once the Berlin Wall fell, there was a sense of jubilation, as expressed in the graffiti on the Wall and people such as my wife, Rosemary Rose, hammering away to get souvenirs

Since the twentieth-century history of Central and Eastern Europe was about anything but democratization, the fall of the Berlin Wall created great political uncertainty. My immediate response was a sense of obligation: I *had* to do something. The obligation came from my commitment to political sociology. I could not ignore the transformation of polity, economy and society within walking distance of my WZB office and spreading across half of Europe. I also had a strong commitment to people who had just gained their freedom.

The question was: What to do? I talked with Hans-Dieter Klingemann at the WZB about producing a series of studies of the first free elections in post-Communist countries and we applied for a grant from the Thyssen Foundation. Hans-Dieter told me that our request only received enough money to allow him to produce a series of handbooks on post-Communist elections. One morning in autumn 1990, I got a phone call in my WZB office saying that two Bulgarians who had created a survey institute had arrived unannounced and wanted to talk about doing a survey there. I agreed to meet them early Sunday morning at their flat. I ate nothing beforehand, thinking it would be a breakfast meeting, but it wasn't. Nonetheless, there was lots of food for thought. Here were two social scientists who could do a survey in a difficult post-Soviet context. What should I do?

In March 1991 I looked out the window of a plane taking off from London for Sofia, wondering what I was doing at the age of 57 travelling to discuss a project in a faraway country I knew little about. Andrey Raychev and Kancho Stoychev met me at the airport and lodged me at a hotel where the old regime had put up distinguished visitors. The refrigerator in my room had the ghost of a mini-bar, an empty can of Austrian beer. The next morning I walked around the city, reading the layers of its history that were in its stones. Ancient Greeks left classical columns. Orthodox Greeks left square churches that had become mosques by the addition of minarets under Ottoman rule and had then returned to being churches again by the restoration of crosses. There was also a monument to freedom: an empty plinth where a bust of Lenin had once watched 'his' people. Times were tough. In a popular hotel to which I was taken for lunch, there were lots of men drinking coffee and smoking in the lounge. However, in the dining room there was nobody but my host, myself and, shades of Prague 1975, a string trio. Bulgarians could no longer afford to pay a market price for the meal that the Party had previously provided elites from its soft budget.

After a few conversations it became clear we belonged to a transnational *landsmannschaft,* because we shared a common interest in finding out how Bulgarians were responding to extraordinary events and an understanding of survey research. We also had common views about freedom. Reflecting on what life was like trying to make a career in a tightly controlled Communist state, a Bulgarian said to me, 'I never want to be beholden to anyone else'. When I told him he was talking like Margaret Thatcher, he did not disagree.

Before going to Sofia I did not have any assurance of funding, nor could I rely on others to do the heavy lifting to find funding for surveys. I was determined to field at least a pilot survey in Bulgaria, even if I had to pay for it from my own pocket. My Bulgarian hosts told me that the British Foreign Office had launched a programme to fund research into transition problems, provided there was a British applicant and Bulgarian partners. By the end of the week my Bulgarian partners and I had prepared a request to the British Foreign Office Know How Fund, endorsed by the chair of the Finance Committee of the Bulgarian Parliament. A £10,000 grant was promptly approved. My next trip there two months later followed a major monetary reform. Instead of people having lots of paper money in their hands and no goods in shops, there were lots of goods in shops but people had no money to buy them.

The informal networks nurtured under Communism began to draw me in. Shortly after returning from Sofia I had a fax from Prague inviting me to do a survey in what was then Czechoslovakia. The directors of a newly created survey institute there had heard that I had money to spend on surveys and, equally important, shared their interest in learning how people were coping with the transformation of their society. I got on a plane to Prague and, thanks to a small seed grant from the National Science Foundation, could commission a Czechoslovak survey too. Writing and fielding a questionnaire in two countries simultaneously in spring 1991 ensured that it was both conceptually and operationally comparative and did not get bogged down in ephemeral details about personalities and events.[1]

An approach from an academic in Poznan with an Oxford link added Poland as a third country. In a seminar room in Poznan I saw photographs of great sociologists who had once worked there such as Florian Znaniecki. In the main square there was a statue to those who had defied Communist rule. Another tourist sight was the open-air Russian market, where people came from up to a thousand kilometres to sell, if they could, such things as a tap for a hand basin. Poles were not yet fully into a modern market economy. I carried several thousand dollars in travellers cheques as a down-payment on a Polish survey. However, my efforts to find a bank or money changer that would accept the cheques was unsuccessful. I ended up paying for the survey through a go-between in Britain who was much more experienced than I was at that time in moving money from Western to Eastern Europe.

To extend surveys systematically across space requires investing a large effort to raise the large amount of money required to survey more than a dozen post-Communist countries and that sort of money does not come from the tooth fairy. To extend surveys over time in order to see how people respond to the consequences of transformation as they unfold requires a continuing flow of lots of money. International organisations offering economic aid did not want to give official recognition to political problems that, in any event, were not included in their training as economists. The Eurobarometer did not want to start surveying non-member states until the worst was past and they could safely be treated as candidates for EU membership. I decided to do what I could to find the money to produce the evidence needed for an empirically based social science interpretation of how people responded to the treble transformation of their polity, their economy and their society.

In May 1991 I went to Vienna in hopes of finding some financial support for surveys of its neighbour countries. The fall of the Iron Curtain meant that the city was no longer cut off from its natural hinterland, places that many Viennese knew from their family history. Christian Haerpfer, who was building a career in survey research there on the strength of his Strathclyde MSc, told me that the Austrian government was offering large grants for studies of societies in transition. We approached Dr. Heinz Kienzl, who had created the Paul Lazarsfeld Gesellschaft to conduct public opinion surveys to inform public policy. The name was inspired by a survey study of the unemployed that Lazarsfeld had done shortly before emigrating to New York in 1934. Kienzl was committed to using social science to promote democracy. He had seen more than enough of the alternatives between the time that Hitler marched into his native Vienna in 1938 and the exit of Soviet troops in 1955.

Kienzl immediately grasped what was needed and pledged that he would raise the money to fund cross-national surveys. Having just retired as General Director

---

1.   For coverage of two decades of surveys, including a very detailed bibliography, see Richard Rose, Understanding Post-Communist Transformation: a Bottom Up Approach (2009). There is a full list of Barometer surveys and questionnaires at www.cspp.strath.ac.uk.

of the Central Bank of Austria, his network of contacts on both sides of the black/ red divide of Austrian politics was extraordinary. Between 1991 and 1998 the Austrian National Bank and the Austrian Ministry of Science and Research contributed many millions of schillings to fund some 50 New Europe Barometer (NEB) surveys covering pre-1914 Habsburg lands, including what is now Ukraine and two post-Yugoslav states. Baltic states formerly in the sphere of influence of the Prussian and Tsarist empires were omitted. In parallel, I put in years of travel to raise additional funding. The British Economic & Social Research Council was the second biggest supporter of research. Internal resources of the Centre for the Study of Public Policy came third. There was also support from scientific and public policy foundations in the United Kingdom, Germany, Sweden, France, and the United States, and from international organizations such as the World Bank, the European Commission, United Nations agencies and the Open Society Institute. The surveys are now available to social scientists (www.data-archive.ac.uk).

Russians and Russia

In May 1991, I also went to Schloss Laxenberg outside Vienna in hopes of finding support for surveys from the International Institute for Applied Systems Analysis (IIASA), a bridge-building institute between East and West. I didn't find what I expected. The director, Peter de Janosi, told me that IIASA was having trouble raising funds, because the fall of the Berlin Wall meant that sponsors saw less need for it, and Soviet finance was especially uncertain. All he could suggest was that I might want to meet a youthful Russian research assistant, Peter Aven. When I told him my plan of doing surveys in Central and Eastern Europe, he asked: 'Why not Russia?' I explained that I didn't know Russian, I didn't know Russians, and Russia was a big country that could consume all of one's time. Aven replied, 'My friends will help you'. Although I repeated my reservations, Aven was insistent. After half an hour I thought to myself: Why am I being so stubborn in refusing so intriguing an offer? I suggested meeting for breakfast the next morning to explore possibilities further. By the time we met I realised that Aven was right. It would be foolish to reject the opportunity to work with Russians who wanted to find what was happening to their society as Mikhail Gorbachev's initiatives were spinning out of control. We discussed what might be done in what was then the Soviet Union and parted with a general agreement to keep in touch.

A month later there was an unexpected visitor in my Strathclyde office, a lecturer in economics at Glasgow University whom I had never met, Ljubo Sirc. He invited me to a conference in Cambridge about societies in transition being held by the Centre for Research on Communist Economics. The Centre was supported by the Institute of Economic Affairs (IEA), which had led a long march to return Britain to market economics as set out by Friedrich Hayek and Milton Friedman and was significant in converting Margaret Thatcher to that cause. Sirc was a Slovene whose autobiography was titled *Between Hitler and Tito*. After years in a Tito prison, he escaped and gained a doctorate writing about Hayek, whom he credited with saving his mind. Many Russian economists who had been trained in managing a centrally planned non-market economy were looking to Thatcher's London for ideas rather than to Keynesians in the two Cambridges, England and Massachusetts. Sirc's Centre was responding to their interest.

The latent function of my conference invitation was that Aven's friends would be in Cambridge to meet me. In July 1991 we began talking seriously there about a Russian survey and they had time to talk to each other about me. We ended up agreeing to do a survey if money could be found. I walked up to Ralph Harris, the founding director of the IEA, and asked if he could find £5,000 for a survey in Russia. He asked a few questions and said he could. It looked like we were in business. However, a fortnight later while I was having difficulty faxing Moscow my wife came in the study to tell me that Gorbachev had just been seized in an attempted Communist coup. I set my fax aside and turned my mind to Central and Eastern Europe. Six weeks later the fax went beep, beep, beep; it was my Moscow contacts. They were ready to go ahead.

Moscow in November 1991 had more uncertainty than food. My collaborator, Viacheslav Shironin, had spent hours the previous weekend queuing for a few eggs. When I suggested he could read whilst standing there, he shook his head. Russian babushkas do not queue quietly. The air was cold but free. Shironin took me to a park where statues of Marx and Lenin and the founder of the KGB had been dumped. He wanted to make sure the statues were where they belonged: toppled. The experience in fielding surveys in half a dozen post-Communist countries was helpful as a starting point for the first New Russia Barometer (NRB) survey. Given the uncertainty about whether the Soviet Union would still exist when we went in the field in January, 1992, political questions referred to 'this country'. It turned out that the name of the country was the Russian Federation.

In June 1992 I presented results of the first New Russia Barometer survey in Moscow and St. Petersburg as part of a delegation from Sirc's Centre that met with Peter Aven's friends and colleagues. Many were now part of the Gaidar government, including Aven himself as Minister of Foreign Economic Relations. Some things remained the same. Ralph Harris was right to bring a bath plug, for this had yet to be introduced in the Party hotel in which we stayed. Western wine of sorts was available, but not a corkscrew. The bartender opened a bottle by using a screwdriver to drive the cork into the bottle. A new restaurant had rock music inside and an armed guard at the door. Our translator followed old customs by diverting bottles of vodka and brandy from the table to the capacious handbag she had brought for that purpose. I asked a Bosnian member of the Centre delegation whether this was his first trip to Moscow. Having been in the mountains with Tito's partisans during the war, he had visited Moscow in 1947 as part of a delegation that had dinner with Josef Stalin. His reply to my question about what Stalin was like was: 'He treated us better than he treated his own people'.

I was approached via fax by a Lithuanian who wanted me to apply for European Union funding for surveys in Baltic states that had just regained the independence that they had lost when Stalin and Hitler divided them. Our common professional knowledge enabled us to put together a successful four-nation grant proposal without having met. In Vilnius the tourist sites included the television mast where in January 1991 Soviet troops had killed 12 Lithuanians demonstrating there for independence. I learned how different each Baltic state was, including the size and location of the Russian minority planted there by Stalin. The result of the trip was the creation of the New Baltic Barometer that asked comparable questions in Estonia, Latvia and Lithuania. The database has made possible many different types of comparisons, including those between Russians in Russia and Russians in the Baltic states.

When I started doing surveys in post-Communist countries I did not know where or when the first country would become undemocratic again. Hence, I ran fast, fearing that the wall of silence would soon be re-imposed. This did not happen. I have now done 20 New Russia Barometer surveys. Knowing Russian and Soviet history, I made no assumption that the Russian Federation was becoming a democracy. Barometer questionnaires asked people whether or not they supported the present regime; this avoided referring to the emotive and potentially inaccurate label of democracy.

By dumb luck the base line for trend analysis of NRB surveys was the first month of the Russian Federation. Questions about regime support — it was 14 per cent in January 1992, — have been repeated in every survey since. Developments making Russia undemocratic according to measures of Freedom House have not made it unacceptable to a majority of Russians. To explain why most Russians have come to support their new regime requires taking into account how the passage of time presses people to adapt to a system that they may not want but which they do not expect to go away. The imaginative skill of my co-author, Bill Mishler, has found a way to demonstrate this statistically (Rose, Mishler and Munro 2011: chapter 6).

When Britons ask me how I do surveys in Russia, the answer is simple: I work with Russians. The maintenance of a trend survey over 20 years owes much to the commitment and skills of the staff of the Levada Centre, Russia's leading institute conducting quality surveys of public opinion. It was founded as VtSIOM at the time of perestroika, when Communist leaders realised that they lacked evidence of how their subjects were reacting to the big changes that they were introducing. In the 1990s its staff showed their commitment to research by concentrating on social science surveys while others turned to more lucrative market research. The Putin administration took over VtSIOM by invoking a legal technicality that was a legacy from Soviet days.[2] The staff I worked with demonstrated their civil courage and commitment to independent social science by leaving it *en masse* and creating the Levada Centre. As I write in autumn 2013, the Centre is once again under political pressure from the Russian state on the grounds that the small amount of funding it receives from abroad to conduct surveys makes it an agent of a foreign power.

---

2. This was the second time that its co-founder, Yuri Levada, had been deprived of a post. In the Brezhnev era he lost his professorship at Moscow State University because of lecturing about the ideas of the American sociologist Talcott Parsons.

What I Did

After the Wall fell the first thing I did was to drink to freedom. The circumstances were unprecedented. Conventional Anglo-American liberals so take freedom for granted that they ignored this fundamental political gain. Some behaved like adolescent Marxists, prophesying that if actions were not taken to stop the rise in officially recorded unemployment and the contraction of the official economy, there would be terrible political consequences. They did not take into account the priceless gain of freedom. Many people I knew could tell the difference. For example, Marietta Nettl had grown up in Budapest, experiencing Hungarian fascism, Nazi occupation, and Soviet occupation. She told me that it was only two decades after coming to England to marry the polymath Peter Nettl that she would say what she thought in front of strangers.

The risk of undertaking research in lands where I did not know the language or people has been rewarding far more than I could ever have imagined in 1991. More than half the post-Communist states in which I have done surveys did not exist in 1989. In different forms, the New Europe Barometer has included ten new European Union members; successor states of the Soviet Union; and successor states of Yugoslavia. In addition, surveys in Korea and Turkey, two countries where political regimes have been problematic, have explored how popular response to authoritarian regimes compares with totalitarian regimes. For the most part, the differences between the legacy of conventional dictatorships and Communist regimes with a totalitarian vocation are greater than the similarities. Surveys in Austria and West Germany have provided standards for assessing the extent to which people who have not been subject to Communist rule differ in their political outlooks from people who have (Rose and Page 1996).

Problem-focused research

The transformation of Communist societies was an interdisciplinary event of an extraordinary kind. Since I had established the Centre for the Study of Public Policy to make use of whatever concepts in the social sciences were relevant to problems confronting government, I was free of the constraints of many Western academics whose professional training had confined their thinking to problems of a single academic discipline (*see* Chapter 11). Moreover, the comparative focus of the CSPP meant that I did not take for granted that peoples everywhere were socialized in a society in which the rule of law, freedom and markets could be taken for granted.

Because science is a method of inquiry and so much was uncertain in the immediate aftermath of the fall of the Berlin Wall, I did not start out to test a single theory of mass behaviour. The flexibility of a survey questionnaire makes it possible to include modules that cover primary interests of political science, economics, sociology and social medicine. Because NEB surveys cover many countries, it is possible to compare how people differ between societies, for example, the once-again democratic Czech Republic and never-democratic Russia and Belarus. Comparisons across a wide range of NEB indicators suggest that the median society has tended to be Slovakia, an assessment consistent with both twentieth century history and geography.

I developed a measure of the gain in freedom based on Isaiah Berlin's (1958) lecture on freedom from the state, which I heard him deliver in Oxford. The thesis was simple: freedom from the state is essential to avoid the risks of authoritarian or totalitarian rule. When an Oxford sociologist dismissed this as a Thatcherite attack on state-funded welfare, I thought him blissfully or conveniently ignorant of the world that Isaiah Berlin knew from his birth in Riga to being a refugee from Petrograd and knowing at first hand the horrors of Nazi Germany and Stalin's Russia. Given the scope of Communist attempts to control the lives of their subjects, it was straightforward to devise a battery of questions that asked people such things as whether they were now more or less able than before to say what they think or choose their own religion. For people who had been subject to compulsory Communist socialization, two questions inverted typical liberal assumptions about political participation being desirable. People were asked whether they felt freer than before to decide for themselves whether or not to join organizations and whether or not to take an interest in politics (*see* Rose 2009: chapter 10).

Building on research I had done on the informal economies of Europe and the household production of welfare in Asia (Rose 1986), multiple indicators were developed to measure household activity in three economies: the official and monetized economy that provides the data input for National Income Accounts; the unofficial cash-in-hand economy; and unofficial and non-monetized household activities. While this sounds abstract, it was easy to collect relevant indicators by asking respondents if they exchanged services such as painting a house or child care with relatives and friends. This bottom-up approach produced a paper that dealt with the Communist inversion of Marx, the introduction of the idiocy of rural life into urban households, since city dwellers could not rely on a non-market economy to provide all the food they needed. 'Who Grows Food in Russia and Eastern Europe?' documented how most people growing food were urban residents wanting to have enough to eat (Rose and Tikhomirov 1993).

The readiness of people to fall back on unofficial means of coping was ignored by conventional macro-economists. Fortunately for me, it was not ignored by the then governor of the Bundesbank, a former French finance minister, and the chief economist of the European Bank for Reconstruction & Development. They were judges for the award of the Robert Marjolin Prize in International Economics. In 1992 I submitted a paper on East Europe's need for a civil economy in place of the amoral uncivil economy of the Communist era. I hoped that I might win one of the $500 prizes on offer. I miscalculated; I won the $25,000 first prize (Rose 1992).

In search of evidence harder than Soviet-style economic statistics, I examined national census data between 1949 and 1989 about infant mortality, life expectancy and the growth in car ownership. The conventional interpretation of statistics about male life expectancy falling in the early days of the Russian Federation was that this was due to the shock consequences of the collapse of the Soviet regime. What this view ignores is the long-term legacy of stagnating male life expectancy in the so-called golden era of Leonid Brezhnev. Even though by 1989 living conditions in the Communist bloc had improved by comparison with the devastation left by war, the improvements were so limited that there was a widening gap with living conditions west of the Iron Curtain. The most dramatic comparisons are between the life expectancy of West Germans and Austrians and their neighbours in East Germany, Hungary and the Czech Republic. These show the many millions of years of human life lost by those subject to the great Socialist experiment (Rose 1994; 2009: chapter 3).

The fall in officially reported life expectancy in post-Soviet Russia attracted the attention of epidemiologists. Meeting a team at University College London, Medical School, led by Michael Marmot made clear the mutual advantage of combining their clinical knowledge of mortality with my capacity to collect data about people still alive in societies in transformation. Working with clinically trained medical researchers is interesting because, unlike economists, they are trained to verify assumptions by systematically collecting evidence rather than ignoring whatever a theory treats as exogenous. This has resulted in many articles in journals with titles such as *Social Science and Medicine* and *Addiction* (*see* www.profrose.eu/writings.php#public_policy).

After conducting repeated surveys in more than a dozen post-Communist countries, in 1995 I had a fellowship at the Max Planck Society's Work Group on Transformation Processes in Berlin. In an office off Unter den Linden I spent weeks probing what I had already published in order to arrive at its underlying theme. My conclusion was that the fall of the Berlin Wall was not the end of history; it offered a choice between *Democracy and its Alternatives* (Rose, Mishler and Haerpfer 1998). To understand change in the *longue durée,* I spent another decade puzzling and publishing more articles. After EU enlargement and Putin's Russia established what the alternative outcomes of transformation were, I integrated two decades of writings in a book, *Understanding Post-Communist Transformation.* Its theme could not have been discerned when I wrote many of the articles that provided its raw materials. Even less was it predicted when the Berlin Wall fell.

Communicating to policymakers

Transformation confronted policymakers with the *hic et nunc* challenge: What is to be done? Barometer surveys created evidence of immediate relevance to policymakers at a time when evidence was scarce. Quantification turned anecdotes into scientific data. Moreover, the numbers produced, for example, about who grows food, were more consistent with observations on the ground than were official statistics. Whereas official data is confined to government records, Barometer data was unofficial. It could take into account activities that did not involve cash, for example, being given a chicken to eat for Sunday dinner by a relative. Moreover government agencies normally do not conduct surveys asking about how many people pay bribes to their officials.

The fixation of policymakers on official data was both impressive and depressing. Everyone working in the region knew that Communist systems had routinely distorted official statistics to make their regime look better. However, the logic of transition required a base line measure based on Communist-era data in order to monitor the direction and scale of change. The methodology followed the guidelines of Samuel Taylor Coleridge writing about the supernatural; he called it 'the willing suspension of disbelief'. This made it possible to give official statistics of historically planned economies from Albania to Laos the appearance of market economy statistics in US dollars at current prices (Marer *et al.* 1992; cf. Morgenstern 1963). When I asked John O'Connor, one of the economists who led this exercise, how it could be justified, he replied, 'Demand creates supply'.[3] In 1991 O'Connor asked me to produce a short paper about the micro-economic uses of Barometer surveys and circulated it within the World Bank. This attracted a series of inquiries and commissions to write papers that, to paraphrase the motto of Heineken's beer, reached economic activities that official statistics did not reach. Along with Jeffrey Sachs and Anders Aslund, I was one of three authors whose papers were kept at hand by the team that produced the World Bank's review of societies in transition.

I wanted to get my data about newly free countries into the hands of the people who lived in the countries where I did research. The *Studies in Public Policy* (SPP) series of the CSPP made it possible to publish immediately evidence of how people were coping with the problems of transition. The first SPP report of Barometer data was number 192; the most recent is number 492 (www.cspp.strath.ac.uk/catalog13_0.html). Lots of books and scores of journal articles have followed with co-authors from Austria, Australia, the Czech Republic, Germany, Hungary, Korea, Russia, Sweden and the United States. In 1992 I volunteered to give week-long seminars to the exceptionally keen multinational graduate students at the Central European University, then in Prague. Their need was not for advanced statistical training but for data about their own country. I placed my data in their hands so they could analyse what was happening free of past constraints. With Claire Wallace, then head of the sociology department, we ran an East European summer school modelled on what I had done in Strathclyde in 1973 to help young West Europeans.

My motto has always been that I will talk once to anyone who wants to talk to me. As word got out that I had unique data about current conditions in societies in transformation, all sorts of people tracked me down by telephone, fax and latterly, email. To complement dissemination in print, I put in tens of thousands of air miles to present results of research to policymakers and PhDs (sometimes the same person, wearing different hats) from Moscow and Budapest to Washington and Berkeley and gave many media interviews. In Vienna Heinz Kienzl saw to it that NEB results were circulated within the Austrian government and Austrian Central Bank and to the press and I appeared in a non-musical role on Austria's Radio Blue Danube. As a recipient of funding from the British Economic & Social

---

3.   A year later O'Connor thought differently. A Hungarian colleague told me, 'John has given up on Gross National Product'.

Research Council, I talked to Foreign Office researchers and its diplomats abroad. In Washington I gave seminars at a wide variety of think tanks, as well as meeting staff in government and international agencies. Although we had never met, the President of Latvia wrote to express appreciation of my efforts in studying and disseminating internationally evidence about his often neglected society. Nothing I wrote was classified and what I said in private was what I would say in public.

While some Western audiences were puzzled because what I said could not be slotted into the disciplinary framework they were taught in graduate school, in countries where the evidence was most relevant the seminars invariably stimulated discussion. In a talk at the Institute of State and Law in Moscow I knew that I had addressed the right topics when the audience spent so much time debating with each other the implications of NRB evidence that I was an hour late for dinner. The Levada Centre translated a number of my NRB studies for publication in their Russian-language Bulletin reaching a wide audience. The comparative dimension in Barometer surveys was specially welcomed because it showed the extent to which the problems a country faced were not unique to it. I left it up to members of the audience to decide what their country should do about this.

When I boarded my flight to Sofia in 1991 I could not have imagined where the forward movement of history would lead. In retrospect, the boundaries of Europe today are much more like those before 1914 than of the Europe that existed for the first half of my career as a social scientist (www.profrose.eu/writings.php#europe; Rose 1996a: chapter 1). *Mitteleuropa* is once again central to Europe and the Danube is once again a great European waterway. There is freedom for people to travel across the continent without facing a distinctive feature of socialist systems, shoot-to-kill border guards. While experiencing history forwards I have also found striking reminders of my roots. In Vienna and Budapest the music of light operas is familiar to me from the St. Louis Municipal Opera. In Schiller's home in Weimar I saw an etching of the American Revolution that he had acquired at the time of the French Revolution. It was a scene from the Boston Massacre that showed British redcoats shooting Crispus Attucks, a black ex-slave. The segregated primary school in my native St. Louis suburb was called Attucks. It too is no more.

Part III

Learning to Compare

Comparison is the oldest form of political science, tracing its roots to Aristotle. In his travels Aristotle observed differences in the constitutions of city states from Macedonia to Asia minor and asked the seemingly simple question: Why? To answer this question required concepts differentiating political systems. Aristotle's concern with observing and explaining similarities and differences between political systems remains relevant for understanding the world we live in today.

I started doing comparative research at the age of eight, studying baseball statistics of the National and American leagues. This also got me into interrupted time series analysis, since in 1919 baseballs were pepped up so that batters such as Babe Ruth could hit lots of home runs, the equivalent of widening football goalposts by half. My introduction to European culture at Johns Hopkins gave special emphasis to comparing differences in architectural forms and styles across both time and space. Renting apartments and signing contracts in different countries has made me aware that ways of doing business vary between countries. For more than half a century comparison has also been part of my daily life. If I want to talk to a foreigner all I need do is chat with my wife.

As a native of a border state, I have always been conscious that there is more than one way of viewing the United States. As an American long resident in Europe, it is easy to spot what is distinctively American in abstract social science theories. Long residence in Scotland and one foot in London ensures awareness of similarities and differences between parts of the United Kingdom. Sixty years of travel across Europe makes me very conscious of the past and present diversity of the member states of the European Union and of their neighbours.

Sticking to the study of one's own country is the default choice of most social scientists, but it is not risk free.[1] It can confuse knowledge specific to a country

---

1. Cf. Mozart's remarks in a letter to his father in 1778: Ein Mensch von mittelmassigen Talent bleibt immer mittelmassig er mag reisen oder nicht — aber ein Mensch von superieuren Talent [...] wird schlecht, wenn er immer in den näämlichen Ort bleibt.

with what is common in many political systems. To gain useful social science knowledge about another country requires combining generic concepts and specific observations. On that count Huck Finn fell short, for when he set out for Indian territory he did not have a clear idea of what he was looking for. All he had was a clear idea of what he was escaping from, school. By contrast, when Lewis and Clark set off from St. Louis in 1804 to explore the unknown territories drained by the Missouri River, President Thomas Jefferson carefully briefed them about what to look for. Drawing on his reading of Enlightenment encyclopedias, Jefferson specified natural, geographical and human phenomena that the explorers should note. The President also gave a useful tip on data base management; he advised backing up notes on birch bark, because it was less vulnerable to climate extremes than notes on paper (Gilman 2004: 15ff).

Decisions about what to compare reflect both conscious choice and opportunistic happenings. My decision to go to Oxford for a doctorate was a conscious choice, whereas two decades of research on formerly Communist countries was a mixture of choice and chance. While I chose to visit Vienna to seek money for research in former Habsburg territories, it was almost pure chance that Peter Aven was in his office the day I stopped by. My studies of Asian politics have been initiated by decisions of Asians, for example, a leading Japanese political scientist, Rei Shiratori, asked me if I would like to collaborate in a book comparing public policy in Japan with countries I knew well. I had to decide whether I was just a European specialist or a student of advanced industrial societies whatever their continent. I chose the latter. Japan showed me that people can achieve high standards of welfare without high welfare state expenditure; it also made me realize the extent to which European welfare states have substituted state for household welfare (Rose 1986).

The number of countries one studies is less important than how they are studied. At one extreme a reliance on abstract models encourages meaningless or misleading universalisms, for example, propositions about all political behaviour being rational. At the other extreme are national studies that reflect false particularization, claiming a country is unique by stressing what is nominal and exceptional in its institutions rather than the many things that are common to lots of countries. The biggest challenge is to understand the first country that is different from one's homeland. If generic concepts are used, an intensive analysis of a single country can have broad significance. Thus, my research on Northern Ireland sought to understand a system of governing without consensus and my Russian research has focused on support for an undemocratic regime. The more countries you know something about, the easier it is to apply meaningful concepts to additional countries. Just because the EU has 28 member states does not mean that there are 28 different ways to educate children or elect MPs. My current research on corruption uses survey data from more than 100 countries to make a worldwide comparison of differences in the individual experience of paying bribes to get public services. My current research on the European Union and its impact on member states shows how multi-level governance and globalization are creating interdependencies that erode traditional boundaries between comparative politics and international relations (Rose 1991b; 2013; 2014a).

Travel is no guarantee of learning if observations are interpreted by a commitment to theories that exclude observations that do not fit prior assumptions. The Chief Economist of the World Bank is likely to be in dozens of countries a year and receive reports about even more. It is a reflection on the narrowness of the economics education that Larry Summers received at Harvard that his experience as the World Bank's Chief Economist did not make him aware of the need for differentiation in prescribing for real economies. Confronted with the collapse of non-market Communist systems, Summers declared, 'Spread the truth ... the laws of economics are like the laws of engineering. One set of laws works everything' (quoted in Rose 2009: 2).

The following chapters discuss three stages in learning to compare. First, it is necessary to have concepts to link specific observations to generic ideas and to guide the systematic collection of quantitative data. Communicating what you learn requires flexibility in how you write about what you have learned, because policymakers view the world differently than social scientists. To make research relevant to public policy, it must focus on the undisciplined problems that face government officials as well as the narrowly defined disciplinary problems that are the stuff of academic journal articles.

Chapter 9

Concepts Are More Than Words

When I started teaching comparative politics at Oxford more than half a century ago, the subject matter was not defined by concepts but by the names of countries. Concepts were treated as alien to the English way of thinking about politics. Textbooks provided useful basic information about political institutions, thus avoiding the subsequent knowledge gap created by concentrating on abstractions without information. The only table a politics text was certain to have was a table of contents. Each country was treated independently of other countries: England was England and the United States was the United States.

Interesting and informative books written by country specialists such as Philip Williams' 1958 study of the Fourth French Republic reflected profound knowledge of its institutions but, in the absence of generic concepts, they were literally incomparable. When reading Tocqueville's *Democracy in America* in my youth, I saw it as a great description of the exceptional character of American democracy. That was also the way it was interpreted in Oxford, albeit students were expected to read it in French. No attention was paid to the author's motive in travelling to America. As Tocqueville (1954 edition: 14) explained, 'I sought there the image of democracy itself in order to learn what we [that is, Europeans] have to fear or to hope from its progress'.

In Nuffield election studies the key terms are not concepts but descriptors, the words British and the year. They are works of contemporary history that rely on interviews with living politicians rather than documents that are left behind by dead politicians. Even though Nuffield studies of each British election have been published since 1945, they have not been summarized to show cumulative trends or discontinuities. Likewise, until nationalist parties won seats in the House of Commons, there was little interest in comparing the nations of the United Kingdom. *Understanding the United Kingdom* (Rose 1982) was the first systematic attempt to examine the extent to which British politics existed, that is, it was the same in Wales, Scotland and Northern Ireland as in England.

Knowledge of concepts and the indicators they require ought to come before technical skill in manipulating what is observed. After all, painters look at objects before they start applying a brush to their canvas. Concepts make it possible to group under a generic heading observations with at least one significant attribute in common. As physics Nobel laureate George Thompson (1961: 4) has explained: 'Science depends on its concepts. These are ideas which receive names. They determine the questions one asks and the answers one gets. They are more fundamental than the theories which are stated in terms of them', Given my lifelong interest in the use of words, I immediately grasped the significance of Giovanni Sartori's (1970) proposition that we must name things before we can count them. The importance of doing so was illustrated when many political observers misinterpreted the collapse of the Soviet Union as the start of a process of democratization. I did not share this view. I saw that new regimes could become either democratic or undemocratic.

Just before starting to teach British politics at Manchester, I wrestled with Gabriel Almond's (1960) conceptual framework for the analysis of political systems worldwide. Instead of asking the journalistic question 'Who runs this country?' or searching for the will of the wisp of power, Almond conceptualized seven functions that every political system must have, such as political recruitment and rule-making. I started teaching this approach to politics students who had previously been socialized to understand British politics in incomparable terms. The chapters in *Politics in England* had conceptual headings suitable for comparison with other countries. The first sentence intentionally echoed Tocqueville: 'In the study of comparative politics England is important as a deviant case' (Rose 1965: 15). There were more index references to France or Germany than to the name of the British prime minister. The care taken to set the analysis of politics in England within a generic conceptual framework has meant that after fifty years the framework is still in use in a global textbook (Powell *et al.* 2014).

By a fortuitous coincidence I began reading the abstract literature of systems theory in the early 1960s at the same time as grappling with the installation of a central heating system in our new house in Manchester. An understanding of central heating requires a flow chart that tracks the movement of hot water from the boiler through pipes to radiators and then feeds back to the boiler for re-heating. A thermostat that takes account of changes in the surrounding environment maintains a stable temperature. Each point in the system involves a number of variables and the amount of heat in the room depends on how they were combined. The heating system can be evaluated by its output in British thermal units and the cost by its input in British pounds. Looked at without labels, a model of central heating has a lot in common with David Easton's (1965) model of a political system, except that it is a lot easier to fix a defective heating system.

Theories provide the justification for hypotheses of cause and effect. Instead of assuming that a single theory offers a complete explanation of political observations, I prefer to test multiple hypotheses drawn from different theories. In this way, if one hypothesis is falsified the other is likely to be supported. This approach avoids the risk of putting all one's eggs in one theoretical basket and wasting efforts in trying to save a theory that turns out to be a bad egg.

Naming What You Observe

My approach is distinctive because it takes into account the fact that the words that name concepts can have connotations as well as a denotation. A lifetime of engagement with music, architecture and applied arts makes me aware that what is not verbalized can still have meanings. As Richard Wagner once said, words are what fills gaps in a narrative told by music.[1] For more than 1,500 years the icons of the Byzantine church have been full of meaning to its communicants. While Microsoft icons have reached more people, they are unlikely to last as long. L'Enfant's design for Washington D.C. placed Congress in a massive Capitol building that looked down on a distant and domestic White House. The symbolism was clear to those who authorized the plans.

Words can be metaphors with broader and deeper meanings. In literary analysis a revealing statement is not what a muckraking journalist can quote as evidence of malfeasance in office but what James Joyce called an epiphany, a quotation that conveys a larger meaning in a sentence or a phrase. Thus, the comment that a leftwing Labour MP made to me in an interview for my doctoral thesis — 'It's hell when your party is in power; you don't know whether to follow your conscience or your party' — came to epitomise a 502-page book about the problem of party government (Rose 1974a). I have scattered epiphanies throughout this text.

The critical philosophical point, which is as old as Plato, is that all words are but approximate indicators of what they are meant to represent. The relationship is even looser when a verbal label is attached to a set of numbers. Wittgenstein added an emphasis on words being subject to a degree of ambiguity. Indicators that are approximate may be evaluated as giving a more or less adequate representation of a concept. However, ambiguous indicators are multi-dimensional in their meanings and have no 'true' or 'best' meaning. At Oxford I learned the gambit — 'It all depends upon what you mean by X'. This was normally used to start an inconclusive discussion about differences in what you may mean, what I mean, and what others may mean. However, social science is not a scholastic debate about what words 'really' mean. At some point a researcher needs to move on. I treat the existence of multiple meanings as an obligation to explain clearly my definition of key concepts at the start of a paper and then show the significance of a concept in a given context.

In comparative research, institutions in countries with different languages usually have different names. This leaves open whether they describe the same thing or whether linguistic differences are a sign of institutional differences. A review of the use of the word 'democracy' found more than 500 different uses, making the key term the adjective that modifies the word (Collier and Levitsky 1997). In a discussion with Japanese social security officials it turned out that I could understand what they were explaining better than my thoroughly bilingual translator because she had no knowledge, in English or Japanese, of how social security systems are funded. I was temporarily flummoxed in reading trend tables because each column had a word and a two digit number as a caption rather than a year. When it was explained to me that the captions represented the years of the reign of each emperor all became clear, for regnal years are also used in some English documents. For example, I started studying English politics in 2 Elizabeth II, the second year of the reign of Queen Elizabeth II.

---

1. Compare the music and the prose text of *Tristan and Isolde*.

Collecting evidence

My training as a newspaper reporter has given me a careful respect for verifying what you think you know. No newspaper wants to run a story about a plane crash that hasn't happened, or be guilty of libel by calling a person a criminal who hasn't been convicted of a crime. An emphasis on specifics, such as the name of a person elected, means there is no need for quantification because each person is one of a kind. Giving a percentage number rather than using a word such as 'many' makes clear whether one is referring to a majority or a minority of instances. If information is taken from a police blotter or official documents, it is reliable even if not always valid. Doing a doctorate at Oxford meant that I could walk to a copyright library to check details relevant to my thesis. The bookshelves nearest to my desk have always been filled with well thumbed reference books.

Newspaper work taught me that there is always a source for information and going straight to the source is the best way to obtain it. That meant figuring out who and where that source should be and picking up a book or a telephone to talk to a person in the know. Face-to-face conversations result in all sorts of unexpected information and insights popping up. Often the most knowledgeable officials are not those who are most prominent; they can be long-serving members of an organisation, including secretaries. When at Oxford it was easy to get to London to interview politicians; for many I was the first academic researcher who had ever asked them about their work. Nowadays the Internet provides ready access to many sources of information.

My first big academic break came through using my newspaper experience to estimate the cost of Conservative Party advertising before the 1959 British general election. Newspaper advertisements are very public documents, and the rates that papers charge for advertising space are also public. Thanks to a tip from a friend in London advertising, I was saved the tedium of spending a month of measuring newspaper advertisements to calculate their cost. The information was obtained from a service that routinely monitored what competing consumer goods companies were spending. It recorded that the Conservatives spent £468,000 on pre-election advertising; this was equivalent to more than £20,000,000 at today's prices. When I invited Conservative Central Office to confirm this figure or say that friendly publishers had not charged market prices, the director of publicity wisely said nothing. The numbers were firm enough to fuel a debate in the House of Commons (Hansard 1960).

Such was the paucity of information in the 1960s about how English people lived that I sometimes wrote articles for *New Society* or *The Economist* in order to have material that I could include in the first edition of *Politics in England*. As my byline and television appearances became more frequent, this opened more doors at higher levels. When people know that they cannot stop you from publishing your views about their activities and you are talking to others about their work too, they have an incentive to give you what they regard as the 'true' facts. In the early days of studies of voting behaviour, there was no archive with European data but those who did surveys, including commercial polls, were often ready to give me boxes of IBM cards of surveys to hump back to Strathclyde to run through counter-sorters and card-fed computers. The heavy boxes became so numerous that I had to design a special trolley to wheel the boxes around.

Diaries are written sources but they must be evaluated in relation to their author; this is not a matter of literary style but of veracity. Whenever I hear someone cite *The Diaries of R. H. S. Crossman* as evidence of how British government works, I ask whether they knew him. I did, and learned that he would not let facts stand in the way of a witty remark. At the conclusion of an interview for my doctoral thesis, Crossman asked if I would send him any notes I had taken so that he could see what he had said. I gladly sent him my 1,000-word summary. It included one polite paraphrase. I wrote that because of his unreliability allies viewed Crossman warily. He crossed out this circumlocution and proudly wrote, 'He became known in Labour circles as Double Crossman'.

Increasingly social scientists present the results of complex statistical analysis without first describing clearly how they measure what they are seeking to explain. Notwithstanding their strengths, inferential statistics can provide an opaque cover for conceptually inadequate indicators and ignore the GIGO principle: Garbage In, Garbage Out. In my work I follow the maxim of Mrs. Beeton's Victorian recipe for jugged hare. It starts with the injunction: 'First catch your hare'. In my cook book of political statistics, the starting point is: 'First catch your dependent variable'.

Quantification is integral to the analysis of elections and electoral data appears unproblematic. However, compiling the *International Almanac of Electoral History* required applying more conceptual judgments than is apparent to users. Tom Mackie and I had to decide when a country held the first election suitable to record as a national election. The starting point was not the introduction of universal suffrage, which normally followed well after the first elections. It was the first election in which the great majority of seats for the national parliament were contested and most candidates stood in the name of parties (Mackie and Rose, 1991: x). Contestation indicated an election was free; without contestation no votes need be cast in a constituency. Without nationwide parties there could not be a meaningful national total of votes. We also had to define what we meant by a political party and when a new party is created, since many are formed as a consequence of splits and/or mergers. We went to official sources in 16 languages to obtain the names of parties and statistics of votes and seats. To avoid ambiguity, we numbered each party and reported its name in the national language as well as an English translation. Draft national chapters were then sent to national experts and to a senior civil servant in the national Parliament responsible for registering the seats that parties won.

Applying rigorous standards in collecting and verifying electoral data required a great deal of time and effort. For this reason, compilers of a number of other election books did not bother to make the same effort. Believing that what we reported was just copied from official publications, they copied from our book. This ended up being to our benefit, for it was easy to prove that they had done so. The money we collected for breach of copyright from five different publishers was more than our royalties from the sale of books.

The push for quantification in political science has led those who pride themselves on their commitment to the methodology of hard sciences to dismiss as mere anecdotes evidence that is acceptable to historians and in courts of law. However, privileging quantification can become mindless empiricism. Data bases may be full of conveniently available economic and social data and have few measures of political interest. For example, a historical data base compiled by a prestigious European university not only recorded the number of horses in each census tract but also their gender, subdivided into three different categories. Quantification is no guarantee of validity. Indexes of democracy and governance can be more concerned with reliability than with validity. A desire to maximize the number of countries covered can lead to weighting equally every UN member state from Andorra to China. A commitment to long-term trend analysis can ignore the extent to which politics interrupts state boundaries, a fact known to every German, Pole and Russian.

Even when a quantitative indicator is clear about what is measured, it may still be inadequate because it does not specify what it is not measuring. While the Freedom House Index (www.freedomhouse.org) is explicit about what constitutes democracy, countries that fail to meet this standard are not differentiated between regimes that are under military rule, controlled by a populist dictator, or run on totalitarian lines. Thus, the majority of regimes in the world today can only be described by what they lack. In my surveys of post-Communist regimes I avoided this problem by asking people their views about four types of political systems: a strong dictatorship, military rule, a monarchy or a system with competitive elections.

Models focus attention on what one needs to know

My education in the streets has made me sceptical of grand theories that achieve breadth by being so vague that it is hard to see how they can be related to evidence of the world as it is. I prefer theories that can be turned into models that clearly and contingently link cause and effect. This choice reflects the influence of reading Robert Merton (1957) on theories of the middle range and Herbert Simon (1969) on the importance of choosing the most meaningful level of aggregation or disaggregation for a problem at hand.

My model of an election result can be summed up in a single flow chart that integrates voting behaviour and electoral institutions rather than dividing these two interrelated phenomena into separate analyses conducted by separate branches of political scientists (Rose 1974: 19). When I first presented it at a seminar at MIT, I was surprised to find that so mathematically sophisticated a professor as Hayward Alker had not noticed that individual decisions about how to vote are intervening variables between rules influencing who can vote, the parties that political elites offer to the electorate, and how the electoral system distributes seats. Hayward immediately applied his fertile mind to suggesting additional variables to be included in the flow chart. When I protested, 'If you do that, you just end up with history', he retorted, 'No you don't; historians don't connect cause and effect'.

A model concentrates attention on what data is needed, whether it is conveniently available or not; its parsimony excludes what is not needed. I began integrating knowledge of voting behaviour and electoral institutions in a prose discussion of how elections are won and lost in *Must Labour Lose?* (Abrams and Rose, 1961) and routinely apply it when translating opinion polls into election results. In a comparative study edited for the Committee on Political Sociology, the model was useful in comparing voting behaviour in countries ranging from Scandinavia to Australia. Following the theory of Lipset and Rokkan (1967), each chapter contained a multivariate statistical analysis of the influence of class, religion, region and ethnicity on individual voting behaviour. Major conclusions of a 753-page book were summarized in a single table that compared the importance of these cleavages for voting behaviour in 15 countries (Rose, 1974a: 9, 17). Subsequently I have developed this as an interactive model of elite supply and mass response (Rose and Munro 2009: 1–57; Rose and Borz 2013).

It is also informative to turn a key dependent variable into an independent variable that has a further political impact. Thus, an article about the consequences of elections has been one of my most frequently reprinted articles (Rose and Mossawir 1967). Consequences are even more important in public policy, for social programmes grow as an unintended consequence of long-term costs increasing faster than the revenue that government needs to finance them (*see* Chapter 11).

In the Field

At Johns Hopkins I was given a very useful travel tip by an instructor who had wandered around Europe for a year after completing his military service there: Travel alone. Travelling with friends or a group encourages talking with people you already know rather than with people who live in the country you are visiting. As a student I travelled alone by train in third-class wooden rail seats and ate and slept where local people did. This was not only cheap but also exposed me to lots not found in tourist guidebooks.

Field work in comparative politics requires a broader set of skills than national politics, since you start with less background knowledge and face challenges to prior assumptions. The degree of specialized knowledge required depends on whether one is writing an intensive study of a theoretically interesting case or making broad comparisons. On my own or with a co-author I have written case studies about more than a dozen countries ranging across continents from Korea to Russia and Ukraine; across Europe from Turkey and Latvia to Portugal and Ireland; and to the United States and Colombia. While the decision to do a case study can be made sitting at one's desk, the understanding required to interpret a foreign country normally requires travel there. Over the years I have had offices in Florence, Vienna, Prague and Berlin as well as in Washington, Illinois and California. One reason I have never moved to an American university is that living on the east side of the Atlantic makes it possible to work in many European countries in a year with far less time and sleep lost in travel than if one tried to cover countries across Europe from an American base.

The greater the number of countries, the more important the language of social science becomes, because it focuses attention on what it is critical to know about a country. I concentrate on understanding words in foreign languages that identify political concepts that have no ready English equivalent, such as *Rechtsstaat* and *raison d'état* and on words needed to find one's way around a city, such as please, where, left, right, how much and thank you. For restaurant menus I start by learning words that describe foods I do not like, such as spinach. Given the influence of Napoleonic and Prussian institutions, French and German are useful European languages to know, and Italian helps one understand *malgoverno*.

A realistic model is specially useful in focusing on what one needs to know in an unfamiliar country. When the United Nations Development Programme commissioned me to go to Bogota in 1990 to advise the President-elect of Colombia about how to organise the office of the presidency, I found that international funds had supported the creation of a computerized cost-benefit data base of the most economically efficient infrastructure investments (Rose 1990a). Applying Dick Neustadt's dictum — No president has economic policies; all his policies are political — I saw that this data base could also be used as a patronage tool to gain support in the national Congress. If a Member wanted a wasteful pork barrel project in return for a vote, it could find the least wasteful project that would satisfy the Member.

While not given classroom training in formal theories of comparative analysis, I did have a lot of experience in finding my way around unfamiliar cities and countries before starting to write about comparative politics. At Hopkins I learned to 'read' the first thing one sees when arriving in a foreign land: buildings. In Paris I chose the Hotel de Cluny as a cheap Left Bank hotel to stay in because it bore the name of tenth-century monastic reformers. My reporter's curiosity makes me wonder what street names are about. In Manhattan they are numbers while in many European cities they identify political figures currently in good repute or aristocratic legacies. The inscriptions on monuments not only identify heroes but also tell you why they were deemed heroes at the time that the monuments were erected. Newspaper headlines call attention to political topics of immediate national interest. The back pages of newspapers offer guidance to what's on at the opera, special museum exhibitions, and ethnic music that can broaden understanding of a country.

Before I knew the term, I was doing what is formally labelled as ethnographic research and what Richard Fenno (1986) has aptly described as soaking and poking. As soon as I got my press card in Baltimore I started hanging out with reporters and politicians. In writing my doctoral thesis I augmented the information obtained from reading what MPs had said in print with interviewing them in the House of Commons. The former Cabinet ministers and MPs that I talked to were a census of politicians participating in the foreign policy debates that my thesis covered. If I had asked a scientific sample of MPs the same questions, the effort would have been largely wasted, since a big majority had little interest or knowledge of foreign policy. The occupational hazard was that sometimes you were expected to soak up more than atmosphere. Quantification took the form of a pint of Guinness and replication could involve another pint or two. The last line in the first interview notes of an Oxford contemporary was, 'I think I am getting drunk'.

Think about what you see and read

The starting point in observation is to interpret what you see people doing in terms that make sense to them as well as in, or in some cases contrary to, what is found in academic texts. Max Weber described this as *verstehen*. Myron Weiner told me that when he was getting nowhere in his research on party politics in Bombay by asking questions derived from theories endorsed by his PhD committee, he asked himself: How would these things get done in Brooklyn? This provided Weiner (1957) with the guidance needed to ask questions that his Indian respondents understood.

Establishing rapport with people you meet is essential in order to learn how they see the world. Good salesmen establish rapport by showing an interest in their customer and talking about common interests. Actors are trained to project themselves into the minds of the characters whose roles they play. Empathy between actors and audience is essential if a play is to succeed. Years of theatre-going have made me sensitive to this. When meeting policymakers for the first time, one needs to establish rapport quickly in order to overcome the barriers that exist between strangers. For example, when I first met a Catholic priest with a Gaelic name for lunch in Belfast, he politely asked about my trip there from Glasgow. I replied by saying that the view of Scottish islands and the Irish sea from the plane was one that the Lord of the Isles would have envied, a reference to the time when his part of Ireland and my part of Scotland were one. Our lunch lasted three hours. Establishing rapport is a challenge for politicians as well as car salesmen, and it is not always done. As Roy Jenkins remarked in his orotund manner, 'Despite the many attributes of the English, a peculiar talent for solving the problems of Ireland is not among them' (quoted in Rose 1971: 42). Today, the same remark could be made about British politicians dealing with Europe.

When a politician assumes you are ignorant and will believe anything he or she tells you, what Bertolt Brecht called the alienation effect is needed. For example, when Emanuel Shinwell, a former British minister of defence, tried to airbrush history in responding to questions about what he had done that was relevant to my doctoral thesis, I broke up his monologue by asking, 'Was that before or after Denis Healey broke with the Communist Party?' Shinwell immediately altered the way he talked to me.

For a comparative social scientist, the test of concepts is whether they are helpful in understanding a country about which you have little or no prior knowledge. In travelling around Brazil after the 1982 IPSA World Congress I knew in advance that there was very high inflation and rightly assumed that Brazilians would prefer dollars rather than rapidly devalued cruzeiros. The one place where this assumption failed was in an Intercontinental Hotel in the heart of the Amazon rain forest. The local staff refused payment in dollars for fear of losing their job. I went to the nearby city of Manaus in search of locals who would engage in local practices. Soaking and poking in a rundown city 2,000 kilometres up the Amazon is a good test of applied sociology. My first inquiry in a mixture of English and nasalised Italian was at the Cedars of Lebanon hotel. While there was no hesitation about changing money, the demand for a 15 per cent commission struck me as greedy and I refused. After poking in a shop selling a bit of everything, including records of *macumba* (witchcraft) music, fortune smiled. A travel agent was happy to give me the prevailing unofficial exchange rate and take a reasonable commission. That evening I learned that two other post-Congress guests, a leading American advocate of rational choice and a senior German professor, had paid for the hotel in hard currencies. I did not embarrass them by reporting the results of my empirical research.

Conversing Through Questionnaires

The language of a social science questionnaire operates at both a conceptual and a conversational level. A question that cannot be linked to a concept has little to contribute to testing hypotheses. However, questions that are not phrased in conversational terms will have little meaning to most respondents. The language used should be direct and have a minimum of abstractions and qualifying phrases. Authorship by a native-speaker is no guarantee of this. My well educated Russian research assistant unintentionally demonstrated this when translating my English-language draft of a questionnaire into Russian with the intention of saving the Levada Centre the effort. His translation was politely rejected because it was written in the style of a well educated Moscow university graduate rather than language appropriate for carrying on a conversation with a worker or a widow in a Russian province.

When I was 10 years old I started interviewing retired baseball players by writing them letters that asked about their career. This invited veteran athletes to reply with a letter as well as an autograph. I continue asking questions in terms familiar to the person I am talking to, whether it is a PhD student, a politician or a plumber. In doing so I allow lots of scope for them to tell me what they think is important about the subject of our conversation. This is not only polite but also illuminating. For example, when I asked a Lithuanian research colleague in Vilnius whether she was born in the city, she replied, 'No, I was born in Siberia'. She explained that her parents were deported there following the Soviet occupation of Lithuania. Many conversations are informal meetings to keep in touch with people with whom I share mutual interests. My inclination is to start with a non-directive statement, such as 'What's new?' It was this question that prompted John Hume's reply: 'They'll be shooting politicians next'.

My introduction to opinion polls was making a bet with a high school classmate that Harry Truman would get at least a hundred electoral college votes even though losing the 1948 presidential election. I won the bet; my classmate more than recouped that loss by making a fortune in Wall Street. Writing the chapter on opinion polls for the 1959 British election study led me to Henry Durant at the Gallup Poll and Mark Abrams at Research Services Ltd. They had information about the British electorate that could not be found in a copyright library in Oxford but could be gained by talking to a representative sample of people. Since I was the first British academic to show curiosity about their work, they were pleased to instruct me in how a survey organization actually works. Durant dismissed

Richard Rose applying his classical Oxford training in methods by consulting the oracles at Delphi about the 1987 British election

academic criticisms of his sampling procedures as an attack on the wrong target; the weakest link, he said, was the low pay and skills of interviewers.

My experience of conducting sample surveys started in Manchester in 1964 with a study of attitudes toward political authority. Students were keen to find out how surveys worked and ready to volunteer as interviewers. Since I did not have a grant, this made me responsible for all stages of organisation, including training the students and piloting the questionnaire myself. The response rate was 77 per cent (Rose and Mossawir 1967: 182). During the 1966 election I prepared a postal questionnaire about campaigning for MPs and candidates that would be received a day or two after the result was known, when winners wanted to talk about their victory and losers wanted to catharsize. To make the cover letter more inviting, I signed each letter myself with an ink pen. The response rate was 83.6 per cent and there was a 1.00 correlation between candidates returning the questionnaire and requesting a copy of the results. When they were published in *New Society*, I got the periodical to post each respondent a copy as publicity for the weekly among opinion-formers (www.profrose.eu/writings.php#england).

My experience of survey work has been expanded over half a century through engagement with all aspects from raising money and negotiating a price for a survey, checking the codes in a final draft of a foreign-language questionnaire and cleaning machine-readable files. I do not pay the last 10 per cent of the cost of a survey until the institute that did it sends a sample report that I can use to verify that the field work has gone as it should.

Scripting a structured conversation

Collecting data from a survey is different from soaking and poking because conversations are constrained by the need to decide in advance what questions should be asked that will produce answers that can be aggregated for meaningful analysis. I start by making a list of the concepts for which the survey should provide indicators. The concepts come from the model that is the foundation of the research.

In every survey both money and time are limited by the patience and interest of respondents. The cuts required have a positive intellectual consequence: they force one to examine each proposed question to see whether it would be useful for testing a hypothesis and, even if it is, whether it is redundant. For example, statistical analysis reduced a list of trust in twelve institutions in the original NRB questionnaire to four government institutions. In addition, questions may be discarded if a large percentage are likely to reply 'don't know'. Occasionally it is useful to document how atypical is some behaviour. When anthropologists generalized from work in a few Russian villages about the widespread use of folk doctors, the question I added to a nationwide sample found that only two of 1,600 Russian respondents visited a folk doctor. This supported my hypothesis that anthropologists are better at producing insightful anecdotes than valid generalizations.

I have been fortunate in being saved the political problems that can arise when a questionnaire is designed by a committee consisting of people differing in their intellectual priorities and understanding of survey research. When Stanford graduate assistants such as Norman Nie vigorously challenged the inclusion of some questions in a multinational questionnaire on political participation, Sid Verba taught them about survey politics. The questions challenged had to be included because of bargains made with multinational partners in Delhi and in Ibadan.

Since ordinary people are much less interested in abstract political science concepts than are political scientists, a questionnaire should begin by asking people to talk about what interests them. In a survey on attitudes toward democracy in Korea, I suggested starting with a few questions about the respondent's health, a topic on which I publish and for which Asian survey data is scarce (www.profrose. eu/writings.php#public_policy). While Doh Chull Shin, my Korean collaborator, thought this of no interest, the survey organization welcomed the suggestion, since ordinary Koreans are much more interested in the state of their health than in the health of the Korean state.

Logically, the unprecedented circumstances of post-Communist societies meant that while some questions asked in democratic market societies would be relevant, others would not. Reciprocally, some experiences relevant in societies in transformation would be irrelevant in Western settings. In designing NEB questionnaires I gave priority to the distinctive experiences of respondents who had lived most of their lives under a Communist regime and were now escaping into an uncertain future (Rose 1992b). When fielding parallel surveys in West Germany and Austria as benchmarks for comparison, a number of questions had to be dropped as irrelevant to the experience of people in established democracies.

Instead of flying into Eastern Europe with a questionnaire photocopied from a Western data archive, I did a lot of soaking and poking in the offices of national survey institutes set up by younger researchers to be free of the bureaucracy and gerontocracy that were a legacy of Communism in academic institutes. Being regularly engaged in national surveys, my collaborators had a lot of useful experience. In Prague the man at the next desk to me was writing a memo for President Havel. Baltic institutes knew how to construct a different sampling frame for Russian-speakers in their countries. My interest in learning from the experience of national institutes created respect and a good rapport with those who did the fieldwork.

The prototype NEB questionnaire was initially written in multi-level English, that is, words that were colloquially familiar and also had conceptual significance. Instead of asking about abstractions such as poverty, there were questions about doing without food or heat or having to borrow money or spend savings. Since the younger staff were avid readers of English-language social science works, conceptual English was the language of the template for translating the NEB questionnaire into more than a dozen different languages. When problems arose in translation, sometimes this was because I had not been clear in specifying concepts. In Vilnius, in 1993, I spent two days with survey staff from the Baltic states going over the text of the first New Baltic Barometer questionnaire, which was fielded in Estonian, Latvian, Lithuanian, Polish and Russian. Since the three Baltic languages are not mutually comprehensible, when my colleagues found their English inadequate to discuss details they switched to their alternative *lingua franca*, Russian.

While demographic categories such as age and gender tend to have a constant meaning across countries, differences in national institutions can complicate comparison. The minimum number of years of legally required education varies between countries and has been rising within each country from one generation to the next. Continental European distinctions between academic and vocational education at secondary level (in German, *Gymnasium* and *Realschule*) have little meaning in England and the American high school has no ready European equivalent. Town size is also a challenge, for a big city in Slovenia is relatively small in Russia. Since one can't change national school systems or urban populations, in order to make cross-national comparisons finer-grained, national distinctions must be combined to create approximately equivalent conceptual categories.

Long before the term social capital became popular among Western social scientists, Communist subjects had used social and political networks to get around or exploit the state that was exploiting them. The anecdotes I heard from collaborators and my own experience in linking up with survey institutes showed that such networks remained important in post-Communist societies. Hence, I wrote questions that asked people what they would do to claim familiar benefits from the state such as health care, a place for a child in a good school, or a good state-subsidized flat. The replies showed that people had a variety of networks they could make use of until they got what they wanted. Their use of social capital not only violated formal bureaucratic rules but also contradicted Bob Putnam's claim that social capital was good for *Making Democracy Work*. Conceptualizing social capital as networks producing goods and services brought me an invitation to join an interdisciplinary World Bank group with open-minded economists such as Kenneth Arrow and Mancur Olson. It also brought a World Bank grant that freed me from relying on secondary analysis of imperfect and indirect measures of social capital such as World Values questions about trust in other people. Instead, I enjoyed the luxury and challenge of writing the first full-length questionnaire that could turn anecdotes into data (Rose 2000). It carefully measured many forms of social capital and mapped the ways in which Russians got things done by hook or by crook.

Chapter 10

Communicating What You Know

Whereas talking is the normal means of communication among philosophers, writing is the normal mode of communicating among social scientists. Before starting my academic career I was already accustomed to writing in many different formats ranging from two-paragraph news stories, to television scripts and lengthy articles. I was high tech because I could type 60 words a minute. Beginning with high school public speaking competitions, I had a lot of experience in talking too.

I started writing journal articles about political behaviour before computers and data archives made the use of quantitative data easy. For an article published in the *American Political Science Review* (Rose 1962), I read and manually recorded on 3 x 5 file cards, information about thousands of motions that activists put to British party conferences. The electronic revolution was far distant. Yet basic principles of writing have remained the same. What is communicated should be set out clearly and systematically and have a beginning, a middle and an end. Moreover, the number of words, tables or citations is not evidence of the amount of thought that an article contains. The art of writing is like diamond-cutting: it is not how hard you hit the diamond but how well.

The information collected in libraries, in the field and databases are but means to an end of communicating what can be learned to others. If you are self-critical when writing, you can educate yourself. Even though I always organise my ideas before starting to write, putting them on paper stimulates both fresh thoughts and the rejection or refinement of notions in the testing process of putting words down in black and white.

My daily reading matter, *The Financial Times* and *The Times*, supplemented by nibbling *The Economist*, is a useful stimulus for an intellectual arbitrageur who wants to connect problems that are bothering policymakers with problems bothering social scientists. My training in writing newspaper stories saves me from wasting time reading more or less speculative stories about forthcoming events. I prefer to wait for news of what actually happens. When I have specialist knowledge in the field, I interpret what is read or seek more information by making contact with those more in the know than the authors of news stories or myself.

A German composer described the source of many of his melodic ideas as *Einfallen*, a word indicating that inspiration is an event that happens rather than being the outcome of reading more journal articles or running more statistical analyses. An author who uses too many tables has no place to sit and contemplate their meaning. Without a modicum of inspiration, much that is written in what is described without irony as social science literature may be useful but uninteresting. When asked his views about banning allegedly immoral books, a mayor of New York commented, 'No girl ever got pregnant reading a book'. The same can be true for a would be author in search of ideas.

Ideas come into my mind at different times of day or night and in different circumstances and countries. I always carry a pencil and paper to make notes when this happens. The topics I write about reflect my eclectic interests and experiences. I chose to write about Northern Ireland, a much ignored part of the United Kingdom, because it required applying the concept of legitimacy in a challenging context. I have written about the American presidency in comparative perspective because this makes use of my knowledge of political systems on both sides of the Atlantic. Ideas that become journal articles may be stimulated by an invitation to contribute a paper to a conference. My current research on the global experience of citizens paying bribes is a logical extension of a lifelong concern with the rule of law and being a long-standing *pro bono* advisor to Transparency International's secretariat in Berlin. I use quantitative data as and when it is relevant to the topic at hand. I prefer to add fresh value to what others have overlooked rather than engage in interminable quarrels about the interpretation of familiar data.

By the standards of musicians, writers take a very long time to become established. While a musical prodigy can give a concert performance at the age of ten, it takes far longer to become a writer of good political science. When I had just turned 21 and wasn't sure what I would do next, I sought advice from a London publisher about going to work there. After describing the unromantic side of publishing, he asked whether I wanted to write a book. I shyly said that I would like to do so one day. He advised not going into publishing but to find a job that would give me something to write about. Working on a daily newspaper guaranteed that there was always news to write about each day; however, the knowledge gained struck me as superficial.

I was fortunate in having two significant books on British politics published when I had just turned 28. While that made me young by the standards of academic authors, I had already been sitting at a typewriter 20 years. Since then my output, though different in style from Enid Blyton or Mickey Spillane, has also been very substantial.

Writing as a Discipline

Unusually among social scientists, I have always regarded writing as a calling, an impulse from within to put words on paper. Like politics, writing a book can be described as the 'strong and slow boring of hard boards' (Weber 1948). For me, the best part of writing is at the beginning, turning something I have observed or puzzled about into the outline of an article or a book. Of course, once I have 'solved' a problem, there remains the task of producing successive drafts of 8,000 to 80,000 words until whatever is written achieves a satisfying shape. This requires both patience and stamina. I have always made time for writing. Instead of going out at the weekend when places are crowded, I prefer to stay at home, where distractions are few. I can then write from 10 am to 10 pm with breaks for meals or strolling in the garden. On a good day I draft 4,000 words or more.

A son once posed the question: 'What's the most boring thing in the world?' His answer was: 'A tape recording of Dad writing a book'. Even though it is a solitary occupation, I enjoy writing and have taken care to turn what was once the billiard room in our flat into a large and comfortable study in which to work.[1] It holds about 2,500 books, thus saving me from walking into five other rooms of the house where another 3,000 or more books are shelved. There are also another 50 feet of shelves with books on architecture, applied arts and music. Walls reaching up to 12-foot ceilings display objects that offer visual rather than verbal satisfaction. I listen to music to avoid long silences.

I specially designed a 6 x 3.5 foot desk to hold books and the bulky print outs that mainframe computers used to generate. There is a stand for keeping in front of me the outline of what I am writing. Having an outline at hand means that I can take interruptions by telephone or email without losing the thread of whatever I am writing. Through the windows in front of my desk there is a view of a large garden and, when the leaves are off the trees, a bit of sea and hills beyond. The chief hazard is intermittent afternoon sunshine that washes out the text on my VDU. Newspaper experience means that I do not need a comfortable setting in order to write. Thanks to the introduction of the laptop, planes and trains now provide an extension of a desk, a critical advantage for anyone engaged in comparative politics. If the idea or occasion arises, I can write almost anywhere at almost any time of day or night.

Putting thoughts on paper

A piece of writing should be like a good pudding: it should have a theme.[2] A good theme focuses the attention of both the audience and the author and answers the question a radio interviewer once put to me: 'Professor Rose, can you tell us in a sentence what your article is about?' The phrasing triggered an alarm bell in my mind and I stated the theme in a sentence. The interviewer thanked me and hung up.

The theme should be clearly indicated in a book's title. A title such as *Representing Europeans* states a generic theme; the subtitle, *A Pragmatic Approach*, indicates that it will have a distinctive point of view (Rose 2013). Nonetheless, it leaves open how the subject will be dealt with. I chose that title because it invites a curious reader to open the book to find out what my views are. Last impressions are equally important: a social scientist who ends an article with a plea for more research emphasizes what he or she has not said. Entitling a book with a question, for example *Can Government Go Bankrupt?*, not only catches a reader's attention but also pushes the author to give a clear answer. In that book the answer was: 'No; governments only get refinanced'.

Starting an article with the sentence 'The object of this paper is...' forces a struggling writer to be clear about its theme. A second sentence starting

---

1. Compare the remark of the opera singer Birgit Nilsson that the secret of singing Brünnhilde is to wear a comfortable pair of shoes.

2. When the head waiter at the Savoy Hotel in London asked Winston Churchill why he did not eat the pudding served, he responded, 'The trouble with this pudding is that it has no theme'.

'Therefore, this paper will ...' should identify the principal points that will be covered in achieving its object. Further steps include the definition of key terms and combining these elements in a convincing model; setting out the steps in developing the book's theme; and writing a conclusion that is not just a summary of what went before but also states implications. The standard format of scientific writing provides a solid structure, but leaves little room for originality. When the subject matter is well known, such as voting behaviour, a familiar format facilitates communication between author and reader. However, when the subject is novel, as in the aftermath of the fall of the Berlin Wall, a standard format can be unsuitable or even misleading.

While no construction firm would start work on a building without an architectural plan of what it should look like when completed, a surprising number of academics start writing without being clear about what their paper will be like if and when it is finished. Newspaper work taught me to organise what I wanted to say before beginning to write. There is no time for second thoughts when the first part of a story is being set in type before you write the last paragraph. Because a book takes so much longer to write than a newspaper story, it is even more important to produce an outline table of contents before keying in the first word. Otherwise, both the author and the reader can get lost well before the final chapter.

Unlike history or biography, political science writing is usually analytic rather than chronological; therefore, organization does not readily follow from the subject matter.

A one-page table of contents gives an overview of what a book should look like when complete, especially if the major sub-sections of each chapter are also specified. Having a first draft table of contents provides the basis for incorporating second thoughts as work progresses. It is much easier to alter lines in a draft table of contents, for example, changing the sequence of chapters, than to rewrite or scrap thousands of words that are out of place.

Since a journal article is much shorter than a book, it should be outlined in more detail, with a line for each paragraph of text. If research can be expressed in a sequence of tables and figures, this can be the starting point of an outline but not a substitute. Since we must name things before we can count them, an article with statistical analysis still requires an introductory section that discusses context, the concepts for which quantitative data provide approximate indicators, and the meaning of statistical output. In a book I sometimes need four chapters to set out the concepts, context and institutions that determine the steps in the statistical analysis that follows (*see* e.g. Rose, Mishler and Haerpfer 1998).

An interest in the arts makes me aware of the importance of presenting ideas in harmony rather than relying on atonal statistics that reveal a tin ear for what is notionally the subject of a study.[3] For me, shaping an article or book has an almost

---

3.   The tell tale sign of a tin ear for subject matter is that an author talks about variables without giving them a proper name and they are described with labels familiar to their computer but not to their audience.

physical quality. I first detail its structure, just as an architect would set out the structure of a building, including details of its facade and interior. The idea is then shaped with my hands, albeit the material is words rather than ceramic clay and the keyboard belongs to a computer rather than a piano. Many years and hours spent looking at Islamic arts has made my eye sensitive to form and function, of special relevance in the presentation of tables and figures.

Like any art, writing requires a knowledge of its rudiments. Many techniques for writing can be learned, for example, how to write a clear entry for a reference book or an accident report for an insurance company. A good newspaper reporter quickly learns to include in a story basic information about who, what, when and where. When dealing with fresh themes and ideas, it is also important to have a sense of when to bend or break rules (Eliot 1919). Louis Armstrong quipped that while he had learned how to read music and understand harmony, it was 'not well enough that it interferes with my playing' (Brothers 2006: 354n).

The paragraph is the basic unit of whatever I write. Each paragraph needs a topic sentence that states its theme. Care in phrasing the first sentence of a paragraph makes it easier to write the sentences that follow. The paragraph can end with either a strong or bridging sentence. A strong ending reinforces the point addressed in the topic sentence. A bridging sentence is forward-looking; it provides a cue to the topic sentence that starts the next paragraph. When doing so, I refer back to the topic sentence of the preceding paragraph in order to make sure that what follows on the page is part of a clear paragraph by paragraph exposition.

Within a paragraph I take care with the structure of sentences in order to increase their clarity and impact. This is particularly desirable in social science writing because of the academic tendency to qualify what is said. Qualifying phrases should normally follow rather than precede the main point of a sentence. Putting the qualification at the beginning of a sentence, for example, starting with the word 'Although', tends to reduce the impact of what follows. My favourite example of the exception to this rule was provided by the late lobby correspondent of *The Times*, David Wood. When Harold Wilson gave him a self-serving briefing, Wood could not refuse to print what the Prime Minister told him. However, he could and did lead an account with phrases such as, 'For what it is worth, highly placed sources in Downing Street are saying ...'

In order to sustain attention, sentences in a paragraph should vary in their length and rhythm. Jelly Roll Morton's maxim is good advice for a writer as well as a musician: 'If you have half a glass of water you can fill it or empty it; that is the principle on which good jazz music is based'. Playing the drums has made me especially sensitive to rhythm (Brothers 2006: 234f). The effect of a sharp, hard stroke on a drum followed by silence can be achieved by a strong upbeat end to a sentence. This is much more effective than the continuous crashing of cymbals or, in social science terms, a crash of abstract symbols. I usually 'listen' to what I write, that is, repeat phrases silently in my mind. A good theme ought to be clear and succinct enough to be understood if spoken on the telephone. Variations in rhythm can be achieved by altering the length of sentences or inserting a semi-colon to create a pause before making a significant point. If technical terms are embedded in sentences that consist of familiar words, they stand out in a kind of counterpoint. This was the approach I followed in writing *Politics in England.* More than 99 per cent of the words were familiar in English, but the key concepts were imported from the model of political systems that Gabriel Almond (1960) had set out in the prevailing German-American style of social science writing.

Precise words are usually preferable to vague words. An author vague about facts should make a reader suspicious, but too many details or numbers can distract attention from the main theme. Describing a politician as consistently having the endorsement of more than half the electorate is more readily remembered than saying that endorsement ranged between 52 per cent and 56 per cent.[4] For this reason, I often use terms such as 'a quarter century ago' rather than a specific number of years.

Unlike numbers, many words have connotations beyond their denotative meanings. I keep at hand an old fashioned dictionary that gives an English word's etymological root in Greek, Latin, Anglo-Saxon or whatever, and adds examples of words that have similar but not exactly the same connotation or meaning. Consulting it helps me select words with the most appropriate connotations and avoids loose thinking, for example, using military metaphors to describe parties as if they were armies clashing with each other. This is usually not the case. When I started writing about British elections, the Conservative and Labour parties were self-referential, charging around the country like knights with their visors down, seeing very little and bumping into their opponents by accident more than design. The introduction of political polling made each party see the field on which they battled for the approval of the electorate. I described this change in an article called 'From Cavalry Charge to Electronic Warfare' (Rose 1985).

As sentences and paragraphs follow, it is a good idea to do a word count to make sure that what you are writing is consistent with the normal length of an article or chapter. In particular, it avoids devoting so much space to a literature review that there is little room left for whatever fresh thoughts or evidence you can add. One reason I like writing books is that space is available to set quantitative evidence in a historical, institutional and conceptual context. Overrunning normal length is a sign of unexpected discoveries. When a research note on the peculiar formula of degressive proportionality used to determine representation in the European Parliament had grown to double the normal length, I turned it into a research grant. Five years later this initiative produced many articles and a book (Rose 2013).

A disciplined writer should always re-read what he or she has written. At Berkeley the assignment that Aaron Wildavsky gave to students, admitted to a second-term class on the basis of a grade A first-term project was to rewrite that paper in order to make it better. Once I complete a draft of anything, I set it aside

---

4. I am always suspicious of reports that give survey data to tenths of a per cent, because it shows that an author is unaware of or indifferent to the fact that sampling error prevents the data from being so accurate.

and turn to other matters in my in-tray or to travel. When I return to the draft afresh, the first step is to outline what had been written. After a break to do other things, it is easier to see what additions, subtractions and amendments should be made. Before word-processing came along, I would keep scissors and a stapler at hand to alter the sequence of paragraphs and handwrite alterations of words or phrases between the lines of double-spaced sentences. The revised draft was then abandoned to a half-time secretary who turned a messy manuscript into a neatly typed document. With this clean draft in hand, I then began a fresh process of outlining and altering paragraphs, sentences and phrases until the new draft needed retyping. With the arrival of word processing, I no longer need a secretary to retype my manuscripts; however, I continue to edit or rewrite everything I key in. The first draft of the book you are reading has gone through more than four stages of revision and polishing before being sent to the publisher.[5]

Working with a co-author makes a difference, since the logic of collaboration is that a co-author should know some things better than I do. Bill Mishler is a long-standing co-author who likes to ponder and probe the meaning of patterns that appear in statistical analysis whereas my preference is to interpret these patterns in words. We exchange complementary documents by email, telephone and face to face dialogue before arriving at an interpretation that matches words and numbers to our mutual satisfaction. When writing about Russia I have relied on Neil Munro for knowledge of Russian-language sources and on Doh Chull Shin for knowledge of Korea.

When the subject matter and a grant makes it appropriate to employ a post-doctoral research fellow, there is dialogue similar to that of master and apprentice. I normally produce a memorandum that specifies what data is needed and evaluates sources, and then scrutinize on a line by line basis how the data is coded. Once this process produces an acceptable database, I write a memorandum about the statistical analyses initially required. First results are more inclined to stimulate curiosity than satisfy it; this leads to iterative analyses to arrive at a set of tables that are not only statistically robust but also conceptually and contextually meaningful. I then write a first draft manuscript with notes to a junior co-author about undertaking further statistical tests and checking textual interpretations. This makes our joint effort better and more accurate. I have had co-authors from more than a dozen countries. Ian McAllister is an outstanding example of a scholar who has learned from this apprenticeship to master the writing of political science articles and books. This book is an exception, for I could hardly get a grant to employ an assistant to research my life.

The transition from a stimulating idea to a published article takes time. While a piece of journalism can appear in print in a matter of hours or a week, a book takes

---

5.   The French poet Paul Valéry said that no poem is ever finished; it is only abandoned. In that sense, each of my books can be seen as an interim statement about a political issue that I or others may subsequently revisit. That is inherent in the progressive development of social science understanding.

me up to two years to write. I find that writing short pieces for prompt publication is a welcome complement to the necessarily slow writing and rewriting of the many chapters that make up a book. Concurrently, talking to audiences about the subject matter of a book makes a good complement to talking to myself while looking at a VDU.

Form Follows Function

The implication of Louis Sullivan's (1896) architectural dictum 'form follows function' is that communication should take different forms — books, journal articles, reports, PowerPoints, seminar papers and classroom lectures — depending on the purpose and audience at hand. People who write fluently in English have the advantage of having a very large potential audience, since the number of people reading English is a multiple of the number who are native-speakers of either the Queen's English or the President's American. However, there is a danger that people who grow up in America or England will talk and write in an introverted manner that ignores the fact that a substantial portion of their audience will be EFL (English as a Foreign Language) readers with a broader, since bilingual, experience than they have (Rose 2008).

Whatever the form chosen, a writer should make sure that it is suited to the audience at hand. I communicate to audiences in many forms. When writing an article or book I try to have likely readers in mind. When it is a person or group I know well, I let this imaginary audience prompt me with questions that my manuscript should answer, and caution me against pushing an argument too far. Without closing my eyes, I can transport my mind to the place that I am writing about, whether it is Westminster, Washington or Brussels. I can also transport myself across time as well, visualizing what Berlin was like before the Wall fell and what Washington was like when it was still a Southern town.

When I started doing radio broadcasts on politics, I was expected to present remarks to an invisible audience for about five minutes. That requires the ability to speak to a microphone but to direct what is said to an audience of unseen listeners. Television soon changed that, making the standard format a live conversation between a presenter and an expert commentator. I was fortunate in being on television in an era in which both partners in the conversation agreed that the object was to inform and entertain the viewing audience rather than providing an under-informed interviewer with a platform for displaying his or her ego.

Giving a talk offers the best opportunity to communicate, since the author and the medium are the same person and the audience is immediately visible. It encourages the clear and pithy expression of one's ideas. Observing how others react to what you say is a helpful reminder that research is not only about thinking things through in your own mind but also about communicating your ideas to other people. When I talk, I listen in the back of my mind to what I am saying and use feedback from the audience to identify points that should be altered before a talk is committed to print.

When invited to give a talk, I ask about the audience in order to relate what I know to their experience. Since I give talks in half a dozen or more countries each

Relaxing with Alastair Burnet during the second day of ITN's coverage of the 1970 British general election

year, this tests the extent to which my ideas have broad relevance. When speaking to an audience that is neither British nor American, I try to make links between my research and the experience of the audience, whether an opening reference to its architectural glories or a political challenge. This is not only courteous; it can also lead to a stimulating discussion in which the speaker as well as the audience learns something. If a talk is to a public policy rather than an academic audience, asking what to talk about seeks a quantitative answer: Should the talk be about 15 or 25 minutes? Policymakers usually do not want a long discourse; they want to put their own views as well as listen.

Pressures on 90-minute 'present or perish' panels at academic conferences increasingly leave little time for discussion among panellists, let alone with an audience. I had the dubious pleasure of participating in an APSA panel in which there was only 30 seconds for discussion after each scheduled participant spoke. The upshot is that papers are presented simply to add one more line to the section of a curriculum vitae that lists conference papers. The Joint Sessions of Workshops of the ECPR, which bring papergivers together for five days, are a far better venue for presenting and discussing papers.

PowerPoints can be an asset for both speaker and audience. Preparing a set of PowerPoints concentrates the mind on organizing thoughts and offering something for the eye as well as the ear. To read the text of a slide aloud implies that the audience is illiterate. Slides lay down the chords of a talk, as it were, while the voice can improvise the melody line that elaborates what the audience reads. Since it takes time for fresh ideas and information to be assimilated, I limit myself to one slide for every two or three minutes of a talk. I use a lot of graphics too, since a good figure communicates better than a table with 50 to 100 cells of numbers. My PowerPoint talks usually follow the Jelly Roll Morton rule: half are text and half are tables and figures.

Publishing social science

Journal articles offer a good way to deal with a very specific point in an established field or to explore an unfamiliar field. Amidst the uncertainties that followed the fall of the Berlin Wall, no one could be sure what would happen in the years between starting a book and seeing it in print. Hence, in the first few years I concentrated on giving talks, producing reports for public policy audiences such as the World Bank, and writing journal articles with fresh concepts and data.

When writing a paper, I always think of the most suitable journal to which it should be submitted. Suitability can be defined in two contrasting ways. For a young academic whose tenure committee will not read what is written but only evaluate the impact factor of the journal publishing a paper, submitting to a high prestige journal has special value. However, as professional interests become more specialized, people who are interested in the content of an article are more likely to read what is published in a specialist journal in which both editors and peer reviewers know the field, for example, *Electoral Studies*.

The definition of an area studies journal is debatable. Rational choice journals assume that the use of mathematics and abstractions makes them globally relevant, although their articles may only be illustrated with stylized facts rather than actual countries. The *American Political Science Review* is not regarded as an area studies journal, even though most of what it publishes is explicitly or implicitly based on American experience. I consider publishing in area studies journals such as *Europe-Asia Studies* and *Post-Soviet Affairs* to be just as important as publishing in methodologically oriented generalist journals, because the former take substantive content seriously, just as the latter are especially concerned with methods and abstract logic.

Professionalization means that many journal articles are written according to a familiar formula that is likely to appeal to its editor and reviewers. Specialisation within political science means that editors lack the knowledge to evaluate articles outside their field and to evaluate conflicting reports from peer reviewers. Editors of the *APSR* have confessed that they felt more comfortable making decisions about submissions when editing *Legislative Studies Quarterly*, because they knew that subject well, than in evaluating the multitude of *APSR* submissions in fields outside their ken (www.profrose.eu/writings.php#studying).

When editing the *Journal of Public Policy,* I made a point of having complementary reviewers of a submission, one a specialist in the particular country or countries covered, and the other especially knowledgeable about its concepts. This provided a test of whether the submission was true to context and also had legs, that is, it could be of interest outside a narrow geographical or intellectual range.

Like TV producers most journal editors claim to seek originality but feel more comfortable with what is familiar than what will surprise or even puzzle their audience. The growing academic fascination with bibliometrics parallels TV competition for audience ratings. However, as Thomas Kuhn (1962) has shown, big advances in science tend to come from paradigm shifts in which 'the professional community has suddenly been transported to another planet where familiar objects are seen in a different light'.

If reading a book educates students, writing a book can educate its author (www.profrose.eu/writings.php#studying). Limitations of space in a journal article force the omission of many relevant points, such as the institutional and historical context of the subject at hand or they receive only cursory attention. The expanse of a book leaves no excuse for intellectual evasions. Four times in my career I have sat down with 40,000 words or more of published journal articles in the expectation that they could be turned into a book in a few months (Rose 1974a, 1989a, 2009, and Rose et al. 1998). However, much more was required than acknowledging the original place of publication and removing duplication in citations and prose. Arraying a collection of articles as a first draft table of contents reveals gaps in the coverage of a subject requiring both thinking and additional research.

Getting a book published requires finding a publisher as well as writing a manuscript. Before approaching a publisher, I look at who publishes books that address the audience for which I am writing. Thus, for a book about the American presidency I approached an American publisher and for a book about the British prime minister, a British publisher. Having written for many different audiences, I have therefore had many publishers on both sides of the Atlantic, including five university presses and profit-making publishers. Given my subject matter and its target audience of political scientists in Europe and beyond, the ECPR Press was a natural choice as the publisher of this book.

Public policy audiences

Communicating to policymakers requires a different style than communicating to fellow academics. Even when talking to policymakers with PhDs, their focus is on conclusions and implications for policy. Questions concerning methodology are usually directed at the sources of one's evidence rather than at the statistical methods used to analyse it. As public officials find themselves facing more and more difficulties in implementing policies and criticisms grow, they increasingly welcome discussion with independent policy analysts.

The development of the World Wide Web has been a great boon to communicating outputs to policymakers across continents. The main CSPP site, www.cspp.strath.ac.uk, has visitors from more than 70 countries. PowerPoints can summarize ideas and data succinctly and posting PowerPoints from talks gives ideas a second life with a larger audience. In collaboration with the Levada Centre, the CSPP launched www.russiavotes.org to communicate with a specialist audience. Because it started in August, 1999, the site offers a unique source of trend data about how Russians have evaluated their regime since Vladimir Putin emerged as Russia's leader.

To overcome the time lag and format restrictions of academic publication that are barriers to rapid communication, I established the *Studies in Public Policy* series. About half these CSPP papers are in the style of journal articles while the other half are much longer and can present valuable tabular data, such as the full results of New Europe Barometer surveys. The papers focus on the Centre's research agenda. Authors are a mix of in house and invited academics, some senior and some junior. Publication within four to six weeks of completion is particularly helpful for younger authors for whom a two-year wait is an agonising period of delay. A copyeditor checks prose and citations, which academics often treat cavalierly. All papers have an ISSN number and are deposited with British copyright libraries and the Library of Congress, thereby gaining both immediate Google recognition and permanency. Since the SPP series was started in 1976, more than 500 papers have been published.

In doing research on the inadequate way in which European Union institutions represent Europeans, I developed a bi-modal win-win strategy to reach both social scientists and policymakers. As the research progressed I prepared PowerPoints and papers for academic audiences from Florence and Lisbon to Harvard. This led to four heavily footnoted journal articles using multi-level multivariate analysis and published in journals of political science, European studies, and mathematical social sciences. Concurrently, I wrote a book to be read by policymakers, *Representing Europeans*, which Oxford University Press published at a price that made it affordable. This has been followed up by short Op Ed pieces for EU-oriented weeklies and websites and presentations to think tanks in Brussels, London and Washington.

Managing a variety of activities requires the disciplined use of time. My literary interest in the passage of time and my social science interest in the dynamics of politics is paralleled by an awareness, in the words of Sir Andrew Marvell, that there is not world enough and time to do everything one would like to do. Hence, at the start of each academic year I make up a time budget that takes into account the number of days required to meet varied commitments. These include about 90 days away from Scotland; 'catch up' days for dealing with emails and household maintenance; days in the University; and about 15 days for taking advantage of activities that crop up at short notice. I do not need to allocate time for holidays, since being at home in Helensburgh is relaxation enough. After half a dozen years of getting accustomed to this discipline I now find that my initial estimate is usually within five or ten days of the iron cage that the calendar imposes. It also makes me scrutinize carefully the opportunity cost of each invitation to travel or write a paper. The opportunity cost of time is often ignored by scholars and their publications suffer. It is also ignored by university administrators who call committee meetings and circulate forms that waste the time of their best staff.

What Would You Tell the President About Iraq in Three Minutes?

My invitation to the White House came out of the blue. It read:

> I am writing to invite you to a small group discussion with President Bush at the White House on May 30, 2007. From time to time the President meets with outside experts who can participate in a live and off-the-record discussion focussed on an issue of importance. In the proposed session we are inviting you and three or four other experts in divided societies who, we hope, would be willing to share their perspective on what their research has to say about the current challenges in Iraq.

After the White House expressed regret that travel expenses could not be paid, I was asked whether a meeting a fortnight hence would work for me. It did.

Iraq is a problem worth thinking about and I qualify as an outsider, never having published anything about Iraq or the Middle East. The invitation to meet the President came because I had written two books about Northern Ireland that could offer a different perspective on divided societies than what the President heard from his advisors. I googled the National Security Council (NSC) source of the invitation, Peter Feaver, and learned he was a Harvard PhD on leave from a chair at Duke University. He had worked in the NSC of President Clinton as well as Bush. Feaver argued that the President needed to convince the American people that the war in Iraq was winnable. This was hardly my view, but at no point did he or anyone else ask what my views were (against the war from before its start) or my politics (a Truman Democrat).

A follow up email made clear what to expect. Prepare a three-minute answer to the question: What are the most important insights from your research about conflict societies that the President may not already have heard and what lessons could be drawn from it that would be relevant to Iraq right now? The key term was 'right now', that is, the problem as it actually is rather than what you would have done in 2003 (not gone to war) or what you would do if you became president in 2009 (hope the strife had ended).

An invitation to talk with the president in the Oval Office makes clear who the audience is but leaves open how to communicate what one wants to say. A lifetime of public speaking meant that I was not frustrated by the need to condense into a few minutes the half a million words that I had published about Northern Ireland. I adapted my speaking style but not my thoughts to the audience at hand and chose an approach that the President would be familiar with as a churchgoer: I told a parable. Northern Ireland was the nominal subject; Iraq was the sub-text.

When the day came, I turned up at the White House gate 20 minutes early. The security guards were far more polite and efficient than at airports. They promptly ushered me to a West Wing waiting room to meet other group members, all senior scholars. Two were specialists on conflict resolution in Africa, two Arabic-speakers familiar with Iraq, and another an expert on constitutions of divided societies. Walking into the Oval Office was like entering a very large suburban living room rather than an office — except for a battery of NSC staffers ranged on one side to take notes. To create a bit of rapport, I mentioned to the President

Shaking hands with President George W. Bush after an Oval Office discussion of broken states that shook America's power

our common link with St. Louis, where his great-grandfather, G. H. Walker, was born and made money. The President responded graciously. I said to Vice President Richard Cheney, who dropped out of graduate work in political science at Wisconsin to go into politics, that it was good to meet a fellow political scientist. Cheney was impassive. The President shook our hands, thanked us for coming, motioned toward two large sofas, offered us a choice of a cola or water, and asked us to share our thoughts with him.

When my turn came, I applied the principle of Ernst Dichter, a Viennese refugee turned marketing consultant. Dichter advised the makers of the first American cake mix to leave something out, such as an egg, so that a housewife could feel ownership of the cake when serving it. I left out mention of Iraq on the assumption that the President would see the relevance of my parable to a problem that he owned. My points were summarized in one-line statements that went like this:

- A divided society can be a stable society — provided that there is a state with institutions having a monopoly of force that can protect itself from foreign incursions and internal insurrection.

- If divisions undermine the authority of a state, it fragments and there is competition for control of territory between multiple armed groups.

- Troops introduced from abroad can support a civil power but cannot substitute for it.

- An army intervening to defend a state that does not exist gets caught in a crossfire between internally warring groups.

- It takes time for armed groups to exhaust their belief that violence serves their ends and consider a political settlement. In Northern Ireland it took more than a third of a century.

The glimmer of good news in the parable was also the bad news — peace and stability are eventually achievable — but warring Iraqis will do more to determine when and how this happens than outsiders, including decision-makers in Washington. Given the situation confronting President Bush, I felt that I was not so much speaking truth to power as speaking truth to weakness.

Others in the group took different approaches. One participant, a constitutional lawyer, spoke in a dull voice and read detailed notes from a legal writing pad without any eye contact with the president. Another took pleasure in the sound of his own voice, emphasizing who he knew rather than saying what the President might find useful. An anthropologist repeated comments about her experience in Iraq long before the war started. Two experts in conflict resolution in Africa presented some rules of thumb for ending a civil war, and gave striking examples from their own experience.

We were told to expect a free-flowing discussion and this happened. After the President made several references to the importance of liberty, I reminded him that Isaiah Berlin was not only in favour of liberty but also of order. The place to talk about liberty, I suggested, was not in a land lacking order but in a land lacking freedom, such as Russia. When the conversation became too academic, the President began leafing through a book of mine that I had given him that ends with a chapter about America's victory over Iraq in Kuwait. That victory left his father riding the crest of a wave — after which there was only one alternative, going down.

The President listened far more than he spoke and when he did speak he made simple points that many critics dodge such as: We had to do something after a small group blew up 3,000 Americans. At another point he remarked that he never wanted to be a war president. I looked at the busts of two war leaders behind his chair, Churchill and Lincoln. I thought that Churchill had the far easier war, for it united his country and ended in victory after six years. By contrast, Lincoln fought a civil war at the cost of half a million lives in an America with a population that was little more than that of Iraq today. Once the war ended the peace was lost, because federal troops could not control the Southern states that the troops occupied.

I realized that my parable had been understood when the President asked me one question that no one else ever had: What would have happened if Britain had not sent troops into Northern Ireland in 1969? My answer was simple: There would have been fighting and deaths but fewer people would have been killed before a new political system was established.

Was it worthwhile? The President seemed to think so, for the meeting ran over its scheduled time. What did my insights add? An emphasis on the paramount need of a state to kill for. If I were being vain, I might claim that his criticism of President Putin for suppressing liberty, voiced when they met the following week, was due to my influence. I hope that he did not need my advice to say that.

Chapter 11

Public Policy and Political Science

Only after I became a political scientist did I learn how much its subject differs from public policy: the former is about what political scientists do, the latter is about what governments do. Having separate institutions and priorities makes it possible for each to go its own way. As a lateral thinker I am interested in the relationship between politics and public policy. The aim of the Centre for the Study of Public Policy is to join the world of ideas with the world of practice. I have been fortunate in being able to keep a hand in both.

A byproduct of the professionalization of political science has been a narrowing of outlooks. Academics now pay much more attention to what other political scientists write than to what politicians say and do, except in response to their questionnaires. Concurrently, politicians have less inclination to talk to political scientists and a lack of statistical training disqualifies them from reading many articles of potential relevance, such as studies of voting behaviour. There are also time lags. In England discussion of electoral change still relies on the one-dimensional concept of the swing of the electoral pendulum, even though electoral competition has not been one-dimensional since 1974. In the United States, while Republicans have held the White House more often than Democrats since 1960, the Michigan paradigm of the primacy of party identification, which favours the Democratic Party, retains a strong appeal to academics.

To deny any overlap between political science and public policy implies that political science has become an asocial science like economics, and that policymakers have no interest in learning about the causes of problems they face in government. Yet it is equally logical to assume that differences in approach can lead to fruitful exchanges. If policymakers claim to know more about government, social scientists can claim to know more about that part of society that does not live and work in the national capital. As government policies have a deeper and broader impact on society, effective policies require more knowledge of what goes on in the world 'out there' than what is offered by the blunt instrument of the ballot or by opaque statistics. Because I have sought to learn from the exchange between these two domains, I have complemented my University post in Scotland with a club in London and a club in Washington rather than a visiting professorship in California or dining rights in an Oxford college.

The idea that policymakers will necessarily be receptive to ideas about how government can do things better shows a naive ignorance of the inertia forces that make it difficult to change policies. Politicians often mistakenly assume that popular election gives them the knowledge to deal effectively with problems that they and their predecessors have helped to create. In my experience, failure is more likely to stimulate policymakers to act than the attractiveness of a fresh idea (Rose

1972). To complain that the views of social scientists about public policies do not receive more attention from government confuses the justification for making political judgments conferred by a PhD and that conferred by winning an election.

I prefer to anticipate problems rather than explain why whatever government is doing at the moment is the only thing that can be done. In the case of Northern Ireland, this meant that for years I was saying in public and private what government did not want to hear or know but later accepted as undeniable. As the concluding section of this chapter shows, climate-seeding can take decades to have an impact. I would rather say the right thing at the wrong time than be in tune with current fashion by saying the wrong thing. My current research is bound to be unwelcome to many policymakers because it is about public officials taking bribes as a condition of delivering health, education and other public services. To make sure that it is publicized to policymakers, I am collaborating with Transparency International, the leading international non-governmental organisation campaigning against corruption.

Disciplined Research and Undisciplined Problems

Public officials and political scientists are each socialized into a discipline, but what each learns is different. A good policymaker is good at doing whatever is valued by superiors and colleagues, whether within the ranks of the civil service or in the cut and thrust of party politics. A good political scientist learns whatever his or her teachers profess, and merit is demonstrated by satisfying peer reviewers who control access to academic publications. In my professional lifetime there has been a substantial broadening in the outlook of public officials in Europe and there is now much greater racial and gender diversity in Washington. Concurrently, political science has been closing down lateral entry from other disciplines and occupations. Increased attention is given to abstractions and less attention to problems of government as it actually is.

There is a cash nexus between political science and public policy, because government funds the universities that employ most political scientists and a substantial amount of political science research. There are also personal and personnel overlaps, for public officials increasingly have a social science background, PhDs can be found in high office, and some political scientists at one time or another have been advisers or employees of government agencies. Notwithstanding this, institutionalized differences maintain an uneasy relationship between the two fields (Rose 1976c).

I did not receive the professional training that makes one think there is a gulf between university research and the non-academic world of politics. On the contrary, Oxford was close to Westminster and an ocean away from political science texts found in American libraries. The fieldwork I did for my thesis — interviewing dozens of MPs — socialized me into talking with elected politicians about matters of mutual interest. Instead of learning how to write questionnaires that created indicators of abstract concepts, the questions I asked probed particular experiences of the people I was talking to. Writing a book about the 1959 British general election meant talking to real politicians about real events. It was the ignorance of politicians and journalists about what motivated voters that led me to become interested in the academic study of voting behaviour.

Miles's law, propounded by a Washington bureaucrat, states: Where you stand depends upon where you sit. Governments and universities each have departments, but they differ in name and much else. Government departments are named after problems in society, such as Finance, Health or Environment, and each department is responsible for conditions that citizens are aware of in their daily lives. By contrast, universities have departments named after intellectual constructs such as Political Science, Economics and Sociology, and the way these subjects are studied tends to be abstract and even remote from everyday experience. Members of different academic departments also tend to live separately from each other and publish in journals with little overlapping readership.

When a policymaker speaks of a problem, it is typically a fire in an In Tray that signals dissatisfaction with an existing policy. By contrast, when an academic speaks of a problem it is typically a puzzle or contradiction between ideas found in books. The problems that confront academics are solved by intellectual reflection and testing hypotheses and they are communicated in journals to fellow academics. The problems that confront policymakers lead to political negotiations within government and are subject to challenge by politicians and interests that dislike their decisions.

When a political scientist investigates a problem, the object is normally explanation, whether statistical or historical. However, statistical explanations are of limited relevance to policymakers if they exclude important influences for lack of appropriate data or theoretical recognition. Excluding inconvenient evidence is not a luxury available to policymakers. Historical explanations emphasize the importance of past events as a cause of current problems. However, retrospective explanations offer limited positive direction to policymakers having to deal with the consequences of past mistakes.

Policymakers want to get a handle on a problem, that is, identify actions that government can take here and now, even if they only treat symptoms rather than causes. Thus, altering an existing tax is preferred to introducing a new tax, because the amount of revenue affected is immediately calculable and people are less surprised by a marginal increase in an existing tax than by the imposition of a new tax. Social science analyses that emphasize diffuse societal causes of problems such as family breakdown do not give policymakers a handle that they can grasp. Even when government can do something to help problem families, its impact is limited compared to that of influences beyond the reach of government.

Dynamic models that explain current problems as the cumulative consequence of past decisions can be useful when influences are persisting. I discovered the power of the long-term compounding of commitments when working on the growth of government. Many big-ticket items of public expenditure such as health and pensions are open-ended entitlements driven by population dynamics that can be calculated with a high degree of actuarial certainty. However, the time frames of policymakers and academics are different. The date of the next election exerts a pressure on politicians to postpone unpopular decisions until that date has passed. A former student discovered this when a junior staffer working on social security reform for the Reagan White House in the 1980s. When he showed Ed Meese, the president's point man, the fiscal challenge that social security costs would create in 2010, Meese explained to him, 'We weren't elected to solve the problems of 2010'.

Academics can take five to ten years to reflect upon the subject of a book, and even longer to achieve an institutional impact. When I met Stein Rokkan in 1960 he had already done more than a decade of transnational networking in what was still the embryonic field of political sociology. A decade later he was the founder-Chair of the ECPR. When Rokkan died in 1979, some things that he had foreseen were evident, such as transnational networks of political scientists across Western Europe. Other developments that he foresaw, such as the establishment of archives of multinational data that could be accessed internationally by high-speed computers through the Internet, were beyond the distant horizon.

I routinely think in terms of deadlines for whatever I write, whether the deadline is before I go to bed, before taking a trip, or the month in which I must submit a book in order to have it published in the following year. When my research is relevant to an issue on the agenda of policymakers, I see no reason to wait for the publication of an academic journal article before setting out conclusions in a form that can be understood by policymakers. However, academics under bureaucratic pressure to attend committee meetings and prepare conference papers now have less opportunity to write for a public policy audience. Moreover, in a world of 24/7 media, policymakers now have far less time to read what others write or think about the longer-term significance of what they say and do.

The statement 'all other conditions remaining equal' is a standing reminder of the lack of certainty in politics and political science. However, it is obscurantist to claim that the alternative is total ignorance of the future. Not even the most misguided policymaker is totally ignorant. Uncertainty is a matter of degree. I think in terms of the probability of alternative outcomes. When someone asserts that we can't know what will happen, I like to offer them an even-money bet on a long-shot outcome. That usually stops the conversation.

In arriving at a decision, policymakers are naturally inclined to prefer evidence that fits their partisan circumstances. Paradoxically, the rejection of an evidence-based policy on partisan grounds holds out hope for its future adoption, since it implies that this rejection is only valid up to the date of the next election. Promoters of causes not associated with parties need to have a strong commitment because their future prospects are more uncertain. When reading parliamentary debates from the late 1940s for my doctoral thesis, I was amused by the speeches of a backbench Labour MP, Dr. Monty Follick, on the merits of a revolving toothbrush and of simplified spelling. When I bought my first electric toothbrush decades later, I realised the meaning of the saying, 'Never say never in politics'. However, three-quarters of a century after Follick began campaigning, English spelling is still not simplified.

Creating a Problem-Focussed Centre

If social scientists are to apply theoretical ideas to the world as it actually is, they must look not only at journal articles and books but also look out the window to see what is happening in the streets. If there are inconsistencies between the two, this is an opportunity to expand knowledge by critically reflecting on what government and what academics do.

Unexpected and often unwelcome events in the late 1960s rekindled social science interest in what government does. In Europe the student revolt of 1968 made governance of the universities a major political issue and youthful demonstrators were proclaiming that their goal was not only (or not even) to understand society but to change it. In the United States, Lyndon Johnson's Great Society programmes provided a banquet of foods for thought. The Vietnam War made students ready to question the institutions and integrity of government and to expect professors to have relevant answers. I needed no push from students to question what government was doing. My involvement in Northern Ireland put me in the front line of engagement with a situation in which failings of governance had fatal consequences.

The response in American universities to the call for relevance was led by senior social scientists who were interested in politics, such as Dick Neustadt at Harvard and Aaron Wildavsky at Berkeley. They helped create Schools of Public Policy offering technical skills and substantive knowledge relevant to the analysis of the problems of government. Aaron's first achievement was to secure a hillside building for the School above the tear gas zone of the Berkeley campus. During a trip to the United States in 1973, I visited Harvard's Kennedy School and Berkeley and became convinced that there was a 'there' there, that is, focusing on problems of public policy through an interdisciplinary lens made intellectual as well as practical sense.

What made institutional sense in the United States did not fit easily in Europe. American public policy schools are one of many postgraduate professional schools along with law, business, medicine, education, and other subjects. Postgraduate professional schools have not been similarly common in Europe. The LSE saw its three-year undergraduate BSc (Econ) degree, in combination with its location, as sufficient to give students an understanding of public policy. Oxford long regarded its status and the confidence and ability of its undergraduates as sufficient to open up a career in government, whatever the subject that they studied.

As I did not want to leave Europe, moving to an American school of public policy was out. Moreover, even when an American programme has many students from abroad its curriculum focuses almost exclusively on American experience. I also ruled out moving to a London think tank, because that would have meant abandoning long-term basic research in favour of writing position papers about immediate issues. Furthermore, some of my views were unlikely to be consistent with the political line of any think tanks.

In 1976 I established the Centre for the Study of Public Policy (CSPP) at the University of Strathclyde. It became the first Centre of its kind in a European university. The idea of the CSPP fitted with the University's definition of itself as a place of useful knowledge, a philosophy matching that of public policy. I had no trouble in explaining this to the then Principal of Strathclyde, Sir Samuel Curran, who was comfortable with backing research of international quality. His successor, Graham Hills, was quite different. The upshot was that the CSPP was left to go its own way at Strathclyde (*see* www.profrose.eu/writings.php#studying). This gave me the freedom of action and incentive to undertake comparative research through a network extending across continents.

The CSPP is university based, but has never been a conventional department. This reflected my own vision of public policy research as inherently problem-focussed and drawing on social science tools from more than one discipline. By contrast with the Committee on Political Sociology, which was a network without an institutional base, the CSPP has the advantage of an institutional infrastructure. The university provides the CSPP with a small core budget that enables it to avoid the interminable scramble for short-term funding that is an obstacle to long-term programmes of research. In return, the CSPP provides the University with internationally visible research, which is well rewarded in the distribution of British government funds.

Location in Glasgow has the disadvantage of being distant from London, whereas free-standing public policy institutes are usually within walking distance of government offices. Their contributions to public debates can be intelligent as well as timely, but so much time is spent in the daily round of speculation and gossip that pervades capital city politics that there is little time to add to social science knowledge. Being in Scotland has the advantage of not wasting a lot of time in ephemeral discussions (www.profrose.eu/writings.php#public_policy). The CSPP relies on a mousetrap strategy: If you build a better mousetrap, the world will beat a path to your door. It has cultivated a comparative advantage in a limited number of areas rather than claiming that it could deal with everything that is currently in the headlines.

The priority that the CSPP gives to comparative research makes it possible to test hypotheses against evidence from a range of national contexts in order to understand the causes and consequences of variations in public policy. While a Centre that concentrates on national political issues has good reason to concentrate its staff in one place, comparative research requires knowledge that is more easily accessed on the ground in multiple countries. Hence, the CSPP has always operated with a network of collaborators in other countries. Its initial programme of work on the territorial dimension in United Kingdom government was supported by the UK Politics Work Group, which I founded as part of the British Political Studies Association (Madgwick and Rose 1982) as well as by Ian McAllister as the CSPP's Research Officer (see Rose and McAllister 1982; McAllister and Rose 1984). Work on overloaded government was supported by an ECPR network and by co-authorship with B. Guy Peters in the United States. Current programmes on the experience of corruption involve Transparency International's secretariat in Berlin as well as the CSPP and research on EU politics involves Alexander Trechsel at the European University Institute, Florence, and collaborators in Lisbon as well as Dr. Gabriela Borz in Scotland.

I have always believed that travelling stimulates fresh thoughts and insights helpful in understanding the circumstances of others with whom one works. Location is unimportant for a comparative centre as long as it is near a good airport, and Glasgow meets that condition. By collaborating with a transnational network of social scientists from Kiel in Northern Germany to Naples and Pittsburgh, the CSPP has been able to produce comparisons of public employment with a common conceptual framework and more national data than OECD or Eurostat have compiled (Rose 1985a).

Comparative research favours the use of quantitative data, which is well suited to systematic cross-national analysis. It also requires care in the construction of indicators presented to policymakers who are concerned with validity as well as reliability. If one understands how programmes work, survey data can be used to produce relevant evidence about how citizens react to the services they receive (Rose 1989a). Experience in designing surveys *and* in public policy has been of particular advantage in examining the collapse of the institutions of Communist societies. Citizens responded by turning their backs on institutions that are the source of official statistics and relied more on informal resources. My work on paying bribes for public services draws on multinational surveys conducted in more than 100 countries.

Distinctive Tools

Public policy analysis requires tools appropriate to the problem at hand. For comparative analysis, concepts are essential to compare and contrast institutions and policies labelled in different languages. Large-scale comparisons benefit from the use of quantitative data in order to group countries according to criteria more meaningful than alphabetical ordering. One way to gain a comparative advantage is by developing distinctive concepts and models with broad applications. The CSPP has done so through work on such subjects as the growth of government and lesson-drawing in public policy.

Growth of government

The unexpected downturn in the world economy in 1975 created a sense of crisis in democracy. Fears were expressed that governments unable to finance increased spending commitments painlessly through economic growth would go the way of Weimar Germany, albeit without producing another Marlene Dietrich. I tried to convince the *Financial Times* writer Samuel Brittan (1975), who thought that economics drove political reactions, that his pessimism was misplaced, pointing out that at that time the only people using guns to challenge political legitimacy were in Northern Ireland. The OECD's diagnosis of the downturn as a cyclical problem justifying deficit spending ignored the cumulative effect of annual deficits.

With a characteristic combination of scientific curiosity and institution-building skills, Rudolf Wildenmann brought together an ECPR group to discuss a response to the economic crisis facing governments. The discussion was lively but very unfocussed. I stopped listening and quietly outlined my ideas; this became a proper cause-and-effect model for understanding overloaded government (Rose 1975). Government became overloaded when the growing cost of public expenditure could not be met by the fiscal dividend of economic growth and deficit financing was no longer possible because it stoked a politically unacceptable level of inflation. This left the alternatives of financing public spending by raising taxes that cut the real take-home pay of workers or by squeezing public expenditure. The topic became one of four ECPR projects supported by a Volkswagen Foundation grant that made possible my first big foray into public policy research and the publication of *Can Government Go Bankrupt?* (Rose and Peters 1978).

To understand the process that produces overloaded government requires an answer to the question: What grows when government grows? In a word, the answer is: programmes (Rose 1984). They package the three resources of government — laws, money and public officials — into policy outputs involving everything from agricultural subsidies to the education of deaf children. Since government does not have a single function, such as maximizing public welfare or securing the re-election of office holders, its activities cannot be reduced to a single number, such as public expenditure as a percentage of Gross Domestic Product. To understand what government does one must understand the different ways in which laws, money and public employees are combined. Some programmes are money-intensive, such as cash-transfer social security benefits; some are labour-intensive too, such as health and education; and law-intensive programmes concern such topics as marriage and divorce. To analyse what was causing the overload, in 1981 the CSPP was awarded a five-year ESRC grant to undertake book-length studies of trends in taxation, public employment, legislation and government organizations since 1950 (www.profrose.eu/writings.php#public_policy).

The focus on programmes led me to venture far from the offices of presidents and prime ministers, who can only influence a few government programmes. The principal cause of the growth of government was the cumulative inertia of programme commitments that the government of the day had inherited from its predecessors (Rose and Davies 1994). The biggest agency in government is not the Department of Waste but long established departments responsible for programmes that produce 'good' goods and services that benefit almost all citizens during their life cycle, such as health, education and pensions. The programme approach makes possible many kinds of cross-national comparisons of aggregate spending, taxation and deficits; the resources that governments give to particular programmes; and the extent to which services are provided by the private or public sector. Insofar as cross-national comparisons show similar patterns due to demographic pressures on open-ended entitlements, this undermines theories of all-powerful presidents or parties choosing what government does (Rose 1984a).

Writing about overloaded government taught me the strength of economics in integrating concepts in cause and effect models. It also taught me a lot about the partisanship of economists offering politically contestable prescriptions to government. The Swedish Nobel Prize in Economics has practised neutrality between the parties of left and right into which many economists divide. In 1974 it named two winners, Gunnar Myrdal, a socialist, and Friedrich Hayek, who saw socialism as an enemy of law and liberty. The Swedes have since encouraged the development of a multi-party system by giving the Economics Prize to political scientists such as Herbert Simon and Elinor Ostrom and psychologists such as Daniel Kahnemann.

My work on overloaded government was attacked by political scientists who did not like the challenge it posed to the spending preferences of Democrats. At an American Political Science Association panel in the late 1970s, a senior professor said it was a shame that I talked like Barry Goldwater. When we next met, after electorates had endorsed Ronald Reagan and Margaret Thatcher, he apologized for having been slow to understand what I had been saying about the existence of limits on public expenditure. The approach was denounced without any subsequent apology by an *APSR* reviewer who thought writing about limits on public spending made me part of a rightwing conspiracy.

My reliance on evidence rather than ideology makes some things I write unacceptable to free-market Thatcherites. In 1986 I was commissioned by the head of the Prime Minister's Policy Unit to write a report on promoting entrepreneurship in Britain. My summary of a large amount of survey data about popular attitudes to economic activity concluded that a large majority of Britons were not entrepreneurially inclined; they wanted reward without risk (www.profrose.eu/writings.php#public_policy). The paper was buried by its sponsors.

Lesson drawing

After more than a quarter of a century studying comparative politics, in the late 1980s I decided that the time had come to see whether the collective knowledge that political scientists had accumulated could be systematically used to draw lessons for public policy. The decision was stimulated by discussions in Paris with officials of OECD, who not only collect statistics but also encourage lesson-drawing by circulating details of successful national programmes to governments. They do not see each country as unique but think in terms of countries having a limited number of options to respond to common problems. This information is used to recommend lessons. The European Union's Open Method of Co-ordination similarly tries to stimulate national officials to learn lessons from each other in order to improve their national performance in such fields as unemployment and poverty. The logic underlying prescriptions to copy another country's programme is often unspecified and so are critical assumptions about comparability.

My work has focussed on the basic social science question: Under what circumstances and to what extent can a programme that works in one country be applied in another country and produce a similar result? The first book I wrote on lesson-drawing set out the basic concepts required for learning lessons (Rose 1993a). The follow up book is a practical guide that identifies two stages in lesson drawing, learning how a programme works in another country and then trying to find out how and whether it can be transferred to one's own country (Rose 2005a).

Up to a point, lesson-drawing has much in common with the study of comparative politics, which seeks to explain why programmes addressing a common problem differ. Insofar as the explanation stresses history and culture as setting countries on different paths, this implies that the only lesson that can be learned is that, even though a programme works there, it won't work here. However, the success of McDonald's in more than one hundred countries is a reminder that even something as seemingly culturally constrained as taste in food is not necessarily a barrier to the transfer of an idea. Lesson-drawing may also be used to study failure. The military have strong incentives to study the strategy of losers as well as victors in war.

When policymakers are dissatisfied with the status quo, they can apply a remedy that worked before. However, if a customary remedy no longer produces satisfaction, then a national government has a choice between adopting a speculative proposal that sounds good in theory but has never been applied anywhere, or looking abroad to see what others do. Japan has been a monumental example of a closed political system that successfully drew lessons from Europe and America in order to modernize its traditional society (Westney 1987). The stimulus to do so did not come from Japanese researchers but from the arrival in 1853 of four American warships demanding that the country open up to foreign trade.

Where policymakers look reflects power, fashion and their comfort zone. As an American long resident in Europe I am always struck by the readiness of European and Asian governments to look to the United States for lessons (Rose 1974b). Its many inimitable political features are not regarded as barriers to applying lessons in other national contexts. Logically, it is more appropriate for one developing country, say China, to look to a neighbour that has pioneered in development, say Korea, to learn what it did to succeed (Rose 2003). When I suggested this to a Chinese social scientist, he smiled and replied, 'But all our best students want to go to the States'.

It is misleading to look to a league table ranking national performance and endorse what the top country does as the best practice that others should emulate. Doing so ignores the extent to which a shortage of resources makes it difficult or even impossible for lower-ranking countries to do what is labelled best practice. My advice to a House of Commons committee reviewing government targets (Rose 2003a) was to think in terms of making progress through better practice. For places that are above-average in performance, this may involve no more than adjustments in what is already being done. For below-average countries, less bad practice is a much more realistic goal to pursue. Lessons aimed at removing faults are more likely to produce immediate gains than an attempt to transform a faulty policy into best practice overnight.

The key step in lesson-drawing is the production of a model in the sense in which that term is used by an engineer trained at Carnegie Mellon University rather than at an Essex or Michigan summer school. To an engineer a model represents how something works. It discards non-essential observations that take up most of the space in a prose description of a policy in order to concentrate on the cause-and-effect relationship of necessary elements. A model can be physical, such as a model railway; a diagram showing relationships between inputs, institutions and outputs; or a system-dynamic computer programme. It is transparent and can be quickly understood by open-minded policymakers (*see* Rose 2005a: 69ff).

The results of lesson-drawing are contingently prescriptive. Careful analysis may conclude that another country's programme cannot be transferred because necessary resources are not at hand, such as the rule of law. This point is often overlooked in prescriptions to deal with corruption by prescribing that governments adopt laws that they can then subvert. Conflicts in partisan values can impose a veto too. A lesson supported by social science evidence can be rejected on the grounds that its object, its means, or both are undesirable. Few social scientists want to face the heat of the political kitchen in which proposals are sliced, diced and seasoned until something politically palatable is produced. Paradoxically, the best chance of having a recommendation adopted promptly is if its means and ends are apolitical. However, a change of government can turn what was once dismissed as 'politically not on' into a policy that the new government embraces.

I put my abstract concepts to the test by drawing a lesson for Britain from the German vocational education and training system. This was the project that took me to Berlin just before the Wall fell. It was chosen because there was British agreement about the need to improve the skills of the middle mass of the labour force and the government explicitly endorsed the German model. The book-length study concluded that to bring British workers up to continental standards first of all required the relatively inexpensive training of trainers (*Meister*), skilled and responsible people in short supply in British work places. Unfortunately, as the title of the book resulting from the analysis made clear, the British government policy was to encourage *Training without Trainers* (Rose and Wignanek 1990).

To promote the lesson drawn I acted as a consultant for a Confederation of British Industry report. I also lobbied the Trades Union Congress, where an official explained that British unions did not like some of their members becoming more skilled because that would increase demands for greater wage differentials or even lead the best qualified to stop being union members. I saw Tony Blair, then the shadow minister of employment. He listened and smiled, but by the time he got into office he had other priorities. Meanwhile, the Conservative government adopted a shortcut strategy: introduce standards one level below continental Europe and let teachers in technical colleges rather than a *Meister* do the training. I can't say that my efforts failed, but only that after a quarter of a century I am still waiting for the recommendations to be put into effect. The problem of low skilled British workers is still there.

Impact Long Term

An engineering approach assumes a consensus about what the problem is and what a solution should achieve; the challenge is to find a technically effective means to this end. When I asked a Glasgow municipal architect what research he would find most useful, he replied, 'How to stop rain penetration around windows in flats at 500 feet'. Officials with other responsibilities were looking for help with

The courtyard of the Reform Club London, where people of all sorts can meet to exchange ideas. Designed by Sir Charles Barry in the republican Renaissance style, in contrast to his Neo-Gothic design for the Palace of Westminster

problems not readily amenable to a quick technological fix, such as how to deal with social problems created by anti-social tenants (Rose 1974c, 115–137).

The relationship between policymakers and social scientists can be seen in terms of a marketplace in which public officials may look for help in dealing with problems and social scientists offer ideas about what to do. The canteen of the British Treasury or the central court of the Reform Club can be bazaars where people meet to exchange information and ideas. However, just as most policymakers spend more time talking to their colleagues in so-called corridors of power, so most social scientists mingle more with fellow social scientists in academic corridors. To do public policy research you need to move between corridors. When in a capital city I try to have at least one meeting with a person in the policy process and one with a fellow social scientist. This helps keep me in shape physically too. The walk between my London and Washington clubs and relevant public offices is about 15 minutes.

The idea that each public policy has a single, identifiable decision-maker is naive in the extreme. Policymaking is a process involving many exchanges over long periods of time between many people in different roles in different networks that collectively make up the grand bazaar of public policy. Any impact an individual has will be partial at best. As a Washington consultant with a doctorate from MIT once explained to me,

> You go to someone with an idea and are told: 'That's a great idea; why don't you discuss it with X and Y'. You then go to them and they tell you to talk to two more people. In the end, you are happy to get 15 per cent of what you initially sought.

Academics engaged in the policy process learn that impact is uncertain and achievements may be minimal. An MIT professor appointed to prepare a social indicators report for President Nixon told me that his main achievement was to get the report published as a White House document.

The appropriate image for transferring ideas comes from meteorology: the outputs of social scientists, whatever their form, can be inputs that seed the climate of opinion (Rose 1977). As professors of meteorology are the first to admit, their theories are only partially successful. Seeding clouds to induce precipitation is even more unpredictable than forecasting the weather. Just as meteorologists continue their work in spite of droughts and psychiatrists remain in practice even if one of their patients kills someone, so social scientists engage with policymakers notwithstanding uncertainty about whether their ideas will be put into practice, compromised or have no effect.

When a policy report is ignored by the government of the day, its argument need not disappear; it can evaporate into the clouds and rain down another day. Changing the intellectual climate does not normally occur within a single electoral cycle or during the short life of a research grant. The effect of a social science idea may be better measured by the time scale of a forester than of a politician or journalist. Keynes' epigram about politicians being in thrall to the ideas of dead economists is a backhanded compliment to the deceased. Fortunately, you don't have to be dead to have influence; however, it helps to have long life. As the following account shows, it can take up to half a century to have an impact.

Influencing election strategy

The first priority of the losers of an election ought to be to understand why they lost in order to win next time. The chapters I wrote in the 1959 Nuffield election study emphasized the strategy of the victorious Conservative Party. The chapters in *Must Labour Lose?* set out what Labour politicians needed to take into account in order to have a chance of winning the next election. The key point in the title was the question mark. It set out a model of how elections are won and lost and the text explained that Labour did not have to lose if it learned to understand how its working-class base of support was changing. Workers were abandoning their cloth caps to shop at Marks & Spencer rather than the Labour movement's Co-operative stores and bowler hats were disappearing (www.profrose.eu/writings. php#england).

Labour's third straight defeat in 1959 was a shock to the Labour Party and to class-conscious British sociologists who, electoral evidence notwithstanding, viewed Labour as the country's natural majority party. Aneurin Bevan, then Labour's deputy leader, had vetoed the party sponsoring Mark Abrams doing a survey before the 1959 election. He placed his hand on the working-class heart that beat beneath his well tailored suit and proclaimed, 'I know what the working class thinks'. I was invited by Peter Shore, then research director of the Labour Party, to give a seminar to his staff on the use of polls. The audience was attentive but not enthusiastic, since the implications went the other direction from the leftwing views of Shore and his friends (www.profrose.eu/writings.php#england; Rose, 1962a).

Trade unions were even more resistant to recognizing changes in British society that were reducing the demand for services of nationalized industries that employed their members. When a railway union leader denounced anti-nationalization campaigns at a Nuffield College seminar, I asked why the unions did not run a public relations campaign in favour of the benefits of publicly subsidized rail services. He was shocked and dismissive of the idea of promoting his members' services to those who paid for them. When we spoke, the rail unions had more than half a million members; since then they have lost seven-eighths of their membership.

In 1962 I wrote a journalistic article setting out electoral evidence suggesting that the Conservative government could be ousted if the Labour and Liberal parties would agree not to compete against each other in constituencies with Conservative MPs. Woodrow Wyatt, a Labour politician in the coterie around the Labour leader, Hugh Gaitskell, rang out of the blue to ask me to lunch. After pouring me a drink he asked dramatically, 'How would you like to change the course of history?' I replied matter of factly that if I wanted to do that I would go back to the United States.[1] He poured another drink and requested a memo that he then forwarded to Gaitskell with his recommendations.

The idea of a Lib-Lab coalition evaporated when Hugh Gaitskell rejected it and Labour took the lead in the opinion polls. Labour did not lose the 1964 election but it had only one MP more than the number required to claim a parliamentary majority, and its vote went up by only 0.3 per cent. Victory owed much more to the demoralized Conservative Party's vote falling by 6.0 per cent. Thanks to the disproportional bias in Britain's first past the post electoral system, the Labour Party has since continued to lose votes although not elections.

The first Lib-Lab agreement was made in 1977 by Jim Callaghan when the Labour government needed the support of Liberal MPs to stay in office. The second was between Labour MPs who broke away to form a social democratic party that allied with the Liberals; it almost pushed the Labour Party into third place at the 1983 election. The next pact brought the Liberals to office in 2010 in coalition with the Conservatives, who had many more MPs than Labour but not enough to have a majority. This was the first but not the last time in which politicians rejected my views, not because they were wrong but because they were not comfortable with them. In retrospect my views about the pivotal position of Liberal voters were simply premature.

Unknown to me, one of the thousands of readers of my writings was the youthful Philip Gould, who embraced the then novel idea that the Labour Party needed to listen to ordinary people if it was to win office. Gould established his own polling

---

1.   Wyatt showed me the grand cantilevered staircase in the Regency house in which he lived with his fourth wife and said impressively, 'I doubt you have ever seen anything like that before?' I again disappointed him, replying, 'Yes I have, in Charleston, South Carolina'.

firm and became active in Labour politics, promoting an election strategy based on polls and his interpretation of focus group discussions. It took three successive Labour defeats and the death of John Smith before a Labour leader, Tony Blair, wanted to listen to Gould. Blair led the Labour Party to three successive election victories with appeals that were a long way from those endorsed by people such as Peter Shore.

My impact on the Conservative Party was indirect. When William Hague took over the leadership of the Tory Party he distributed copies of Gould's 'How I did it' book (1999) to every shadow Cabinet member with the inscription: 'Know thine enemy'. Like Labour predecessors in Opposition, *über* Thatcherites resisted the message that elections are won by listening to the electorate. Such Tories were in thrall to simple rightwing doctrines that brought the party another defeat. After three successive election losses, Conservatives under the leadership of David Cameron got the message. To win an election the Conservative Party needed to stop making an introverted appeal to its hard line base and instead adopt positions in harmony with more voters.

Like global climate change, changes in the intellectual climate do not meet the deadline of a weekly periodical. A policy recommendation may appear dormant and yet achieve a sleeper effect when policymakers wake up to its value. However, patience is required to wait for this to happen. My own experience of seeing radical political changes in American race relations, in a divided and embattled Northern Ireland, and the fall of the Berlin Wall makes me willing to be patient and rely on the maxim 'Never say never in politics'.

L'envoi

Several readers of the manuscript in draft have asked that I offer advice to younger academics. I do not believe in telling other people what they must do with their lives, but I am willing to make comments that may help inform their decisions. For example, Ed Page, who had a 1st class degree in Politics and German from Kingston Polytechnic, sought my view about whether to accept a grant for postgraduate study at Strathclyde or at St. Antony's College, Oxford. I told him that St. Antony's was the place to go if he wanted to become a historian of contemporary Germany, whereas if he wanted to become a political scientist then Strathclyde was the place and to let me know what he decided. Page decided to turn down Oxford in favour of Strathclyde. His choice worked out well: he is now a professor of government at the LSE.

In going through a file of old articles when completing this manuscript, I found that I had once broken my rule about giving advice in an interview for an ECPR Newsletter, so here goes again:

Do what interests you. The PhD is the start of an education, not its end. Don't begin writing a thesis if you are not interested enough in its subject matter to give it several years of your life.

Go for bear, that is, pursue a subject that is important. Don't waste time writing a conference paper if all you will get is one more line for your curriculum vitae and the pebble it may add to the beach of knowledge is well back from the foreshore. After getting my doctorate, I published relatively little for more than half a dozen years because I was busy learning more.

If you criticise, be constructive. Peer reviewers of papers for journals are too often me-ers, criticising authors who do not think like me. Such arrogance may boost a reviewer's ego but it doesn't help an author. A reviewer ought to consider the intent of the author before identifying shortcomings in failing to achieve his or her purpose. If I can't think of anything constructive to say about a paper, I say nothing. I once heard this maxim applied to the paper that a well known American political scientist presented to an international conference. When the discussant was asked whether he had ignored the paper in his remarks because he hadn't read it, the reply was, 'No, it was because I have read it'.

Learn to put yourself in other people's shoes. Don't reduce the people you study to the one-dimensional actors found in abstract theories. A self-aware social scientist should try to be a mind-reader, understanding other people well enough so that you can think as they do. You don't have to be Sherlock Holmes in order to notice small details that can be telling or to see significance in what people avoid saying as well as what they choose to talk about.

Lesser evils are preferable to greater evils. People who think that a loss of trust in government is the worst thing that can happen to their country are substituting hyperbole for history. You don't have to know people, as I do, who have endured racial discrimination, civil war, being a political refugee or a Holocaust survivor to realize that a loss of political trust is not the worst way in which politics can go wrong.

The hardest part of statistical analysis is saying what statistics mean. As computers make it increasingly easy to produce high-level inferential statistical analyses, it becomes increasingly difficult to connect what is shown on a computer screen and what can be observed by walking down a street. Even if there is no language requirement in a PhD programme, this does not remove the need to translate into understandable words the quantitative output that computers produce.

Don't think in career terms. There are plenty of other occupations where being a careerist is normal and they usually pay better than being a scholar. When writing the first draft of *Politics in England* I realized that this might make me the author of a profitable textbook if I fit it into a conventional marketing formula. I decided against this because it would remove what was original in the text and wrote the book to suit myself. In various editions it has now sold upwards of 200,000 copies. Although the sales of my subsequent books have not been so big, I still write books to suit myself.

References

Publications solely by Richard Rose[1]

1960   The Relation of Socialist Principles to British Labour Foreign Policy, 1945–1951, Oxford: Oxford University DPhil thesis.

1961   'The Bow Group's role in British politics', Western Political Quarterly 32(3): 275–283.

1962   'The political ideas of English party activists', American Political Science Review 56(2): 360–371.

1962a   'Political decision–making and the polls', Parliamentary Affairs 15(2): 188–202.

1964   Politics in England, Boston: Little Brown & Co, and (1965) London: Faber and Faber.

1965a   'England: a traditionally modern political culture', in L. W. Pye and S. Verba (eds) Political Culture and Political Development, Princeton: Princeton University Press, pp. 83–129.

1966   Studies in British Politics: A reader in political sociology, London: Macmillan and New York: St. Martins, 1st edn, 1966; 2nd rev. edn, 1969; 3rd rev. edn, 1976.

1967   Influencing Voters: A study in campaign rationality, London: Faber and New York: St. Martins.

1968   'Class and party divisions: Britain as a test case', Sociology 2(2): 129–162.

1969   'Dynamic tendencies in the authority of regimes', World Politics 21: 612–28.

1971   Governing without Consensus: An Irish perspective, London: Faber and Faber, Boston: Beacon Press.

1972   'The market for social indicators', in A. Shonfield and S. Shaw (eds) Social Indicators and Social Policy, London: Heinemann, pp. 119–141.

1974   Electoral Behavior: A comparative analysis, New York: Free Press.

1974a   The Problem of Party Government, London: Macmillan and New York: Free Press, 1974; Penguin edition, 1976.

1974b   Lessons from America, London: Macmillan.

1974c   The Management of Urban Change in Britain and Germany, London and Beverly Hills: Sage Publications.

1975   'Overloaded government: the problem outlined', European Studies

---

1.   For a full list of academic publications see the curriculum vitae at www.profrose.eu/about.php Journalism referenced in the text can also be found at that website.

Newsletter, Council of European Studies, Columbia University, 5(3): 13–18.

1976 Managing Presidential Objectives, New York: Free Press and London: Macmillan.

1976a 'On the priorities of citizenship in the Deep South and Northern Ireland', Journal of Politics 38(2): 247–91.

1976b Northern Ireland: Time of choice, Washington DC: American Enterprise Institute and London: Macmillan.

1976c 'Disciplined research and undisciplined problems', International Social Science Journal 28(1): 99–121.

1977 'Implementation and evaporation: the record of MBO', Public Administration Review 37(1): 64–71.

1982 Understanding the United Kingdom: The territorial dimension in government, London: Longman and Chatham, NJ: Chatham House.

1984 Do Parties Make a Difference?, 2nd edn, Chatham, NJ: Chatham House.

1984a Understanding Big Government: The programme approach, London and Beverly Hills: Sage Publications; (Italian and Spanish translations).

1985 'Opinion polls as feedback mechanisms: from cavalry charge to electronic warfare', in A. Ranney (ed.) Britain at the Polls, Durham: Duke University Press, pp. 108–38.

1985a Public Employment in Western Nations, Cambridge: Cambridge University Press; republished digitally, 2009.

1986 'The state's contribution to the welfare mix in Britain', in R. Rose and R. Shiratori (eds) The Welfare State East and West, New York: Oxford University Press, pp. 80–106.

1989 'Whatever happened to social indicators: a symposium', Journal of Public Policy 9(4), pp. 399–450.

1989a Ordinary People in Public Policy: A behavioural analysis. London and Newbury Park, CA: Sage Publications.

1990 'Institutionalizing professional political science in Europe: a dynamic model', European Journal of Political Research 18: 581–603.

1990a 'La Presidencia al servicio del pública', Reforma Administrativa: Informe del Presidente de la República, Vol. 13, Bogota: Government Printing Office, pp.165–96.

1991 The Postmodern President, 2nd edn, Chatham, NJ: Chatham House; (Spanish and Portuguese translations).

1991a 'Is American public policy exceptional?', in B. Shafer (ed.) Is America Different?, New York: Oxford University Press, pp. 187–229.

1991b 'Comparing forms of comparative analysis', Political Studies 39(3): 446–462.

1992 'Eastern Europe's need for a civil economy', in R. O'Brien (ed.) Finance and the International Economy 6, Oxford: Oxford University Press, pp. 4–16.

1992a 'Escaping absolute dissatisfaction: a trial and error model of change in Eastern Europe', Journal of Theoretical Politics 4(4): 371–93.

1993   'Evaluating presidents', in G. Edwards III, J. Kessel and B. Rockman (eds) Researching the Presidency: Vital questions, new approaches, Pittsburgh: University of Pittsburgh Press, pp. 453–84.

1993a   Lesson-Drawing in Public Policy: A guide to learning across time and space, Chatham, NJ: Chatham House.

1994   Comparing Welfare Across Time and Space, Vienna: European Centre for Social Welfare Policy and Research, Eurosocial Report, 49.

1996   What is Europe? A dynamic perspective, New York and London: Longman.

1996a   'Political science, ideas and government in post-war Britain', Contemporary British History 10(2): 178–190.

1997   'How patient are people in post-communist societies?', World Today 159(3): 130–144.

2000   'Getting things done in an anti-modern society: social capital networks in Russia', in P. Dasgupta and I. Serageldin (eds), Social Capital. Washington, DC: The World Bank, pp. 147–171.

2001   The Prime Minister in a Shrinking World, Oxford: Polity Press.

2003   'When all other conditions are not equal: the context for drawing lessons', in C. J. Finer (ed.) Social Policy Reform in China, Aldershot: Ashgate, pp. 5–22.

2003a   'What's wrong with best practice policies—and why relevant practices are better', in On Target? Government by Measurement, London: House of Commons Public Administration Select Committee HC 62-II, pp. 307–317.

2005   'Giving direction to government in comparative perspective', in J. Aberbach and M. A. Peterson (eds) The Executive Branch, New York: Oxford University Press, pp. 72–99.

2005a   Learning from Comparative Public Policy: A practical guide, London and New York: Routledge.

2007   'Political behaviour in time and space', in R. Dalton and H.-D. Klingemann (eds) Oxford Handbook of Political Behaviour, New York: Oxford University Press, pp. 283–301.

2008   'Political communication in a European public space: language, the Internet and understanding as soft power', Journal of Common Market Studies 46(2): 451–475.

2009   Understanding Post-Communist Transformation: A bottom up approach, London and New York: Routledge.

2013   Representing Europeans: A pragmatic approach, Oxford: Oxford University Press.

2013a   'Do words have meanings?', European Political Science, http://www.palgrave-journals.com/eps/index.html.

2014   'Politics in Britain', in G. B. Powell Jr., R. J. Dalton and K. Strom (eds) Comparative Politics Today, New York: Longman.

2014a   'Responsible party government in a world of interdependence', West European Politics, forthcoming.

Articles with Richard Rose as senior author

Rose, R. and Borz, G. (2013) 'Institutional stimuli and individual response as explanations of turnout', Journal of Elections, Public Opinion and Parties (JEPOP), in press.

Rose, R. and Davies, P. L. (1994) Inheritance in Public Policy, New Haven: Yale University Press.

Rose, R. and Garvin, T. (1983) 'The public policy effects of independence: Ireland as a test case', European Journal of Political Research, 11(2): 377–97.

Rose, R. and Haerpfer, C. (1997) 'The impact of a ready-made state', German Politics 6(1): 100–121.

Rose, R. and McAllister, I. (1982) United Kingdom Facts, London: Macmillan and New York: Holmes and Meier.

Rose, R. and McAllister, I. (1983) 'Can political conflict be resolved by social change?', Journal of Conflict Research 27(3): 533–557.

Rose, R., Mishler, W. and Haerpfer, C. (1998) Democracy and its Alternatives: Understanding post-communist societies, Baltimore: Johns Hopkins University Press.

Rose, R., Mishler, W. and Munro, N. (2011) Popular Support for an Undemocratic Regime: The changing views of Russians, Cambridge: Cambridge University Press.

Rose, R. and Mossawir, H. (1967) 'Voting and elections: a functional analysis', Political Studies 15(2): 173–201.

Rose, R. and Munro, N. (2009) Parties and Elections in New European Democracies, Colchester: ECPR Press.

Rose, R. and Page, E. C. (1996) 'German responses to regime change: culture, economy or context?', West European Politics 19(1): 1–27.

Rose, R. and Peiffer, C. (2012) Paying Bribes to Get Public Services: A global guide to concepts and survey measures, Studies in Public Policy No. 494, Glasgow: Centre for the Study of Public Policy.

Rose, R. and Peters, B. G. (1978) Can Government Go Bankrupt?, New York: Basic Books.

Rose, R. and Shiratori, R. (eds) (1986) The Welfare State East and West, New York: Oxford University Press.

Rose, R. and Suleiman, E. (eds) (1980) Presidents and Prime Ministers, Washington, DC: American Enterprise Institute.

Rose, R. and Tikhomirov, E. (1993) 'Who grows food in Russia and Eastern Europe?', Post-Soviet Geography 34(2): 111–126.

Rose, R. and Wignanek, G. (1990) Training without Trainers? How Germany avoids Britain's supply-side bottleneck, London: Anglo-German Foundation.

Other references

Abrams, M. and Rose, R. (1960) Must Labour Lose? Harmondsworth, Middlesex: Penguin.

Almond, G. A. (1960) 'Introduction', in G. A. Almond and J. S. Coleman, The Politics of Developing Areas, Princeton: Princeton University Press.

— (1997) 'A voice from the Chicago School' in H. Daalder (ed.) Comparative European Politics, London: Pinter, pp. 54–67.

Bassett, R. O. (1935) The Essentials of Parliamentary Democracy, London: Macmillan.

Beetham, D. (1970) Transport and Turbans, Oxford: Oxford University Press.

Berelson, B., Lazarsfeld, P. and McPhee, W. (1954) Voting, Chicago: University of Chicago Press.

Berlin, I. (1958) Two Concepts of Liberty: An inaugural lecture, Oxford: Clarendon Press.

Bonham, J. (1954) The Middle Class Vote, London: Faber and Faber.

Brittan, S. (1975) 'The economic contradictions of democracy', British Journal of Political Science 5(2): 129–156.

Brothers, T. (2006) Louis Armstrong's New Orleans, New York: W. W. Norton.

Brown, C. G., McIvor, A. J. and Rafeek, N. (2004) The University Experience, 1945–1975: An oral history of the University of Strathclyde, Edinburgh: Edinburgh University Press.

Budge, I. (1994) 'Blondel and the development of European political science', in I. Budge and D. McKay (eds) Developing Democracy, London: Sage, pp. 6–23.

Butler, D. E. and Rose, R. (1960) The British General Election of 1959, London: Macmillan.

Butler, D. and Stokes, D. (1970) Political Change in Britain, London: Macmillan.

Campbell, A., Converse, P. E., Miller, W. E. and Stokes, D. E. (1960) The American Voter, New York: John Wiley.

Chapman, B. and Potter, A. (eds) (1974) W.J.M.M.: Political Questions, Manchester: Manchester University Press.

Chester, D. N. (1986) Economics, Politics, and Social Studies in Oxford, 1900–1985, London: Macmillan.

Clark, W. (1967) Guns in Ulster, Belfast: Constabulary Gazette.

Collier, D. and Levitsky, S. (1997) 'Democracy with adjectives: conceptual innovation in comparative research', World Politics 49(3): 430–451.

Cuoco, L. and Gass, W. H. (eds) (2000) Literary St. Louis: A guide, St. Louis: Missouri Historical Society Press.

Daalder, H. (1961) 'The plethora of polysyllables', reprinted in European Political Science, 2013.

Dogan, M. and Rose, R. (eds) (1970) European Politics: A reader, Boston: Little, Brown and London: Macmillan, 1971.

Donnelly, J. B. (1978) 'The vision of scholarship: Johns Hopkins after the war', Maryland Historical Magazine 73(2): 137–162.

Easton, D. (1965) A Systems Analysis of Political Life, New York: John Wiley.

Eliot, T. S. (1919) 'Tradition and the individual talent', The Egoist, 6, 54–55 and 72–73.

Epstein, L. (1954) Britain: Uneasy ally, Chicago: University of Chicago Press.

Eulau, H., Eldersveld, S. and Janowitz, M. (eds) (1956) Political Behavior: A reader in theory and research, Glencoe, Ill.: Free Press.

Farrell, M. (1983) Arming the Protestants, London: Pluto Press.

Fenno, R. (1986) 'Observation, context, and sequence in the study of politics', American Political Science Review 80(1): 3–15.

Gilman, C. (2004) Lewis and Clark Across the Divide, Washington and St. Louis: Smithsonian Books and the Missouri Historical Society.

Gould, P. (1999) The Unfinished Revolution: How the modernisers saved the Labour Party, London: Abacus.

Grant, W. (2010) The Development of a Discipline: The history of the Political Studies Association, Chichester: Wiley-Blackwell.

Green, V. H. H. (1957) Oxford Common Room: Lincoln College and Mark Pattison, Oxford: Oxford University Press.

Gutheim, F. and Washburn, W. E. (1976) The Federal City: Plans and realities, Washington DC: Smithsonian Institution.

Hansard (1960) 'Political expenditure', House of Commons, Debates, Vol. 627, Cols. 733–803, 21 July.

Hanson, A. H. (1972) 'Peter Nettl: a memoir', in T. Nossiter, A. H. Hanson and S. Rokkan (eds) Imagination and Precision in the Social Sciences, London: Faber and Faber, pp. 1–12.

Hayward, J., Barry, B. and Brown, A. (eds) (2003) The British Study of Politics in the Twentieth Century, London: British Academy.

Headey, B. (1974) British Cabinet Ministers, London: Allen & Unwin.

Kadushin, C. and Rose, R. (1974) 'Political sociology', in Current Sociology: VIIth World Congress of Sociology, The Hague and Paris: Mouton, pp. 229–266.

Kimbrough, M. and Dagen, M. W. (2000) Victory without Violence: The first ten years of the St. Louis Committee of Racial Equality (CORE), 1947–1957, Columbia, Mo.: University of Missouri Press.

Kornai, J. (2006) By Force of Thought: Irregular memoirs of an intellectual journey, Cambridge, MA: MIT Press.

Kuhn, T. S. (1962) The Structure of Scientific Revolutions, Chicago: University of Chicago Press.

Kyle, O. R. (1957) Abraham Lincoln in Decatur, New York: Vantage Press.

Lijphart, A. (1997) 'About peripheries, centres and other autobiographical reflections', in H. Daalder (ed.) Comparative European Politics: The story of a profession, London: Pinter, pp. 241–252.

Linz, J. J. (2000) Totalitarian and Authoritarian Regimes, Boulder: Lynne Rienner Publishers.

Lipset, S. M. (1960) Political Man, New York: Doubleday.

Lipset, S. M. and Rokkan, S. (eds) (1967) Party Systems and Voter Alignments, New York: Free Press.

McAllister, I. and Rose, R. (1984) The Nationwide Competition for Votes: The 1983 British Election, London: Pinter and New York, Columbia University Press.

McKenzie, R. T. (1955) British Political Parties, London: Heinemann Educational Books.

Mackie, T. T. and Rose, R. (1991) The International Almanac of Electoral History, 3rd edn, London: Macmillan.

McKittrick, D., Kelters, S., Feeney, B. and Thornton, C. (1999) Lost Lives, Edinburgh: Mainstream Press.

Madgwick, P. and Rose, R. (eds) (1982) The Territorial Dimension in United Kingdom Politics, London: Macmillan.

Marer, P., Arvay, J., O'Connor, J., Schrenk, M. and Swanson, D. (1992) Historically Planned Economies: A guide to the data, Washington DC: World Bank.

Merton, R. K. (1957) Social Structure and Social Theory, revised and enlarged edn, Glencoe, Ill.: The Free Press.

Morgenstern, O. (1963) On the Accuracy of Economic Observations, Princeton: Princeton University Press.

Munck, G. L. and Snyder, R. (eds) (2007) Passion, Craft and Method in Comparative Politics, Baltimore: Johns Hopkins University Press.

Nelson, S. (1984) Ulster's Uncertain Defenders, Belfast: Appletree Press.

Neustadt, R. E. and May, E. (1986) Thinking in Time, New York: Free Press.

Newton, K. and Boncourt, T. (2010) The ECPR's First Forty Years: 1970–2010, Colchester: ECPR Press.

Northern Ireland Convention (1976) Reports of Debates, No. 34, 3 March, cols. 1009–13.

Powell, G. B., Dalton, R. J., Strom, K. (eds) (2014) Comparative Politics Today, New York: Longman.

Purdie, B. (1990) Politics in the Streets: The origins of the civil rights movement in Northern Ireland, Belfast: Blackstaff Press.

Putin, V. (2000) First Person, London: Hutchinson.

Rallings, C. (1975) 'Two types of middle-class Labour voter', British Journal of Political Science 5(1): 107–112.

Redcliffe-Maud, J. P. R. (1981) Experiences of an Optimist, London: Hamish Hamilton.

Riesman, D., Glazer, N. and Denney, R. (1950) The Lonely Crowd, New Haven: Yale University Press.

Rippley, L. J. (1984) The German-Americans, Lanham, Md: University Press of America.

Rokkan, S. (1970) 'International cooperation in political sociology', in E. Allardt and S. Rokkan (eds) Mass Politics: Studies in political sociology, New York: Free Press, pp. 1–20.

— (1979) 'The ISSC programme for the advancement of comparative research', in S. Rokkan (ed.) A Quarter Century of International Social Science, New Delhi: Concept Publishing, pp. 17–26.

Rolph, C. H. (1961) The Trial of Lady Chatterley, Harmondsworth: Penguin.

Rose, C. I. (1923) 'A proposed method for studying the attack of molten slags and glasses upon refractory materials', Journal of the American Ceramic Society 6(12): 1242–1247.

Rubin, L. D. Jr. and Jacobs, R. D. (eds) (1953) Southern Renascence: The literature of the modern South, Baltimore: Johns Hopkins University Press.

Sartori, G. (1970) 'Concept misformation in comparative politics', American Political Science Review 64(4): 1033–53.

Scarman, L. (1972) Violence and Civil Disturbances in Northern Ireland in 1969, London: Her Majesty's Stationery Office.

Sharp, Thomas (1952) Oxford Observed, London: Country Life.

Simon, Herbert (1969) The Sciences of the Artificial, Cambridge, Mass.: MIT Press.

Simpson, R. (1983) How the PhD Came to Britain, Guildford, Surrey: Society for Research into Higher Education.

Stepan, A. (2007) 'Democratic governance and the craft of case-based research', in G. Munck and R. Snyder (eds) Passion, Craft and Method in Comparative Research, Baltimore: Johns Hopkins University Press, pp. 392–456.

Sullivan, L. (1896) 'The Tall Office Building Artistically Considered', Lippincott's Magazine, No. 57.

Thompson, E. M. (1943) Leg Man, New York: E. P. Dutton

Thompson, G. (1961) The Inspiration of Science, London: Oxford University Press.

Tocqueville, A. de (1954 edition) Democracy in America, Vol.1, New York: Vintage Books edition.

Traubel, H. (1959) St. Louis Woman, New York: Duell, Sloan and Pearce.

Tunstall, J. (1970) The Westminster Lobby Correspondents, London: Routledge.

Veblen, T. (1919) 'Why are Jews pre-eminent in science and scholarship?', Political Science Quarterly 34(1): 33–42.

Weaver, R. K. (1986) 'The politics of blame avoidance', Journal of Public Policy 6(4): 371–398.

Weber, M. (1947) The Theory of Social and Economic Organization, Glencoe, Ill: The Free Press.

— (1948) From Max Weber, H. H. Gerth and C. Wright Mills eds, London: Routledge.

Weiner, M. (1957) Party Politics in India, Princeton: Princeton University Press.

Wellek, R. (1960) 'Leo Spitzer, 1887–1960', Comparative Literature 12: 319–334.

Westney, E. (1987) Innovation and Imitation: The transfer of Western organizational patterns to Meiji Japan, Cambridge, MA: Harvard University Press.

Wildavsky, A. (1971) The Revolt Against the Masses and Other Essays on Politics and Public Policy, New York: Basic Books.

Willetts, P. (1972) 'Cluster bloc analysis and statistical inference', American Political Science Review 66: 569–582.

Williams, P. M. (1958) Crisis and Compromise: Politics in the Fourth Republic, London: Longman.

Brief Curriculum Vitae

Professor Richard Rose DPhil (Oxford) BA (Johns Hopkins)

Academic Employment:
University of Strathclyde, Director, Centre for the Study of Public Policy, 1976–; Professor of Politics 1966–2005, 2012–. Formerly at University of Aberdeen; University of Manchester; visiting appointments and fellowships at Wissenschaftszentrum Berlin, Oxford University, Cambridge University, European University Institute, Florence, Stanford, etc.

Honours:
Honorary doctorate, European University Institute, Florence
Sir Isaiah Berlin Prize for Lifetime Achievement, UK Political Studies Association
Dogan Foundation/ECPR Lifetime Achievement Prize in European Political Sociology
Lifetime Achievement Award, Comparative Study of Electoral Systems.
Honorary doctorate, Orebro University, Sweden,
Richard E. Neustadt Award, as contributor to the best book on the presidency.
Lifetime Achievement Award of UK Political Studies Association
Lasswell Lifetime Achievement Award, Policy Studies Organization
Honorary Foreign Member of the American Academy of Arts & Sciences
Fellow of the British Academy
Robert Marjolin $25,000 AMEX Prize in International Economics
Foreign member, Finnish Academy of Science and Letters

Fellowships:
Associate Fellow, Nuffield College, Oxford, 2002–2005
Wei Lun Visiting Professor, Chinese University of Hong Kong, 2000
Max Planck Arbeitsgruppe für Transformationsprozesse, Berlin, 1996
Visiting Fellow, Central European University Prague, 1992–95
Ransone Lecturer in Public Administration, University of Alabama, 1990
Harding Visitor in Political Science & Economics, University of Toronto, 1989
Visiting Fellow, Fiscal Affairs, International Monetary Fund, Washington, 1984
Japan Foundation Visiting Scholar, Tokyo, 1984
Shell Oil Distinguished Scholar, 1981
American Enterprise Institute, Visiting Scholar, Washington, 1980
Brookings Institution, Washington, DC, Summer, 1976
Woodrow Wilson International Center Fellow, Washington, DC, 1974
Guggenheim Fellowship, 1973–74
American SSRC Fellow, Stanford University, 1967

Professional activities include:
Transparency International, Index Construction Committee, Berlin
Specialist advisor, House of Commons Public Administration Committee.
Consultant, Council of Europe Venice Commission on Democratic Elections
World Bank Consultant
OECD Consultant
Chair, European Science Foundation Citizens in Transition Network
National Endowment for Democracy, International Forum Washington DC
Research Associate, UN European Centre for Social Welfare Policy and Research, Vienna
Scientific Advisor, New Democracies Barometer, Paul Lazarsfeld Gesellschaft, Vienna
Creator, New Europe Democracy, New Russia and New Baltic Barometers, post-Communist society surveys www.cspp.strath.ac.uk.
Consultant, International Institute for Democracy and Electoral Assistance (IDEA), Stockholm
UN Development Program Consultant, President of Colombia
Founding Council member, Society for Advancement of Socio-Economics
International Political Science Association, Council, 1976–82; Co–director, World Congress Programme, Rio de Janeiro
Northern Ireland Constitutional Convention, Consultant to Chair
Chair, Work Group on United Kingdom Politics, Political Studies Association
Home Office Working Party on the Electoral Register
Council of European Studies, Choice in Social Welfare Policy Committee
Co-Founder, British Politics Group USA
Director, International Social Science Council European Summer School
Co-Founder, European Consortium for Political Research
United States–United Kingdom Fulbright Educational Commission
Secretary, Committee on Political Sociology, International Political Science and International Sociological Associations.

Editorial Boards:
Current:
Demokratizatsiya, Social Studies Review, SWS Rundschau (Vienna)
Past:
Journal of Public Policy, Comparative Politics, Comparative Political Studies, East European Constitutional Review, Governance, Political Studies, Policy Studies Journal, Sage Papers in Contemporary Political Sociology.

Seminar and conference papers:
Papers to hundreds of national, European and international meetings in political science, sociology, public finance, public administration and public policy, etc., in Albania, Australia, Austria, Belgium, Bosnia-Herzegovina, Brazil, Bulgaria, Canada, People's Republic of China, Colombia, Czech Republic, Denmark, Egypt, Estonia, Finland, France, Georgia, Germany, Greece, Hong Kong, Hungary, Ireland, Italy, Japan, Korea, Latvia, Lithuania, Luxembourg, Mexico,

The Netherlands, Norway, Poland, Portugal, Romania, Russia, Slovakia, Slovenia, South Africa, Spain, Sweden, Switzerland, Taiwan, Turkey, the United Kingdom and the United States.

Translated into:
French, German, Italian, Spanish, Portuguese, Romanian, Greek, Swedish, Norwegian, Polish, Russian, Ukrainian, Arabic, Japanese, Chinese, Korean and Samizdat.

Media:
Over the decades contributor to *The Times, Sunday Times, Financial Times, Daily Telegraph, New Society, Economist, Times Higher Education,* and dailies, weeklies and monthlies in Britain and the United States. Election psephologist and broadcaster for BBC, ITN, STV (Scottish Television), RTE (Radio Telefis Eireann), etc.

Research grants from:
World Bank, UNDP, UNESCO, European Commission, European Science Foundation, National Science Foundation, Ford Foundation, American Social Science Research Council, United States Institute of Peace, Exxon Education Foundation, American Enterprise Institute, British Economic & Social Research Council, Foreign Office Know How Fund, Nuffield Foundation, Survey of Race Relations, Joseph Rowntree Social Service Trust, Outer Circle Policy Unit, Northern Ireland Community Relations Commission, Public Finance Foundation, Canada Council, US Embassy Cultural Affairs London, French Embassy London, Volkswagen Foundation, Hans-Böckler Stiftung, Anglo-German Foundation, Wissenschaftszentrum Berlin, Agnelli Foundation, Austrian National Bank, Bank of Sweden Jubilee Fund, Swedish Ministry of Foreign Affairs, Japan Foundation, Institute for Political Studies in Japan, IDEA Stockholm, Open Society Institute Budapest, European Foundation for the Improvement of Living and Working Conditions Dublin, Fundaçao Francisco Manuel dos Santos, Lisbon.

Books since 2001:

2013   *Representing Europeans: A pragmatic approach*, Oxford: Oxford University Press.

2011   *Popular Support for an Undemocratic Regime: The changing views of Russians*, Cambridge: Cambridge University Press, (with W. Mishler and N. Munro).

2009   *Understanding Post-Communist Transformation: A bottom up approach*, London and New York: Routledge.

2009   *Parties and Elections in New European Democracies*, Colchester: ECPR Press, (with N. Munro).

2006   *Russia Transformed: Developing political support for a new regime*, Cambridge: Cambridge University Press, (with W. Mishler and N. Munro).

2005   *Learning from Comparative Public Policy: A practical guide*, London and New York: Routledge.

2003   *Elections and Parties in New European Democracies,* Washington DC: CQ Press, (with Neil Munro).

2002   *Elections without Order: Russia's challenge to Vladimir Putin,* Cambridge: Cambridge University Press, (with N. Munro).

2001   *The Prime Minister in a Shrinking World,* Oxford: Polity Press.

Articles and book chapters since 2010 include:

2013   'Institutional stimuli and individual response as explanations of turnout: the 2009 European Parliament election', *Journal of Elections, Public Opinion and Parties (JEPOP),* with G. Borz, in press.

2013   'Aggregation before representation in European Parliament party groups', *West European Politics* 36(3): 474–497, with G. Borz.

2013   *How Size Matters: Portugal as an EU member,* Glasgow: U. of Strathclyde, *Studies in Public Policy* No. 500 with D. Cremona and A. Trechsel, and in Portuguese.

2012   'Evaluating competing criteria for allocating parliamentary seats', *Journal of Mathematical Social Sciences* 63: 85–89, with P. Bernhagen and G. Borz.

2012   'Representation in parliamentary democracies: the European Parliament as a deviant case', in U. Liebert, T. Evas and C. Lord (eds) *Multilayered Representation in the European Union,* Baden-Baden: Nomos, pp. 73–90.

2011   'Political trust and distrust in post-authoritarian contexts', in S. Zmerli and M. Hooghe (eds) *Political Trust: Why context matters,* Colchester: ECPR Press, pp. 117–140, with W. Mishler.

2011   A micro-economic responses to a macro-economic crisis: a Pan-European perspective', *Journal of Communist Studies and Transition Politics* 27 (3–4): 364–384.

2011   *The Allocation between EU Member States of Seats in the European Parliament,* Brussels: European Parliament Directorate General for Internal Policies: Policy Department C: PE 432.760, co-author with G. Grimmett *et al.*

2011   *The Internet Goes EFL* (English as a Foreign Language), Washington DC: Brookings Institution Issues in Technology Innovation Report No. 5. January 2011 http://www.brookings.edu/papers/2011/01_efl_rose.aspx

2010   'Under what circumstances could maximizing turnout alter an election result?', *Representation* 46(2): 119–138, with U. Kohler.

2010   'A supply-demand model of party system institutionalization: the Russian case', *Party Politics* 16(6): 801–822, with W. Mishler and in Russian.

2010   *Evaluating the Quality of Society and Public Services,* Dublin: European Foundation for Living and Working Conditions, with K. Newton, 77 pp.

2010   'Experience versus perception of corruption: Russia as a test case', *Global Crime* 11(2): 145–163 with W. Mishler. In Russian and in D. Pfister and H. Moroff (eds) *Fighting Corruption in Eastern Europe: A multi-level perspective,* London: Routledge.

2010   'Stresses and opportunities of transformation: the impact on health',

Journal of Communist Studies and Transition Politics 26(1): 80–100, with M. Bobak.

2010   'United Kingdom' in D. Nohlen and P. Stover (eds) *Elections in Europe: A data handbook*, Baden Baden: Nomos, pp. 1991–2034, with N. Munro.

2010   'The impact of macro-economic shock on Russians', *Post-Soviet Affairs*, 26(1), 38–57 with W. Mishler.

2010   'Associations between different dimensions of religious involvement and self-rated health in diverse European populations', *Health Psychology* 29(2): 227–235, with A. Nicholson and M. Bobak.

For a full curriculum vitae and list of publications, see www.profrose.eu/about.php.

Index

Lightning Source UK Ltd.
Milton Keynes UK
UKOW03f0113171213

223148UK00001B/78/P